MOM,
I NEED YOUR HELP

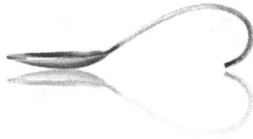

A Story of Love and Bent Spoons
Heartbreak, Healing, and Hope

A Novel By
Jess Gallant

Printed in the United States of America

First Printing, 2014

Kindle Printing, 2014

Mitzu Publishing Service

MitzuPublishing@aol.com

Mitzu Publishing Service
ISBN-13: 978-0-692-21287-5
ISBN-10: 0-692-21287-6

To my husband Paul, I couldn't have done this without you. To my son, James, and my daughter, Kylie, you know who you are. I will hold you close to my heart always.

Mom, I Need Your Help

A Novel By

Jess Gallant

Preface

In the middle of December, 2013, my husband announced he was writing a book.

"I've been writing it for a few weeks," Paul said. "You've probably noticed."

I hadn't.

We've joked about some bad books we had read over the past few years. One just recently, but I won't mention the title. Paul was famous for saying, "Even I can write better than this," so it didn't come as a complete surprise.

He had a way of just jumping in with no fear of failure. If it didn't work, it didn't work, at least he tried. There was no mistake that couldn't be fixed in his mind. No failure that couldn't be overcome.

So now he was writing a book.

"I don't want you to read it," he said. "And don't tell anyone. If it's no good, it's no big deal. I figure I've got the time, so I might as well give it a shot."

We've bought some waterfront land this year instead of a project house, so we're at a loss as to what to do with ourselves. You can't really fix up a lot of land. So why not write a book? He had a point.

I, on the other hand, always feared making mistakes, so I didn't try as many things as I wish I had. I've been thinking of writing my story on and off since that day in 2005 when Kylie said, "You should write a book, you can't make this stuff up."

I had written the first chapter in my mind many years ago. I even knew the title. I also knew I wouldn't write it without a happy ending, but the happy times just didn't last long enough.

I questioned my ability and wondered if anyone would be interested in my story. I thought maybe I could help someone going through similar circumstances. I decided to try. If no one liked it, maybe it would still be good therapy for me.

For a few weeks, Paul had been joking about his book. "Maybe I'll let you read it if you're good," and, "Oh, I have to put that in my book," then pretending to write about something stupid I had done.

"I don't care." I'd say. And then quietly, "I think I'll write my own book."

He never heard me. I'm not sure I wanted him to. I think I only wanted to start a conversation. I was afraid of his reaction, but after the third time of quietly trying to say I wanted to write a book, I just started.

On Christmas Day, after "FaceTime" with the kids and grandchildren, I sat down and wrote the beginning of my story. The first six pages. I had already written it hundreds of times in my mind. The words flowed as I relived every minute. I got choked up and fought back tears. I guess Paul thought I was searching the internet for our next project home or curtains or something. He was writing his own book.

At 3:30, Paul stopped writing, and I was finishing up my sixth page.

"Seven pages today, only three hundred more to go," he joked. He figured he needed to aim for three hundred and fifty pages. "Do you want to read it?"

"No," I said. I knew he wouldn't let me anyway. "But

I want you to read mine."

"What? You're writing a book?" He was smiling.

"Yes, I told you."

"No you didn't."

"I told you three times. You just didn't listen."

"I never heard you. You're kidding, right? Are you really writing a book? What's it about?"

This was all in fun, but I wasn't sure he would be laughing when he found out the subject matter.

"You'll have to read it. Then you'll know what it's about."

"Really? You want me to read it?" He was having fun. "I get to read your book?"

"Well, it's only the first six pages. Read it, then tell me what you think."

I was getting nervous. By now I knew I wanted to write this. I had to write it. Would he be okay? Would I be "airing our dirty laundry in public" as they say?

"Oh goody," Paul said as he rubbed his hands together like a critic getting ready to dissect my story. "This should be fun."

I wasn't so sure about that. I puttered around in the kitchen and waited trying not to bite my fingernails. I was about to be judged not only on my subject matter but also on my ability to convey it in a way that someone would want to read it. I trusted Paul's opinion, but could I stop now if he asked me to?

He was taking forever!

He finally stopped reading and stood up. This was it. Would he want me to continue?

"Are you sure this is what you want to do?"

"Yes, I think I have to. You know where it's going, right?"

"Yes," he said as he walked over and gave me a hug.

3

"If you want to do this, you should. I think it's great, the writing and the story."

"It will be a hard story to tell," I said.

"I know."

So that was it. I was going to write a book.

Although based on true events, I will call this fiction, but again it is my story. The names and places are fiction as well to protect the privacy of the people involved.

Chapter One

"Mom, I need your help." Five little words. I've heard those words often over the years, so it was no big deal when I heard them from my nineteen-year-old daughter on this sunny afternoon, a Saturday, in early June of 2003. Little did I know I was about to begin a long journey, and I was totally unprepared.

"Mom, I need your help!" I was relaxing with my husband and some friends when she yelled down over the hill to where we were sitting.

"I better see what she needs," I told my husband. "I'll be right back."

I walked up over the hill and up the stairs to our garage apartment. My daughter had claimed it as hers when we bought the house a year ago.

My mind wandered. She probably wanted to move the sofa again. Or maybe she's going to ask my opinion about an outfit. Or she might need a button sewn on something or pants hemmed. I wasn't overly concerned.

Life was good. Our business was finally supporting us and both our kids. My twenty-one-year-old son had come to work for us last fall, and my daughter had never worked anywhere else. We were able to buy a new, larger building for the business and all the equipment that went with it. There was plenty of room for my son and husband to have their own private offices while my daughter and I shared the large front office with two work areas.

Life was indeed good. Not great, but good. The kids had a lot of growing up to do, but we had hopes that they would eventually take over the business, and as my husband would say, "pay us to stay home." My son was already married with an infant daughter, our first grandchild. We had a nice life, and summer, our slow time, was just beginning. We were looking forward to a few afternoons off to enjoy the lake we lived on. My daughter would run the office alone during that time. That was the plan. No long vacations, the kids weren't ready for that, but a few afternoons a week to relax. That's all we wanted. That's all I wanted, and it was all about to change.

"Mom, I need your help," she said again as I entered the apartment.

She stood in the middle of the room. Cute as ever in a short jean skirt and top. I always think she looks great. So different from me. She has her father's dark hair and eyes, almost black. At about five foot three, she's certainly not tall but still taller than me. She's my baby, always has been and always will be, and I love her dearly.

I could hear a little crack in her voice this time. I was getting concerned. I suddenly had that little feeling you get in the pit of your stomach when you know something is not right. My daughter didn't take life too seriously. She was usually happy, and she had her father's great sense of humor. I enjoyed being around her. I knew right away this was serious.

"Kylie, what's wrong?" I asked my daughter.

She started to cry. She didn't cry often. Something was very wrong.

"I need you to go with me to the New Beginnings Rehab Hospital. I need help," she blurted out between sobs.

"Why? What do you mean?" I was totally confused. Kylie didn't do drugs.

"I've been taking pills, and I can't stop."

"What kind of pills?" I was starting to panic. Was she all right? What had she done to herself? She looked and acted normal. I saw her every day.

"Pain pills," she said. "Oxys."

"What are those? Why would you take them?" I was still trying to hold it together.

"Oxycontin, you've heard of them. I took some for fun a few times, and the next thing I knew I was taking them every day. Now I can't stop. I don't know what to do. I need help." She was crying harder now, embarrassed and scared.

I hugged her and held onto her until she stopped. She was my baby, and I would do anything to help her, to fix her problems, and make everything all right.

"We don't have to go right now," she continued. Kylie didn't want to be a bother. She knew I had been enjoying our company. "They're open early tomorrow. I'll be fine until then. Go back to Dad and relax. Can we head out early?"

The rehab hospital was about forty-five minutes away on the outskirts of the nearest city. I had heard of it. We made plans to leave at eight the next morning, and I left to rejoin my husband and our friends. Was she going to be all right until morning? How? Did she have more pills? Would she take more? I didn't want to know.

I have helped my children through many difficult times caused by their own bad choices. They always came to me, not their dad. I think because I didn't get angry often. Some things we fixed without telling Dad. They didn't want Dad to be disappointed in them. I heard the pleas often. "Please don't tell Dad," and "Does Dad need to know?" were the most popular. If I told on them, would they continue to come to me for help? My husband worked long hours, and if I could fix things without bothering him, I did. As the kids got older, we had a running joke among us that Dad was on a "need to know" basis. But there were times when Dad did need to know, and this was one of them. I was not going to do this alone. Our daughter needed our help, and I especially needed my husband's support.

    I tried to explain things to Paul the next morning. He was supportive but as confused as I was. I had no answers to his questions. I didn't know how long I'd be, or what they could do to help her. I'd stay in touch. Kylie showed up at the house at eight, and after an awkward goodbye to her father, we left.

    The long ride gave us a chance to talk, but the conversation was difficult. I was glad she wanted help and was courageous enough to ask. I asked how she got the pills. She said she bought them from someone off the street and didn't know his name. She didn't want to talk about it. Was she protecting someone?

    Kylie had done her homework and knew where she needed to go. I didn't ask how she knew. I tried not to dwell on the "Why?"... "How could you?"... "What were you thinking?"... and my all-time favorite, "I thought you were smarter than that." It would do no good now. The damage was done, and we would get her fixed. It was that simple. These people would help. She would be better, and we would put this behind us and move on. Boy, was I naive.

    The New Beginnings Rehab Center was in an old hospital that had seen better days. It had been converted to an emergency center and then to its current use as a medical center for offices, x-rays, and other outpatient services as well as the rehab unit. We made our way inside and checked in with the receptionist. We gave them Kylie's insurance card and waited. It wasn't busy on this Sunday morning, so before long we were called into a small office.

The nurse was very nice and did not appear to judge my daughter's irresponsible actions. She took the typical pulse and blood pressure readings. Then started asking questions. I would learn a lot of new words and phrases that day.

"What have you taken?"
"Oxys."
"Which ones?"
"80s."
"How often?"
"Once a day."
"For how long?"
"A couple of months."
Had it been that long? How could I not have known?
"Is that your drug of choice?"
Drug of choice?
"Yes."
"Have you done heroin?"
Heroin! No way! Please say no!
"No."
"Never?"
"Never."
Thank God!
"So no needles. Never shot up anything?"
"Absolutely not!"
"She's terrified of needles. We have to hold her down for shots," I said somehow thinking it would help. I was given a look that said, "I'm not talking to you." I kept quiet. I listened. I wanted to help but didn't know how.

"Okay," the nurse said, "this is how it works. We're going to take you through those double doors over there.

They remain locked at all times. We'll get you comfortable. Dr. Stevens will meet with you, and we'll put together a plan of action to get you clean. You'll meet in groups and individually with the councilors. We should have you ready to go home in three to five days."

"My mom can stay with me, right?" Kylie said in a panic.

"No, Honey. No one is allowed back there but the patients."

"I can't do it! I don't want to stay. I'll be fine. I can quit on my own." She was terrified.

What had just happened? She had begged me to bring her here, now she wanted to leave as fast as possible. The nurse tried to comfort her, but Kylie wasn't staying without me.

"Let me get Dr. Stevens. Please wait here."

I'm sure she thought Kylie was going to run. We waited. We had driven all the way down here and would at least talk to the doctor.

Dr. Stevens was a soft-spoken, short, round, black man. I mention his color only because we live in the Lakes Region of New Hampshire, and unfortunately, people of color are rare. He was extremely nice and genuinely caring. I could tell right away he had a passion for helping, and he would help us any way he could, but it had to be Kylie's choice, and those locked doors scared her to death.

Was there anything else we could do? Outpatient? Medication?

Kylie even mentioned the methadone clinic. Another new term for me. How did she know about that?

"Absolutely not!" was Dr. Stevens response to the methadone question. "That is only as a last resort, and you do not need that kind of help."

He left us to make our decision. He was sure he could

help Kylie, but she had to stay. Without me! After all, she was an adult. That would not be the last time I heard those words, "She is an adult." At nineteen, she had to make her own decisions about her medical care. I had no say.

We sat in the waiting room. I was trying to talk her into staying. I'd call often. I was sure I could visit as long as I didn't stay. I would have said anything to get her through those doors, but she wasn't budging, and she was an adult.

The nurse came over when she knew I was losing steam.

"Look," she said, "you haven't been taking the pills for that long, and it's not that high a dose. You can get off them yourself. You will feel awful, like you have the flu. Your bones will ache, and you will feel twitchy. Take some aspirin for the pain. Hot baths for the body aches and tough it out. You should be better in a few days. That's what we'll do for you here. You do need counseling, but we offer that as an outpatient." The last thing she said was, "Dr. Stevens is right about the methadone clinic. Stay far away from that place."

Armed with brochures and pamphlets, my daughter and I left to begin our first detox (another new word).

Three days and two very long nights later, Kylie was feeling better. I never let her out of my sight. I slept with her in our guest room, but I know she didn't sleep. Neither did I. She twitched, jumped, tossed, and turned. I ran hot baths for her every couple of hours even during the night when I knew she wasn't able to sleep. I didn't care if either of us slept. I only wanted to get through the next few days while the drugs left her system. We talked, we cried, we hugged. I never got mad. I just wanted her better and this behind us. It would be over, and no one else would ever know. I said my first prayer in years.

It would be a long summer.

Less than a week after our trip to rehab, Kylie told us she was going out with friends.

"You can't let her go out yet, she's not ready," Paul whispered to me behind her back.

"What can I do?" I whispered back.

"I don't know, but do something!" He was still whispering but getting louder.

"Kylie, do you think it's a good idea to go out so soon after umm…you know, last weekend?" I didn't know what to call it. Your drug use? Trip to rehab? Three days of detox? What do you say? "We're scared."… "We don't want to let you out of our sight."… "We don't trust you not to do it again."

She turned to face us. All I could say is, "We love you, and we're concerned. We want to be sure you've put this incident behind you and won't be tempted again."

"I'm fine, Mom, Dad. What I did was stupid, and I'll never do that again. I'm only going to hang out with some friends. I'll call you later." She hugged us and left.

"Nice job!" Paul yelled as he stormed out of the room.

I followed him. I knew he was scared for his daughter and needed to vent, so I tried not to be angry with him. I understood where he was coming from.

"Paul, she's nineteen. She'll be twenty in three months. I can't ground her and send her to her room. She doesn't even live with us."

"You could have done something!" That was the end of the conversation. He walked off again.

Could I have done something? Could I have changed her future?

I didn't know.

She did come home to her apartment early that night, and for a few weeks after that, things were pretty normal. But it was summer in New England. Fourth of July was right around the corner, and she had new friends. People I didn't know. It started slowly.

A phone call in the evening, "Mom, I just wanted to let you know I'm going to stay overnight at Vanessa's."

I knew Vanessa, but I wasn't entirely sure that was where she was staying. The calls came once or twice a week at first, but before long she rarely came back to her apartment.

The more she stayed over somewhere, the later she showed up for work. She knew it was slow at work this time of year, and I would be there anyway. I had hoped for her help in fixing up our new office space. I thought it would be fun and was looking forward to it. But now I was just hoping she would show up. There was always an excuse, "I overslept."..."My alarm didn't go off."... "I had a migraine." The migraine excuse worked best because I knew she got them a lot. Migraines run in the family, and the medication she had to take for them left her feeling sleepy and groggy. I tried to believe her. I wanted to believe her, and if I acted like I didn't believe her, she would cry. She wasn't normally like that. I was getting nervous.

Summer was flying by, and I was not getting any afternoons off. Paul had given up on me. He had done his job of making sure his work was covered. James, our son, was around, and we had a couple of other employees. Paul could get them going in the mornings and head home after lunch for that much needed time off.

Kylie was my problem. If I couldn't get her to cover

13

for me and do it well, I was just going to have to stay until we closed. I had no choice because I didn't trust her. Not that I thought she would steal or close the office and leave. She was usually responsible, but she just didn't seem herself. She was on edge, easily confused, and absentminded. She was also very depressed and cried often.

"I hate my life," she said a lot.

"Then change it," I would respond. She had a new boyfriend by now, and I think he had a lot to do with it. I had never met him, but I already didn't like him.

When Kylie did talk to me, it was about getting her boyfriend out of the house he was living in. She called it a party-house and was tired of hanging out there. I think Kylie thought she could save him if she could find him an apartment. What she wasn't saying was that he had no job and couldn't afford one. My daughter knew better than to bring him to her apartment. That was made quite clear before she moved in.

Was she seriously thinking of renting a place with this loser?

It was about this time that I noticed the weight loss. Kylie tried to hide it, but it was becoming very obvious and not only to me. Others commented on it. I kept asking if she was eating. What? When? How much?

"I'm fine, Mom. Don't worry."

But she wasn't.

I thought she was sick, maybe even cancer. I was so worried that I asked her to make an appointment with her doctor. She was still seeing a female pediatric nurse practitioner. Debbie had helped Kylie through some rough patches in high school, and they were close. She would keep Kylie as a patient until she turned twenty which was coming up fast. Kylie made an appointment.

My granddaughter was turning one in August, and James asked if we could host a party. We lived on the lake and his house was too small, he said. Reluctantly I agreed. Many of our family members hadn't seen Kylie in months, and I knew they would be concerned. She hadn't seen the doctor yet, and I didn't have any answers.

Well, Kylie showed up in baggie clothes weighing all of ninety pounds fully dressed. I know because I made her step on the scale. She also had the biggest, darkest, black eye I had ever seen. She was wearing dark glasses and tried to cover it up with make-up, but it didn't fool anybody.

"Start talking, now!" I was angry. Someone had hurt my little girl, and I wanted to know everything. I was pretty sure I knew who. The no-good loser boyfriend. I had finally met him once over the summer, and if I had any doubts about not liking him, they were erased back then. Now, I hated him! But she defended him, saying it was all her fault. What was happening to my daughter? She had always been the one in control in her relationships. If she asked a boy to jump, he asked how high? I used to be worried she was too controlling. Now she was letting this no-good loser abuse her, and he certainly wasn't much of a catch. What was going on? What did she see in him?

The party went just as I expected. The questions weren't only about the weight loss but also the black eye. Needless to say, her father was furious. It was a good thing he didn't know where the jerk lived. But Kylie kept defending him. She never told us how it happened, only that it was all her fault. No one could believe she would go back to him, especially me.

My husband's sister and brother along with my good friend, Alex, cornered me before the party was over.

"Jess, do you think Kylie's doing drugs?"

"No." I confided in them about the incident in June and said I was sure she would not do that again.

"We're not talking pills. We think it might be heroin."

"No way. She wouldn't go near a needle. She's deathly afraid of them." I was sure I was right.

"Check her arms," Alex said.

I looked over across the lawn at Kylie and that's when I noticed she had on long sleeves. It was eighty degrees. My heart sank. I couldn't believe it. I thought back to what she had been wearing for the past couple of months. I couldn't remember a tank top or sleeveless shirt. Wait, she did wear a short sleeved shirt the other day. She had tied a two-inch strip of material around each of her arms just above the elbows. "A fashion statement," she'd said. "I'm starting a new trend." We laughed. I thought it was cute. How could I be so stupid? I suddenly felt sick.

"I will," I said, not letting on that I already knew the answer. I didn't need to check. It was so obvious now.

I thanked them for their concern and told them about the doctor's appointment next week. If she was doing drugs, wouldn't that show up in tests? If she tested positive for drugs, I would talk to them again. Ask for their help. Advice. Right now I just wanted to change the conversation.

How did they know to look for needle marks? Drugs were not rampant where we lived. As far as I knew, none of my friends or family had ever done drugs. Alcohol was another story. I always worried about drinking but never drugs. I was worried now.

Alex stopped by the office on her way home from work about a week later. Kylie had come in late again and was not herself. She cried easily and often that day. "I hate my life," she said over and over. When Alex walked in, Kylie was sitting under a desk in a corner of the back room in tears. Alex went to talk to her. They had always been close, but after a few minutes of trying to console Kylie, Alex got up, took me aside, looked me square in the eyes, and said one word....

"Drugs."

I started to make excuses, but Alex always had a way of telling it like it is. She would be blunt and to the point.

"She's almost twenty and she's hiding under a desk. Open your eyes for God's sake!" She walked out. She didn't need to say anything else.

The physical came and went. I wished I could have been there, but someone had to be at the office, and after all she was an adult. I wanted to let the doctor know what I suspected but didn't know how. Doctor/patient confidentiality rules and the whole "adult" thing. She was on her own.

"How did it go?"

"Fine. They took blood for tests," Kylie answered. "She'll let me know when the results come in." She was being vague.

Would Kylie confide in her doctor? Could a medical doctor help if she was doing drugs?

I waited. It would be a few more weeks and a lot of, "Have you heard from the doctor?" comments before she finally told me her plan.

Kylie said she needed to go to the methadone clinic. Only for a few months, maybe six. Debbie said it was the best thing for her now. I didn't believe that for a minute, but I struggled to keep calm and listen.

"Dr. Stevens said you didn't need that," I finally said, still fighting to keep my cool.

"That was before, but it's worse now."

She didn't go into detail. But I knew, and she knew that I knew. We didn't talk about it then. It would all come out slowly over time, but not that day.

"I think you should go back to see Dr. Stevens. They have the outpatient clinic. You never did go to counseling."

I did not want her to have anything to do with the methadone clinic. A few months ago, I didn't even know there was one in the state. I thought they were only in big cities, and the only people who used them were homeless addicts who lived on the streets, shared needles, had diseases, and were dirty and disgusting. Now my daughter was saying she needed to go there. She was too good for that. Wasn't she? She had a job (if her father didn't fire her), a place to live (the apartment if she wanted it), and most importantly a family who loved her. I had helped her to detox before (I was getting used to the terminology), I could help her again. We'd get her clean, then into the outpatient clinic. It was every morning for two weeks (I had done my homework). I would cover the office and give her the time off, with pay of course. Anything! I would do anything to keep her away from that place. That place made it all too real.

Was Kylie really a drug addict?

"I know I can get clean," she said. "But I can't stay clean. I need the time to get the cravings under control."

What did she mean by cravings? My education was continuing, and my head was spinning. What could I say to talk her out of it? I should have done research on it. I didn't know much about how a methadone clinic worked. I only knew it wasn't for her, but she had answers to every protest I came up with.

It broke my heart when she said, "I just want to sleep. I want to be normal like you and Dad. I watch the sun come up and know you and Dad are getting up, and I haven't slept. You guys are taking the dogs out and working out or going for a run. You're getting ready for work, and I haven't even gone to bed. I'm such a loser. I don't want this life. I hate this life. I hate myself."

"It won't be for too long," she continued. "I promise. Counseling is mandatory. Once a week. They make you pee in a cup to test for drug use, and if you're not clean you get kicked out. It's the best thing for me right now. Please support me. Please help me. Mom, I need your help."

Those five little words again. She was wearing me down.

"Noel goes there," Kylie blurted out.

"Your friend from high school? Noel who lives by the bus garage? That Noel? You're kidding me?"

She hadn't been a close friend, but I knew who she was. And she was normal. Kylie mentioned a few other names of people who had gone there or were still going there. Some I knew, most I didn't. How did she know that many people who went to the methadone clinic? How did she know that many drug addicts?

She would have to make the hour and twenty minute round trip every day to get her "dose."

"I'll leave early and be back by eight for work." Kylie was eager to get started.

She wanted her life back. She wanted to be and feel normal again. I didn't understand. I didn't get it. Kylie was fighting demons only people who had been there could relate to. I had never done any drugs. Not even pain medication for childbirth. Could I judge her for something I didn't understand?

And what would I tell her father?

***

19

I lost that battle, but I was determined to win the war.

Kylie and her loser boyfriend went to the methadone clinic for their initial intake (new term) interviews. They were both accepted into the program but were given a long list of rules. They had to show up every day, there would be random urine tests, methadone must be present in the urine and no other drugs, once a week counseling was mandatory, and oh yes…it cost $85 a week, prepaid, in advance, and in cash! Did I mention this was a "for profit" clinic?

Loser boyfriend didn't have a job, so he qualified for state aid. Kylie's cost was not covered by insurance and was coming out of her paycheck.

"Don't ever ask me to pay for it," I said. After all, she was an adult.

And so, three days before her twentieth birthday, just three months after she first asked for my help, my all grown up daughter took her first dose of methadone. Somewhere along the line, I had failed her, but she was now "in recovery" as they called it (I was learning). Would it work? Would it last? Would she ever be normal again?

Well, it didn't work for loser boyfriend. He lasted less than a week.

After Kylie's first dose, she did indeed show up for work at eight. That was a good sign. She was determined to make this work and prove me wrong. She sat beside me at her desk, working for a change. But she was different. Her hands shook. Her words were a little slurred. Maybe no one else would notice.

"What's wrong with her? I thought she was getting help." That was Paul. He noticed.

I had told him what was happening but skimmed over the details. I never mentioned the word "heroin," since Kylie had never used that word either. Like I said, she knew that I knew, but it was never said out loud. I was afraid Paul would disown her if he knew all the details. For the same reason, I never used the word methadone. Kylie was going to a place to get medication to help her stay off the drugs. That was it. After all, he was on a "need to know" basis, and that was all he needed to know. I hoped.

"I think it's a reaction to the medication," I said. "They may have to adjust the dosage." It really wasn't a lie. "Please give her time."

He had been great, but he was losing patience. We had a business to run, and we needed good dependable employees. She would shape up or be replaced. Kylie was walking on thin ice, and our busy time was right around the corner.

Paul was right. Our company was growing, and we were busier than ever. If she didn't do her work, I had to do it. I had been covering for her all summer, but I knew I couldn't run the front office by myself during the winter. I had done it for years, but we had grown. It was definitely a two person job now. Would she make it? Could we depend on her? I would always be there too, but I needed her help. "Please, God, make this recovery work, help her beat this addiction, please give me back my child,".... I would say this prayer over and over again for many years to come.

Kylie did improve. After a few days, her hands didn't shake as much and her speech was better. She showed up for work every day on time. She eventually left loser boyfriend and moved into our guest room. She never moved back into the apartment. It was not year round, and she knew she would have to move out when it got too cold, she said. I think there was more to it than that, but I didn't press the issue.

She was home and getting better, but my daughter

was not the same person she had been six months before. Gone was the confidence and quick, easy sense of humor I loved. It was replaced by paranoia and self-doubt. She became obsessive about order and routine. She always had that perfectionist personality trait, but this bordered on OCD. I tried not to notice as Kylie over-plucked her eyebrows or organized the paperclips for the fourth time in two days. Was this all part of recovery? Was it from the methadone? Would she ever be normal again? I didn't like it. I bit my tongue. She was alive, safe, and gaining back some of the weight she had lost. I should have been happy.... I wasn't.

When family asked how she was, I told them she was on medication to help her stay off the drugs. We didn't lie about the drug use. Everyone knew anyway. But Kylie didn't want them knowing about the clinic, so we agreed to leave that part out. She looked so much better that eventually it was not an issue. To everyone else, she was better.

I had the opportunity to view the methadone clinic first hand in November. It was snowing on a Saturday morning, and my vehicle was all-wheel drive. Kylie's was a sporty white Celica she bought before the drugs. It fit her personality to a "T" back then. Now, she just needed to get to the clinic. I volunteered to drive her.

I wasn't allowed inside, so I sat in the car and watched the line of people form outside in front of what looked like a small, white, two story house with clapboard siding. Inconspicuous. The people came from all walks of life. One gentleman even wore a suit and tie. There was a pretty woman in a tailored skirt and jacket, obviously a professional on her way to work in an office. Was I wrong about the clientele? Not completely, the bums far outweighed the normal looking people. When had I become so judgmental?

After that incident, Kylie got nervous about making the round trip to the clinic in bad weather. She decided she was going to rent an apartment near the clinic, forty minutes from work. She had a friend who needed a place anyway, and he would help with the rent. Not a boyfriend, she assured me. I believed her. He made loser boyfriend look like a saint. Where did she find these people?

They rented an apartment in a pretty little complex overlooking a park. Loser roommate lasted less than a month. Kylie was all alone in the city. She bought a kitten and seemed okay, but I was concerned. Her life revolved around the clinic, her cat, and her job...in that order. Her days consisted of going to the clinic, going to work, and going back to her apartment. She even brought the kitten to work every day. She never went out. She never left the apartment on the weekends except to go to the clinic. "I can't leave the kitten alone," was her excuse. We never saw her outside the office. Was this good for her? Did she just need time to heal? Was this all part of recovery?

Kylie was also getting counseling every week, and she learned a lot. She learned about the workings of the brain.

"The receptors in the brain are damaged by the drugs," she told me once after a counseling session.

"But isn't the methadone continuing to destroy them?" I asked.

"Good question. I don't know, the counselor didn't mention that."

Kylie hadn't thought of that, but I had. I did not want her on any drug. I was sure this methadone was not good for her. In my mind, it only replaced the heroin. It didn't cure her. It was just prolonging the inevitable. But she was "stable" (new terminology) as they called it. Somewhere between normal and high, I called it.

She learned about "triggers" (new meaning) and temptations. Maybe that was why she didn't go out. Was she afraid of the triggers?

She learned about "hitting bottom." I thought she had. It was time to get up.

I asked when she would start weaning off the methadone. I knew she couldn't just stop. She was now addicted to this new drug. It was going on six months, and she had been the best little methadone patient there was. She never missed a day, never had a bad urine test, and made all of her counseling sessions. But most importantly to them (I thought anyway), she never missed a payment.

I encouraged her to talk to her counselor about getting off methadone for good. She did but was given vague answers. "You need six months to a year at least," they told her. Kylie talked like this was a lifetime commitment.

"Not many people ever get off and stay clean," she said.

Was this becoming a lifestyle choice?

"Kylie, you can't stay on this forever. What kind of a life would you have? What about a family, vacations, any kind of travel? This was supposed to be short term, not a lifetime. You made a mistake. You used drugs for less than six months. Strong ones for less than three. This should not affect the rest of your life."

We were having the same argument over and over. I wished I could talk to the counselor. Kylie really liked her. Maybe she could put together a plan to get her off eventually. But the counselor was the one who was stalling. "We don't want any stress in your life when you start to wean off," the counselor told her. She used anything Kylie said as an excuse to keep her coming. They didn't want to lose a good paying customer. I was furious.

I stood by helplessly and watched as my once vibrant and fun loving little girl became more and more distant. She had been the one who walked the halls of the middle school with her friends "like they owned the place," a teacher had told me once. She was confident and sure of herself all through high school. She had some very nice boyfriends, and she broke a lot of hearts.

Now I watched as the obsessiveness and paranoia engulfed her. She would constantly check and recheck everything, sometimes locking her car five times before she was sure it was locked correctly. I was concerned about what she was doing at her apartment. She mentioned once that she constantly worried about her stove being off when she left for work or went to bed, so she would make up routines. If things were done in a certain way or order, she could remember it in her mind and be sure she had turned the stove off or locked the door. It was very unsettling.

She constantly fidgeted and couldn't sit still for long. She cleaned with a passion I had never seen. And she organized everything over and over again. First by color, then by size, then by something else. It broke my heart. But she would also doodle beautiful designs full of pretty pastels and curlicues when she was restless. She began doodling as a little girl so this was nice to see. A sign my Kylie was still there somewhere.

Chapter Two

As winter turned into spring, Kylie continued to be the perfect little methadone patient. She kept to the same routine, but now occasionally she would visit with her brother after work. James loved his sister very much and was worried about her almost as much as I was. Her brother had moved into the apartment behind the office as soon as the original owners of the building moved out. They had stayed on as tenants for four months after we purchased the building. My husband and I had helped James buy a house when he was nineteen. One of those good deals with a very low down payment. The mortgage was less than his rent payment, and we thought it was a good investment for him. We had been buying real estate off and on for years and encouraged him to do the same. The house, however, was a one bedroom, and he was now married with a toddler. The apartment was a two bedroom with a fenced backyard, and the fact that it had an in-ground pool had nothing to do with it, so he said. We agreed on a rent. This was not a company perk. We had planned on the rent from the apartment to cover some of the mortgage, and he needed to understand that. He said he did.

James is my oldest. Now at twenty-two, he stands six feet tall and one hundred sixty-five pounds, same as his father. But that's about all they have in common. James has brown hair and eyes, but they are much lighter than his dad's, and he has my fair skin. He does not have his dad and Kylie's easy sense of humor, and he certainly did not inherit their perfectionism. But he is very sweet and loving, and very, very smart.

We didn't realize how smart he was until he came to work for us. I can't deny I was happy the first time my son realized he knew more than his father about a certain job. He always looked for approval from Paul and never thought he measured up. James was telling his father he was all wrong about an installation. When Paul finally realized James was right and had to admit it, they laughed and James gloated for days. I smiled every time James rubbed it in. I was lucky to see my children and granddaughter almost every day. I was happy. Life was good, not great, but good.

Paul and James constantly butted heads over details. Paul tried to teach James about the need for organization and the inner workings of running a company. Pricing jobs was always a challenge. James would throw out a price we should charge for a particular installation without ever writing anything down. Paul wanted details. He wanted to know what parts were needed, the cost of those parts, how long the installation would take, and how many people were needed. James did it all in his head and was close more often than not, but when he was wrong, it was usually in a big way.

We bid on a couple of large jobs and were thrilled to be chosen to do the work. One was an installation in a big five bay garage with offices. It was right next to our building, and we knew the owner fairly well. It would be a good job for our growing company. James designed and priced the job himself. He did a great job with the design, and the installation went fairly well, but when all was said and done, we lost money. A lot of money. We lost money on the other job too, but not as much. Paul tried to explain that it made no sense to get a job if we couldn't make a profit.

Paul tried to get James to make lists, and when he wouldn't, Paul made lists. Lists of every part imaginable, along with their prices. He made copies of the lists, so James would only have to check off what he needed for a job. Paul would do the math and price the job. But James was scatterbrained. He still forgot to mark off half the parts, usually just the small ones, but they all added up.

We wondered if James would ever understand about the financial end of our company. He was not the one paying the bills. He still had a lot of maturing to do, and we had our work cut out for us if we ever wanted to have the kids "pay us to stay home." Our dream, our retirement, depended on these two kids, and at times, it did not look very promising.

The kids were coming around, we would say to each other. They just need time. They're still young. Kylie was showing up every day. Still not normal in my eyes, but she was there and she tried. James was a terrific salesman. He brought in a lot of work for the company, if we could only get him to price the jobs right. He was also a great troubleshooter. He could often tell you what was wrong with a system without even looking at it. He could get it up and running in no time. Save the day! But trying to get him to finish a job correctly and not just the quick fix was often difficult. He didn't have the patience, and he was most definitely not a perfectionist. We plugged along and hoped for the best.

We should have planned for the worst.

As much as I enjoyed seeing Renee, my adorable granddaughter, every day at work, I eventually had to admit to myself that renting the apartment to my son was not the best idea. I was struggling to get him to pay the rent. He would give me a little bit here and there, always promising the rest shortly, more often than not trying to barter with me over it. "I worked ten hours overtime last week," he would say. "That should count for something."

We paid him a good salary along with a company van and a credit card which he was using to fill both his and his wife's vehicles with gas. We bought him lunch most days, and that usually included his wife if she was in the apartment. We paid for full health insurance for his entire family. The rent wasn't high, and we even paid for the heat and hot water. He should have had plenty of money to pay it.

Being tired of chasing him for the rent wasn't the only reason I had regrets. My daughter-in-law, Lauren, was not the best housekeeper, to say the least. Actually, she did not keep house at all. The door between the apartment and office was often left open. It was great to have little Renee toddle on out to give Grammy and Auntie a hug or a kiss before nap time. She was such a cutie, and if customers were there, they raved about her. She was good for business. We were a family business in a small town. It was almost expected. Customers would ask "Where's the baby?" But I would run to close the apartment door whenever someone entered the building. Lauren didn't seem to notice. Small hints and well-intentioned advice went unheeded.

This was not your typical untidy home. Dishes would pile up in the sink for a week, even though they had a dishwasher. Fortunately, we provided uniforms for my son because laundry was rarely done, and the apartment had its own washer and dryer. I don't think she even knew what a vacuum was.

After six months, the filth was an inch thick covering everything. If I watched Renee for a few hours, which I did occasionally, I would clean her room, her little rocking chair,

29

and her high chair, wondering how they could live like this. My son was embarrassed and tried to help his wife keep the place clean, but he was fighting a losing battle. Lauren didn't get embarrassed. She just did not see the mess and filth. I worried about Renee, but she was a happy and healthy little girl. What could I do? It was their life. I had to let them figure it out. My mother-in-law never interfered, and I loved her for it. I was determined to be the same way. They could live any way they chose, but not under my roof.

When James mentioned a customer's house was up for sale, Paul and I suggested he buy it. It was a two bedroom raised ranch with a daylight basement they could eventually finish if more children came along. We sincerely thought purchasing a home would be good for them. Better than paying rent and getting nothing in return, we explained. In 2004, real estate was still a good investment. He would easily qualify for a mortgage since he had a good paycheck, rental income from his first home, and good credit. It would make him more responsible. He would have to budget, we said, but he could do it. It would be their own. It would be great!

They reluctantly agreed and started the process. It was June. They could enjoy the pool for the summer and move at the end of August. We had done it. We had eased them out without a fight or ultimatum. It was a good thing, right?

Kylie waited, watched, and listened, saying nothing. She didn't always get along with her sister-in-law, but she loved her brother and niece very much. At this point in her life, they were her only social contacts. She was staying after work to visit with them more often now. There was no doubt things would be different. I was still worried that Kylie was becoming more and more isolated, locking herself away from the world when she wasn't at work. My heart broke for her, but it was what she wanted.

I talked with Paul before mentioning it to Kylie.

"Could we rent the apartment to Kylie?" I asked him.

Could I persuade her to move back to town? The methadone clinic had rewarded her good behavior with two "take homes" (new phrase) a week. She would not have to make the round trip to the clinic on the weekend.

"I manage her money," I told my husband.

I had put her on a budget when she first rented the other apartment.

"She can afford it if she's careful," I continued.

Besides her car payment and the clinic, she had no other bills.

"I will take the rent out of her pay weekly." I wanted my daughter back home.

I was hoping she would begin to live again. Paul understood. He was worried about her too. I mentioned to Kylie that since her brother was moving out, she could rent the apartment if she wanted to. I waited for her reaction. She was thrilled. I was happy.

So Labor Day weekend of 2004, my son and his family moved out of the apartment and into their new home. My daughter and I spent a week cleaning and painting the apartment. It was the first time I had really seen it. It was adorable and Kylie was excited about decorating. She moved in and for her twenty-first birthday, my husband and I bought her a queen size bed, pillow top mattress, and a three-inch memory foam topper. "Just what I wanted!" she screamed. I knew sleeping was an important part of her recovery. All was good.

It wouldn't last.

I tried almost daily to talk to Kylie about her

recovery and the methadone clinic. They were now giving her a week's worth of "take-homes," rewards for being so good. Was she a puppy in training? I think they were trying to make it easy for her, so she wouldn't ask to lower her dose. "Why change what is working for you?" I could just hear them say to her. "We won't even make you come in every day.".... "You can still live a normal life.".... "Just medicate yourself up so you don't feel anything and give us $85 a week, and we'll all be happy." I hated them.

She showed me her "supply" once. Little containers with stick on covers about the size of single-serve coffee cream containers. She wanted to open one to show me the liquid dose. I don't know why. I didn't want to see it, but she insisted. It tipped over and the methadone spilled out on the counter. Kylie was in a panic. She needed the exact amount to get her through the weekend. She called the clinic but they didn't care. She would not be getting any more until Monday, period. She was just going to have to survive on her own. So much for the lovey/dovey relationship. I knew she was only a dollar sign to them. They didn't care about her. She had been going there for over a year, the perfect little patient, but it didn't matter. She was still a nobody. She was on her own.

Kylie hung up the phone and cried.

"What will I do? I can't go a day without a dose. I'll be so sick," she said through the tears.

I hugged her and said, "Everything will be okay. I'm sure it won't be that bad."

"You don't understand, I'm up to 150mgs. I'll be sooo sick." She was sobbing even harder now.

"I thought you were at 80mgs?" She had told me that when she started.

"They bring you up. They want you addicted so you'll stick with it and not go back to heroin."

She hadn't told me that. All the time I was hoping they would bring her dose down, they were increasing it. She was more addicted now than ever. I was crushed. What else did I not know? I was so upset. This kid was trying so hard to beat this addiction, and they were literally making it impossible.

I was afraid she would buy pills or heroin to get through the weekend, but I knew if she did, she would fail a urine test. Then she would be in more trouble, and they would kick her out. "Maybe not such a bad idea," I thought for a second. But I knew that would be worse. We concentrated on how to get her through the weekend.

"What if you don't take the only dose you have left first thing Saturday morning? Could you wait until you felt like you needed it? Afternoon or even later? Then maybe it will last through most of Sunday."

Who was I kidding? I had no idea how this all worked or how long a dose lasted, but I had to say something. Give her some suggestions. Maybe this would open her eyes. Maybe she would realize how much this controlled her life. Would this be a turning point? I hoped so. I prayed it would be. "Please, God, help her through the weekend and please help her to see this isn't good for her."

It was a very long weekend for me. I left her Friday at five o'clock with a hug and words of encouragement...

"It won't be so bad."

"Space out the dose."

"I'm sure that will work."

"I bet this happens all the time."

"You'll be fine." And most importantly, "Call me if you need me, and I'll be there for you."

I waited, I checked in, I prayed. She was fine. I'm not sure what she did. She never told me. I never asked.

One crisis averted. Another on the horizon.

Chapter Three

I was about to hear those five little words again, the ones that give you the sinking feeling in the pit of your stomach, but they didn't come from my daughter this time.

"Mom, I need your help." I froze. I cringed. It wasn't the "Mom, I need your help moving the sofa." It was the "Mom, I need your help with something very, very serious." And it was coming from my son.

My first thoughts were of Renee. Was she all right? Lauren? Was his marriage in trouble? I was over thinking, but I knew the tone, and I knew it wasn't good.

"What is it, Hon?" I asked.

What can I say, I always called him Honey or Hon. He was my first born and would always be the toddler with the beautiful blond curls and the infectious laugh. We used to joke that we only had Kylie so James would have someone to play with. He was my Honey then and that would never change. It didn't matter that my husband was Honey, too. They were the men in my life, and I loved them both immensely. There were times when I didn't like either of them very much, but I always loved them both, and I always will.

When James pulled me aside and whispered again, "Mom, I need your help," it wasn't for help to get off drugs.

I would soon learn he wanted help to stay on drugs.

"I made a big mistake, and I owe some not very nice people money," James said. His hands were shaking, and his voice quivered just a little.

"How much?" I asked.

"Six hundred dollars," he whispered.

"What kind of mistake did you make?" I was in shock. How could he owe someone six hundred dollars for a 'mistake'?

"I owe a guy money for drugs," he blurted out in a whisper. "I don't know what I was thinking. I will never do it again. I know how much you worry about Kylie, and I'll never put you through that. I will never be like Kylie. This was a one-time thing. I have to pay this guy. I don't know what he'll do if I don't. I'm scared. I'm so sorry. Please, Mom, I need your help."

James was rambling on, but he was saying all the right things. He was my son. He made a mistake. He wanted to fix it. He was sorry, and he was scared. What was a mother to do?

He kept on talking, "I'll pay you back. I promise. You can take it out of my pay."

I had stopped listening. I was in shock. No way. Not again. Wasn't he smarter than that? He was twenty-three years old now. He had a family, a great job, a mortgage.... Why? Why would he take a chance like that?

But he said he'd never do it again, and I wanted to believe him. We got along great most of the time, and I believed he never lied to me. Okay, maybe sometimes, but not about anything important. He was a good kid and a nice person. Funny in a sweet, awkward kind of way, and I loved him unconditionally. I could help him, I told myself, and that would be that. We would never mention it to anyone. It would be over, behind us, and he would pay me back. I would make sure of it.

"If I loan you the money," I emphasized the word loan, "you will pay me back every cent, and you will never do this again." I almost screamed the word "never!" I would help but only this one time. I told him, "If it happens again, you are on your own."

"Thank you, thank you, thank you! It will never happen again, I promise."

I gave him the money from the company deposit in cash (it had to be, drug dealers don't take checks) and told him I wanted him to pay the company one hundred dollars a week. As his mother, I knew he couldn't pay it all at once, or he wouldn't be able to pay his other bills. His credit was good, and I wanted to keep it that way.

It was late October of 2004. It would be a very long winter.

Chapter Four

Things were pretty normal for a few weeks. We were gearing up for a busy winter. The cold had started early that year, with January temperatures in November. Indications of a long winter ahead. As much as I hated the cold, it was good for business. We delivered heating oil. Actually, that's how we started back in 1988 when my husband bought an oil truck and announced we were going into the oil business.

He had worked for an oil company for a few months shortly after we got married. He had been working for a construction company, and knowing a lay off would come as the weather turned colder, he took a temporary job delivering oil. So he had been thinking about starting his own company ever since.

We started with heating oil, then added kerosene, then diesel fuel, and now we were heavily into the service end of the business. We used to contract out the service calls, but when we had too many unanswered calls, and Paul had to go out in the middle of the night to fix furnaces without the proper knowledge, we began to think about adding service to the company. The final straw came when the company we contracted to do our service work decided to start delivering heating oil. Quite a conflict of interest.

James had gotten his heat tech license and was working on his plumbing license as well. He had a decent job in the city and was learning every day, but did he know enough? Was he ready to be the sole heat tech in a company our size? Paul would help, of course, since we had finally hired our first driver a few years before. Paul had worked two jobs until the company could support us. He had been the only driver for more than ten years, but now he had some help. We took a chance and asked James if he wanted to work for us. It was the fall of 2002. He was barely twenty-one years old.

James had done well through two winters. When I called him at two in the morning for a no-heat call, he was always right there. He thrived on saving the day. The customers loved him, so we had expanded into the plumbing end of the business and had even done a few whole-house installations. We had high hopes.

Kylie and I handled most of the delivery end of the business by then. Paul was concentrating on the service end along with keeping three oil trucks and two service vans on the road and in good working order. Not always easy in the ice and snow. Our area had some steep hills and sharp curves. We had some treacherous driveways to navigate as well. We never turned anyone down. As long as they were in our delivery area, we would get oil to them. Paul was very firm about our delivery area, though. We turned many people away who were less than a mile past our invisible markers. He knew if we went a mile for one customer there would be another one just past them. A mile was a long way in an oil truck, and he wanted to keep our customers close to home. We'd fill in within our boundaries, Paul would say. That decision made years ago would play an important role in the near future.

So all was normal and busy with each of us doing our individual jobs in the company. Kylie was now writing letters to a young man in jail. She would never date him, she assured me. He was just someone she had met years before, and they had a lot in common. He'd had issues with drugs himself but was now clean (obviously, he was in jail). At twenty-five, he was doing one year in jail for something he had done at twenty. He wanted the roller coaster ride of probation to be over and that was the only way he could walk away from it, she said. I kind of understood, but I wanted my daughter to have no part of it. She was, however, coming out of her shell a little, and she had fun reading his letters to me. They were heartwarming and funny, and he would often include poetry. What could I say?

Something, though, was not quite right with James. He was distracted more than usual. He called in sick a few times, which he had never done before. He was looking a little thinner. Not too noticeable at first, but he just wasn't himself. Something you couldn't put your finger on. We never talked about the earlier incident. He tried to pay me back, but more often than not he would ask to borrow the money again a few days later.

I worried about his finances. He should have been able to make ends meet, but he was struggling to pay his bills. His wife hadn't worked in a long time, so when she got a job at a diner down the street from the office, I thought it would take some pressure off James.

She worked ten hours a week. It should have helped pay the bills, but Lauren had a funny way of looking at things. She put Renee in daycare full time and expected James to pay for it out of his check along with all the other household bills. After all, Renee was his daughter too, she would say. Her check would be her play money. So her job ended up costing James over one hundred dollars a week.

As much as I didn't want to interfere, I did try to talk to her once about cutting the hours Renee was in daycare or using some of her paycheck to buy groceries.

"That's what I did when I was your age with young

kids," I said.

Shortly after she left, my phone rang. James was asking in a slightly raised voice what I had just said to his wife. I learned to mind my own business when it came to their marriage, but I knew the stress was taking a toll on my son.

At about that same time, James and Paul were working on an installation at a school for at-risk kids in the area. It was a big job, and they had set aside a week to finish it. Paul called me at the office and asked if I had seen James.

"No, I haven't seen him all day," I answered. "Isn't he with you?"

"He was, but he left to get a part. He's been gone for three hours." Concern and frustration were in his voice. "I can't do anything else until he comes back with the part. I'm dead in the water here, and we have to get this done."

"Did you try his phone?" I asked.

"Of course I did!" he shouted.

It seemed every time one of the kids messed up, it was my fault.

"I'm sure he'll turn up," I said holding back the tears that stung my eyes. "Someone's coming in, I have to go," I lied and hung up the phone. I couldn't handle his yelling while I was trying to do my own job. I told myself James was his problem.

James eventually showed up with some kind of excuse about his phone being dead and having to go to a bunch of different suppliers to find the part. It was a common part everyone usually had. Paul let it slide. They had a job to get done.

Things went along like that for a while. They would need a part, and James would volunteer to get it and be gone for hours. Paul tried to make sure they had every possible part they might need, and when James still found something he needed in town, Paul had Kylie drive in to get it. She was usually gone less than an hour and a half.

Paul was trying everything he could think of to get James to be more responsible and productive. He worked side by side with him. He talked to him about sticking with a job until it's done.

"Take pride in your work," he would say. And of course, Paul's old standby, "Do it right the first time so you never have to do it again."

When James didn't listen to his pleas, Paul yelled at him. It still didn't work.

It seemed that James just didn't care like he used to. Was the job too stressful, we wondered? Maybe his marriage was not going well. Money problems? What was turning our normally happy, dependable, and capable son into a stranger who would avoid work and us? He would find excuses to leave or lock himself in his office for hours.

As he came out of his office one day to go home, I asked if he was feeling okay.

"You look tired. Is everything all right?"

His eyes were half closed, and he tripped as he walked by my desk.

He gave me the typical brush off. "I'm fine, I just didn't sleep well last night." Then he left.

My gut told me something was wrong. My daughter told me what it was.

"He's high," she said. Point blank. She didn't beat around the bush. No... "Maybe he's high," or "He could be high," or even, "Do you think he's high?" There was no question in her voice. She knew.

I felt like someone punched me in the stomach.

"How do you know? Are you sure? How can you

41

tell?" I asked, but deep down I knew she was right.

All the pieces of the puzzle fell into place. Leaving for hours at a time, locking himself in his office, calling in sick, distracted and moody, not caring about the work. It all made sense. My son was doing drugs.

I had never seen Kylie high. I had only seen her the next day, sick, upset, and ashamed. I had just seen my son "high." I didn't like it. It wouldn't be the last time.

"Pain pills?" I asked. "Oxys?" I was a pro now, I thought, depressed.

"I don't know. Come with me."

I followed Kylie to James' office. The door was locked.

"I'll be right back." She left and quickly came back with an old beat-up credit card. She opened the door in less than thirty seconds.

"Where did you learn how to do that?" I asked in disbelief.

How much did I not know about my daughter?

She smiled that mischievous smile of her dad's that I adore.

"Dad taught me." She suppressed a laugh when she saw the shocked look on my face.

How much did I not know about my husband?

"He wanted to make sure I never got locked out of my apartment. He even gave me the card," she explained, twirling the beat up card through her fingers.

She was definitely her father's daughter. And he loved her. What other dad would teach his daughter how to break into a home?

James' office was a mess, although it was never very neat. There were parts manuals and proposals spread all over the desk and file cabinets. Trash littered the floor. Two empty coffee cups sat in the middle of the desk on top of the newest proposal he was supposed to be working on.

Kylie started rummaging through the papers, looking under them all. I stood by the door and watched wondering what she was looking for.

She found it in the bottom right-hand drawer of the desk. She lifted out a spoon.

"Exactly what I was afraid of," she said.

"A spoon?"

"A bent spoon," she corrected me.

It was indeed bent at an awkward angle.

She sat the spoon on the desk to show me why. The bend in the handle caused the bowl of the spoon to remain level keeping anything in the spoon from spilling.

"Drug users do this so they can mix the powdered heroin with water in the bowl of the spoon and have two hands free to use the plunger on the needle to suck it up. Then they inject it into a vein in one of their arms."

I was getting another lesson.

"He's definitely doing heroin," Kylie continued. "If it was coke, there would be two spoons, and one would be all black."

"What?"

"Never mind. It's heroin, just what I thought. I could tell by his eyes."

"What about his eyes?"

"All sleepy looking. Half closed. They look like they're rolling in the back of his head," she explained.

I had seen it.

"Heroin and oxys are opiates," she went on. "They're downers. They make you sleepy."

"Why would someone want to be sleepy all the time?" I asked my teacher.

"They don't only make you sleepy. They make you feel good. Like everything is all right with the world. No

43

worries or stress. All will be fine. Sort of like that."

As I listened to her, I wondered if she had known or suspected before. Had she confronted him? Had she kept his secret? I wouldn't put her on the spot. I wouldn't ask. I had been there.

We stood in silence. Staring at the spoon sitting on the desk as if it was the enemy. There was no doubt. My son was using heroin.

"What do we do now?" we said at the same time.

"I don't know," I answered for both of us.

We walked out of James' office together, locking the door behind us. I took the spoon.

We quietly closed up the office. I said goodbye to Kylie and headed home. As I drove, I asked myself, how could this happen? How could both of my seemingly normal children get involved in drugs? What causes them to potentially throw away their futures? Especially James. He had a family, a great career, and a sister who was still struggling with her own addiction. Why would he even start? What was he thinking? I was angry and hurt. How could he do this to himself? To us? To me?

James is the brains behind the service end of the business. We have just hired Sam, my stepson. He is six years older than James, but James is definitely more educated about the installation and repair of furnaces, our bread and butter. Sam is a plumber. We are hoping to expand and become a full-service plumbing and heating business. We need both boys to do this.

How was I going to tell my husband? "Guess what, Honey, both our kids are drug addicts." I wanted to run away. This was not a conversation I was looking forward to.

As I pulled into the driveway, I saw Paul out with our dogs.

"I was thinking of taking them for a walk. Do you

want to come?" he asked as I got out of the car.

"Sure, I'll grab the leashes. Do you want a beer?" I waited for the usual response.

"Yes. Actually, I think it's a two-beer walk!" he yelled over his shoulder as I walked past him and into the house. It was a running joke between us.

We had fallen into an evening routine years ago. We had two little Shih Tzu dogs. They were our babies. We got Shadow, our all black male, when Kylie turned five. I think I was having that "empty lap syndrome" and needed a baby. We felt at five and seven the kids were old enough to take care of a dog, and Paul's brother and sister had Shih Tzus. So it was decided we would get the same breed. I'll never forget the day before I headed up north to pick up Shadow from the breeder. Paul pulled me aside and said, "I'm not sure about this. Don't you think we should get a real dog?" We still laugh about that today long after their passing. They both lived for more than eighteen years.

Shadow was the runt and fit in the palm of Paul's hand when we got him. I watched as the other dogs in the litter peed on him, but I fell in love immediately. His bigger litter mates also chewed on the end of his tail causing the hair to fall off. The breeder actually said if it didn't grow back we could return him. I gave Shadow a quick bath before Paul got home and hoped for the best. Would he be "real" enough for Paul? He looked more like a rat than a dog at that point, but it was love at first sight. Shadow was Paul's dog, and no one else's.

A year and a half later we would get Pebbles, our female, for the kids we said, but really it was for Shadow to have someone to play with. For the first few years, Kylie played with Pebbles a lot, on many occasions dressing her up in baby clothes and diapers and pushing her around in a baby stroller. But in reality, Pebbles was my dog, my new baby.

45

So, we would come home after work and take the dogs for a walk. Not just an average walk, these were great times. Our yard was fenced so they could go outside anytime, but when we got the leashes out, they went crazy. We lived on a long dirt road that was pretty much deserted except in the summer, so we would grab a beer or two for the walk. Paul would often look at me and ask, "Is this a one beer walk or two?" He usually took two, just in case.

Shadow would run as fast as his little legs would take him. He looked like superman with his front and back legs stretched out parallel to the ground, his tail pointed straight back as well. We walked, or should I say ran, about a half mile up the road, then back. Shadow would not slow down even going up the very steep hill at the end. He was a trooper and he loved it. He ran straight through puddles, and if he had to poop, he did while he ran, never stopping. Paul would yell back to me, "Land mines, look out!" He was referring to the three or four little poops I was about to step on in the middle of the road.

Pebbles couldn't keep up with him, but the walk back was much slower, and they played with each other, stopping to sniff everything in their path and chasing the occasional squirrel the way dogs do. We had many long conversations during this part of the walk. It was a great time, and we did it as often as possible. As long as there was no snow on the road and it wasn't too cold, we took them for a walk.

As we walked the slow walk back, I contemplated telling Paul about James. I couldn't. The words just wouldn't come out. How could I ruin this beautiful, peaceful evening? How could I break Paul's heart? I knew he would be heartbroken. Just like me, he would have the whole range of emotions. Anger, fear, let-down, pity, helplessness, embarrassment, and on and on. And then there would be the questions... What was he thinking? Why? How could he?

Finally, and most important... What can we do to help him?
I'd tell him tomorrow.

"Paul, we need to talk." No one ever wants to hear those dreaded words. They invariably signal something you don't want to be told, and I knew Paul did not want to hear this. I couldn't put it off any longer.

"Oh no, I hate those words," he mumbled under his breath as he followed me into his office the next morning. He had just come in after getting the drivers off for their oil deliveries.

He sat down behind the desk he used for running what had become his end of the business. Ordering parts, scheduling installations, and coordinating all the service calls. And now he would say "putting out fires."

I sat in the chair in front of the desk and waited while he put a few things away. I wrestled with the words. I had been thinking of how I was going to tell him all night. I hadn't been able to sleep, my mind running in a thousand different directions. What would we do? Could we still run the business? Would he get better fast once we confronted him? Could he beat this thing? Was he addicted? Could he stop? The same questions I knew Paul would soon have. I didn't have any answers. How do you tell someone his son is shooting up heroin? I had never discussed the details of Kylie's addiction with him. I tried to sugarcoat it. Should I do the same now? Could I? Would that only make it harder if it all came out at a worse time?

"Well?" he said.

I didn't realize I had been in another world.

"I've got work to do so if you need to talk, talk," he continued, already in a bad mood. Stress. It was about to get worse.

"James is shooting up heroin." I blurted it out. No sugarcoating I guess, the words just came out. So much for trying to prepare him.

I waited for his reaction. He didn't say anything for a while, letting it sink in I figured. I knew he was hurt. How could his son let him down like this? He had such high hopes.

"I knew he wasn't right, but I never imagined that," he finally said. "Are you sure?"

"Yes. Kylie and I found a bent spoon in his office. By the way, thanks for teaching her how to break in with a credit card. It came in handy." A small attempt to lighten the moment.

He smiled for a second, but now wasn't the time for humor. "A bent spoon?"

"Never mind, I'll tell you about it some other time. It's just proof he is shooting up, and it's heroin. He has all the signs, too. It explains a lot."

"That's great! What do we do now?" Reality was sinking in.

"I don't know," I said quietly.

"What do you mean, you don't know? You've been through this before. You should have all the answers. You ALWAYS have all the answers! Can't you fix this? Can't you fix him?"

"I don't have all the answers. I never did." I was getting a little louder myself. We were both trying to keep our cool as we felt ourselves fighting a losing battle with drugs. We were still hoping for the best with Kylie. She was nearing the end of her treatment, I hoped. How much longer could she stay on methadone? Now we were faced with the beginning of another battle against unknown forces. Evil forces that had attacked our son.

"Is he here yet?"

"I haven't seen him this morning. I was hoping he was with you." I was hoping he was with his father, but I was not surprised he wasn't.

"Call him! Get him in here now!" He put his head in his hands as I walked out of the room.

"Great job," I told myself. "You could have handled that better." But how, what is the best way to tell a father his son is a heroin addict?

I picked up the phone to call James, knowing he probably wouldn't answer. He was either at the office really early or not at all. The phone rang several times until his voice mail picked up. "James, call me as soon as you get this." I hung up knowing there was a good chance it would be hours before he called. I might not hear from him until tomorrow. That's how bad things had gotten.

"How did it go?" Kylie whispered from her end of our long workstation.

Paul and James had built the workstation for us this past summer. It was about ten feet long with a lower section for us to sit at, desk height, and an upper part, bar height, for customers to write checks on. It kept a lot of the office equipment concealed under the top counter and gave the office a neater, more professional look. There was plenty of room for two computers and a shared printer in between.

The workstation was made of knotty pine tongue and groove boards with black laminate counters. James had worked briefly for a countertop maker, so he and Paul laminated the tops. We had a lot of laughs during that time, especially when the laminate would not stay down. We were getting areas where it would lift up, so we'd set books or anything heavy on the spot hoping to fix it. Then, sure enough, it would lift in another area. We didn't tell James at

49

first because he was so proud of the laminate job, and we didn't want to hurt his feelings. When he finally saw a lifted spot a few days later, he was able to fix it easily by rewarming the glue underneath with a blow dryer. Then he put some heavy books on the spot, and it never lifted again. We loved it!

Kylie and I then went and picked out pictures to go on the wall behind the workstation and on the opposite wall above the small sofa and chair. We decided on black and white pictures of flowers. They had black frames with white matting. I had hoped to do all of this the summer Kylie was struggling with her addiction. I wanted her involved so I waited. Our new office finally looked great. It was a family accomplishment.

So now I leaned over that lovingly made station and whispered back to Kylie, "Not good."

"What are you going to do?" she asked, no longer whispering. There was no need. Paul had left.

"I don't know, any ideas?"

"How about the outpatient clinic at the New Beginnings Rehab? He may have to detox first. It all depends on how much he's been using and for how long."

There were those words again, detox and rehab. And the questions. How long? How much? It had been only a year and a half since I had been at the New Beginnings Rehab with Kylie. It hadn't worked for her.

Maybe it would work for James. I was trying to stay positive, but I was drained. I did not want to go through this again. It wasn't fair. I was about to have a pity party. I had to snap out of it. As I sat there staring into space, Kylie came over and gave me a hug. One of the perks you get when you work with family.

Then the phone rang, and it was back to business. The problems of my son put aside for now. I would deal with him when I could catch him, but we had a business to run.

I didn't see James until the next morning. Lauren had called later that morning to say James was sick. I wasn't surprised.

When James walked into the office the next day with an apology and some lame excuse about the flu, we ushered him into his dad's office and told him to sit.

"We need to talk," I said. I hoped that made him nervous.

How do we start? We had closed the office door for privacy. Kylie could handle the customers.

"What's going on, James?" Paul began.

"I had the flu."

Nice try I thought. It was not going to work.

"The flu, that's all? For the last couple of months?" Paul had told me last night he thought it may have been going on a lot longer than that. Not always, like now, but there had been times when he suspected something was not quite right. Then he'd come out of it.

"Not the last couple of months, but yes, the last few weeks I've had the flu," James said defensively.

"That's it, nothing else is going on?" For some reason, Paul wanted James to tell us himself.

"No, nothing else. I have to go now." He started to stand.

Paul glared at him and said, "Sit!"

He did.

"You are not leaving this room until we figure out what's going on with you, and if you still have a place in this company." Paul didn't mince words. It needed to be said, and it certainly got James' attention.

He sat a little straighter. He took a drink of the coffee

he was still holding. I knew he was trying to stall for time while he pulled himself together. His emotions often betrayed him just like mine. He was a sensitive kid. I should say adult, but he was still a kid to me. My heart ached for him. We waited.

He tried one more time. "I don't know what you're talking about."

Paul quietly said, "Yes, you do."

And that was it. His lip quivered and he started to cry. Nothing more needed to be said right then. He had said it all. Now we needed to figure out how to move forward.

At that time, Kylie knocked on the door. There was a call for Paul that couldn't wait. Probably another fire to put out. James grabbed the opportunity to sneak off to his own office. I let him. He needed to pull himself together, so we could talk some more now that everything was out in the open.

After a few minutes, I sent Kylie to talk to him. They have always been close, sometimes closer than others, but working together had brought them even closer recently. Now they had something else in common. Would she be able to help him? Maybe he would open up to her.

"Tell him we need to talk when he's ready," I said as she left.

"Kylie is smart about this stuff," I told myself. "She has been in counseling for over a year. Her favorite TV show is 'Intervention.' I'm sure she can help. She can teach him about the triggers and the receptors in the brain. He'll listen to her. Won't he?"

Kylie was gone a long time. She wasn't smiling when she came back.

"How did it go? Did he talk to you? Is he going to

quit?" Please just tell me something positive, I wanted to scream.

She sat down, took a deep breath, and said, "I don't know, I'm worried."

Not what I wanted to hear. "That bad?"

She shook her head yes.

It was mid-morning. The day was flying by, and it was December. The phones were ringing, bills had to be paid, tickets printed, schedules made, deposits taken to the bank, and so on. Business did not stop. James was in his office, hopefully working on a proposal. We would deal with him later. I didn't know what Paul was going to do without his help. But Paul was very smart and a quick learner. He'd been working with James on and off for a couple of years now and with Sam to help, I was sure he'd manage. I couldn't think about that now.

A little later, Kylie went to the post office and came back with a stack of bills, checks, and a letter from Tom, her convict friend (not boyfriend, just friend). She was getting two or three letters a week and responding to every one, all the time assuring him and me they were only friends. I was beginning to doubt her resolve. I think she was starting to melt a little, and I wasn't sure how I felt about that.

She read the letter aloud when the office quieted down. It was comical and endearing. He was getting out the first of January and would be staying at the Tranquility House in the city for three months. He could come and go as he pleased, but he had to be there every night and attend many classes and meetings, especially AA meetings. Tom wrote that they wanted him to attend ninety meetings in ninety days. That was their goal for the people who stayed there. He would do it. He was determined to turn his life around. He knew Kylie didn't want to be more than friends, he said, but he hoped she would come to visit him. I thought he hoped for more.

"What do I do?" she asked me. "What do I tell him?"

"What do you want to do?" I asked back.

"I don't knooowww," she whined and buried her head in her hands.

I laughed. She was so dramatic. She laughed with me. It felt good. We may have laughed too long. We still had a major problem facing us.

Paul and I went to James' office later that afternoon. He hadn't come out much. I was sure he was embarrassed and afraid of what we were going to do. At this point, we didn't know the answer to that question ourselves, but we had to start somewhere. We hoped we could figure it out together, now that there were no secrets.

"Hi, James. Can we talk?" Paul asked as he knocked on the door.

"Sure, Dad. Come in."

Paul stepped into his office.

"Hi, Hon," I said as I followed Paul through the door. "How are you doing?" I gave him a hug.

"We can't go on this way. You can't go on this way. What do you suggest we do?" Paul was putting the question directly to James.

"I don't know. I didn't mean to do this." His hands were shaky. He may have been withdrawing. "I will stop, I promise. Please give me another chance? I swear I'm done."

"Do you need to detox?" I asked him using my new vocabulary I was beginning to hate.

"I think I can do it myself. Give me the weekend. I'll be fine by Monday."

It was Friday afternoon. We could wait until Monday, but he was going to have to straighten out. He was put on notice, and we would be watching.

"Do you need counseling? The rehab center has

outpatient services. Half days for two weeks." I was not convinced he could do this on his own. Kylie hadn't been able to. If I could get him into counseling, perhaps we could keep him from reverting back to the drugs. I hadn't mentioned to anyone about the incident in October. He had already failed once.

"I can't lose him for two weeks," Paul insisted. "We're so far behind now because of the last few months."

"I don't need the rehab. I'll be fine. You'll see." He stood up to leave. "Can I go home now?"

"Show up Monday morning, clean and ready to work. If you can't do that, don't show up at all," Paul said sounding tired but firm.

We left his office together. James grabbed his coat and said goodbye to Kylie.

As James was walking out the door, Paul yelled from where he stood in the back of the office, "Don't let me down!"

"Don't worry, I won't," James yelled back as he closed the door behind him.

"Do you think he can do it?" The question came from Paul directed at both Kylie and me.

Neither of us answered. We looked at each other with a slight shrug.

"That's what I thought." Paul walked into his office and closed the door.

"What do you really think?" I asked Kylie.

"It's anybody's guess. Some people can stop on their own. Just like that. But you have to be incredibly strong and have a lot to lose. Most people will justify just one more time. 'Nobody will know.'... 'I can handle it.'... 'I deserve it.'... 'One last time.'.... And it goes on and on."

We sat in silence for a while finishing our individual jobs, getting ready to close the office.

"I don't think he's strong enough," Kylie said as I was leaving for the weekend.

"Neither do I," I sighed. "Neither do I."

Driving home again, I realized it had only been forty-eight hours since Kylie had found the spoon. That awful bent spoon that would erase all doubt. It felt like a lifetime ago. The reality was also setting in that I never should have bailed him out in October. I should have gone straight to Paul then. Maybe we wouldn't be in this position now. Would Paul have given him the money? If he didn't, would James have gotten beat up or worse? If they had beat him up, would he have stopped and never done it again? Too many questions, what if's, and if only's. No answers. I wanted a drink.

Chapter five

It was a long weekend. We tried to enjoy it as best we could. It was mild so there weren't any no-heat calls. Christmas was two weeks away. I loved shopping for Renee. Having a two-year-old grandchild at Christmas was going to be fun. But my heart wasn't really into it yet. Thanksgiving had been a disaster, and I was worried about the next get-together.

Kylie and Lauren were not getting along. I think Lauren blamed Kylie for having to move out of the apartment. Lauren had loved it there. She loved being in the middle of everything, but it was ultimately her and James' own fault they weren't still there. Part of me wanted to tell her the truth. Maybe it needed to be said. "If you had cared a little about the place, taken the time and effort to keep it clean, and paid the rent, you may still be there!" I wanted to scream, but that would have made matters worse. She still would have resented Kylie for being there and hated me at the same time.

Kylie was not exactly fond of Lauren either. She resented the way "she pushed herself on the family," as Kylie put it. "She's trying to take my place. I'm your daughter, she's not," she would often tell me. "Lauren's doing the same with my aunts and uncles too. She has her own family. She doesn't need mine."

Lauren did have a way of rubbing people the wrong way. I often felt sorry for her. I thought she meant well but lacked the social skills necessary to carry on a conversation. Like with her housework and her finances, she just didn't see things the way others did.

So Thanksgiving had been a disaster. James and I played referee or tried to keep the girls separated. I was dreading Christmas.

I was also worried about James. Paul and I talked about it some over the weekend, but we mostly just wanted to forget about work and James for a couple days. We knew we would probably be working six or even seven days a week pretty soon, and we were always on call, so we valued what little time we had.

On Saturday, late in the afternoon, we sat on our deck in the Adirondack chairs I had painted green to match the trim on the house. Paul had painted the house a very dark brown with a forest green trim last summer. We loved it. It made the house blend in with the woods and added to the natural setting. The lake looked like glass this afternoon, so we grabbed a couple glasses of wine to watch the sunset. This time of year, the sun sets so early in this part of the country we rarely got home to see it setting over the lake.

Paul and I have been together so long that more often than not, we can enjoy the scenery and peacefulness in complete silence without that awkward feeling of needing to fill the silence with words. This was one of those times. The sunset was breathtaking across the glassy water. I will never forget how lucky we were to be able to enjoy it all year round from our home.

However, my thoughts still drifted back to my children. How could both of my children get involved in drugs as adults? I thought once they were past those rough teen years everything would be fine. What happened? Where did we go wrong?

***

Monday morning James showed up for work on time. He looked normal. Maybe a little thinner but pretty good, and his easy smile was back. Maybe this was the end of it. I wanted to believe.

"How are you this morning?" I asked as he passed by on his way to Paul's office with a handful of papers.

"Better. I told you I could do it myself."

"Make sure you keep it up. We missed you."

"Welcome back," I said to myself, "now please stick around."

I hadn't realized how much I'd missed him. He had become a different person, a stranger. But he was back, and he would be okay. Again, I dared to hope.

By Wednesday my hope was dwindling. I was seeing a little stress in his manner. I couldn't put my finger on it exactly, but I knew he wasn't as happy as he had been. And then it happened.

"Mom, I need your help."

"Not again," I whined to myself. Those dreaded words. Somehow they're different when they come from your twenty-three-year-old child. It's one thing to have a three-year-old ask, "Mom, I need your help. I can't tie my shoe." I was finding it very unsettling coming from my children now. They were adults.

"Sure, Hon. What do you need?" I asked. I wanted to scream, "What is it now?" But I kept calm and followed him into his office.

It was a little tidier than the other day but not much. He closed the door behind me. Not good. This can't be good.

It wasn't.

He was fine, he said, "Don't worry, I'm not doing drugs."

I must not have been as calm as I thought.

"It's just that… I haven't paid my mortgage," he said stumbling over the words.

"How late are you?" We had preached to the kids from an early age about the importance of good credit.

"I haven't made the November payment yet."

He had been able to buy his first house before his twentieth birthday because of his credit. Now he was closing in on a "sixty-day late" blemish on his credit report. The bank extended him a huge line of credit on that home less than a year after he bought the house. He never asked for it. They just sent him a letter saying he qualified for it. Paul and I didn't even know about the credit line until after all the paperwork had been done. We were furious. That was like giving someone a blank check. We talked and talked about not using it. "Save it for a rainy day."… "Use it responsibly."… and so on. I knew with the wedding, the baby, and the moves, he had used some but surely not all of it.

"Can you borrow from your credit line just this one time until you get back on your feet?" I was wondering why I hadn't thought of that the last time he asked for money.

"It's maxed out," he told me.

I knew he was embarrassed to say so, and he knew I was shocked.

"There's none left?"

"No."

He went on about the closing on the new house, the baby, daycare, furniture, and other things, but I was barely listening. Kylie mentioned they went out to dinner a lot, too. Lauren didn't like to cook almost as much as she didn't like to clean. I had watched Renee when Lauren went to Cancun with her sister. Had that come out of the credit line as well? I was sure it was something like twenty-five or thirty thousand dollars. How could it all be gone? Had he spent it on drugs?

I had to restrict the amount he could charge on the company credit card because he was charging expensive dinners out, and both boys, Sam and James, had charged up over a thousand dollars on snowmobile parts last month, always promising to pay it back but never following through. The last straw was when I had a receipt signed by Lauren for dinner at an expensive restaurant, and I knew James was not even with her that night. They were taking advantage of us. The amounts had been reduced to cover only gas and only for the company vehicles. We had credit at most of the places that carried the parts we used. If they abused the cards again, Paul told them, we would cancel them completely and figure out someway to gas up the vehicles before they left the shop.

So, I stood in that office face to face with my son, who was proving he was not handling money very well, and I had to make a decision. If I gave him money for the mortgage, would he even pay it? Would he pay me back? I didn't think so. If I didn't give it to him, would the stress of not paying his mortgage add to the stress he was already under and lead him back to drugs so he would "feel like everything is all right with the world, no worries, no stress" to use Kylie's words? The counselors had told Kylie she needed to be stress free to be successful when she came off the methadone. Would I be contributing to my son's failure?

Then I thought about my granddaughter. What would happen to her if they lost their home? I couldn't put Renee out on the street. I knew that wouldn't exactly happen. They would always have a place to stay, but it wouldn't be home. She wouldn't have her room and the big girl bed I had already bought her for Christmas. I had the headboard, frame, mattress, box spring, waterproof mattress pad, sheets, pillows, and even an adorable little girl quilt. I caved.

"Look, James, I don't know what you think, but we

are not made of money." I think I had said this before many times when he was a teenager. "I know you see the money coming into this company, but you don't see it going out. When all is said and done, we make a very small profit. We can't bleed money from this company and have enough to survive the slow times. Sometimes, our margins are so small we barely break even. We have put so much of our own money into this company. I can't just hand you money every time you make a bad decision."

Who was I kidding? I had already made my decision, but I felt a lecture was important. At least it would make me feel better. He was shaking his head with the right amount of "I knows." He wasn't listening. I should have tried to trip him up, I thought afterward. Say something ridiculous and see if he just kept shaking his head. But it wasn't a time for jokes.

"I'll pay you back, I promise. I know I said it before," he said, adding the last part knowing I was about to say it. "But this time is different."

"How is it different, James? You and Lauren have been spending money like crazy."

"Lauren has nothing to do with this. It's all my fault." He always defended her.

"Okay," I said after a long moment of silence. "I will pay your mortgage this one time, but you have another payment coming right up. You will have to pay that yourself. I'll write the check out to the mortgage company. If you stay sober and drug-free, you don't have to pay me back. Consider it a Christmas gift, but this is absolutely the last time." I was trying to be firm, but I knew if he tried to pay it back he would not be able to pay the next one. I wanted so much for him to stay drug-free that I probably would have paid all his bills.

"Thanks, I won't let you down," he said quietly, not

quite as exuberant as the last time.

"You better not. I'm sticking my neck out for you." I agreed once more to not tell Dad as long as he followed through with his end of the deal. He promised again, gave me a hug, and I left feeling I may have made another big mistake.

I reasoned that if he was productive, the business would make that up in no time. If he failed to stay clean, I would talk with Paul. I wanted to give him the chance to save face. I loved him.

When I came back to sit at my desk, Kylie asked what was going on. Now I had to lie to my daughter. I was not going to tell Paul unless James failed, but Paul would have no reason to ask. So it wasn't really a lie. Right? I hate to lie, and I'm not good at it. What was I getting into?

"Nothing, Sweetie, we were just talking." She was always my Sweetie. I hated keeping something from her, but I hoped James would make it, and I didn't want her to think less of her brother. "Did I miss anything important?" I said, changing the subject.

"No, but I got another letter from Tom."

She proceeded to read it to me. He had written another poem for her. Tom certainly had a way with words, and we laughed again. He was keeping us entertained. She was falling for him. I knew that even if she didn't.

I would not interfere. I would not push her towards him or away. She was an adult. I had no way of knowing if he would be the best thing for her or the worst. She would have to make that decision, and I would stand by her choice.

It would be another week before I started to worry about James again. Little things at first. Staying in his office longer than usual. Unexplained trips to the store. I didn't notice anything different in his eyes, but I was getting that sick feeling telling me something wasn't right. He was looking thinner especially in his face.

"Mom, I hate to say this, but I think something's going on with James," Kylie whispered to me one morning at the office.

"Do you think it's drugs again?" I asked already knowing the answer.

"I don't know for sure. Maybe he's sick. Maybe depressed. I know I would be if I lived with that...." She looked at me and bit her tongue. "Woman."

She and Lauren were still not getting along although Lauren pretended to get along fine with her when I was around. Kylie told me recently about some pretty disturbing things going on between James and Lauren.

"She never cooks or cleans and she goes out with her friends all the time leaving Renee with James. She's always yelling at him, and he just takes it. He doesn't deserve to be treated that way."

Kylie could be extremely protective of her brother. Even though he was older, she has always been a little more worldly. They had a unique relationship. He was always there to protect her physically, so no one messed with Kylie if he was around, but Kylie protected James' feelings and tried to guide him in social situations. Kylie was sure Lauren was only using James and was not really in love with him. I was beginning to worry the stress in the marriage was turning him back to drugs.

"Can you talk to him?" I asked Kylie.

"I can try, but if he is doing drugs, he's not going to tell me. Unless he's caught red handed, he'll continue to deny it."

"He won't be able to deny it much longer. Your father's getting pretty frustrated with him. He said he messed up a big job, and we're going to lose our shirt. Your dad thinks it could be an honest mistake, but I'm not so sure."

So I was left feeling that James may be sick, depressed, distracted by his home life, or doing drugs. I felt it was probably a combination of all those things and was at a loss as to how to help. Giving money and threatening had not worked.

As I was lost in my thoughts, Kylie decided to find proof. She searched his office, his coat pockets, and even his laptop case. Nothing. He was either clean or getting smarter.

He was getting smarter.

Christmas was Saturday, two days away. I had decided not to have a sit-down meal but rather finger food. I was concerned that the tension at the table would be too much to handle. Paul was sure that James was back to using drugs. Kylie was sure that Lauren was the cause, and James was denying both. I just wanted to get through the day.

Kylie was continuing to search for evidence with no luck. We were both watching his eyes. After he talked to us and left, we would look at each other and shrug. Maybe, maybe not, but he was continuing to get thinner.

And then it happened. Kylie found a needle. James was indeed getting smart. The needle was in his jacket but not in the pocket. He had put a small hole in the lining of the coat and was able to put a needle through it. The needle fell to the bottom of the coat inside the lining. Searching only his pockets didn't result in anything, but if you felt along the bottom of the coat, you could feel the needle. Kylie showed me where it was. There was our proof, but what do we do with it?

James had been in the bathroom, his coat laid over a chair. He returned before I had a chance to gather my thoughts. Kylie, on the other hand, jumped right in.

"I found a needle in your coat," she confronted James.

"There's no needle in my coat. What were you doing with my coat anyway?" He recovered quickly.

"I was looking for proof because something is definitely going on with you!" Kylie was not one to back down.

"Well, I'm fine, I'm not doing anything! Mind your own business!"

"So explain the needle! What's it for?"

They were yelling at each other now, and the phone rang.

"Shh! Go in the other room and talk," I interrupted.

"There's nothing to talk about!" James grabbed his coat and slammed the door on his way out.

"That went over well," I said to Kylie as I grabbed the phone.

"No one likes to be caught," Kylie quietly replied as she sat back down to work.

Chapter Six

Our concern over James was taking a toll on the quality of our work. I could see it happening. We were never done at the end of the day. We were making mistakes. A ticket that didn't get printed, a service call overlooked for hours, addition mistakes on deposits. Fortunately, Paul had insisted we write each call down in a separate square in a notebook. Kylie had taken two notebooks and drawn a line down the middle of each page and eight lines across. We could document sixteen calls per page. Of course, the lines were all different colors, mostly pinks and purples, but the system worked. We were able to go through all the pages at the end of the day to make sure everything was taken care of. This system saved us from having many dissatisfied customers, but it was not fail-proof.

It seemed more and more things were overlooked, and we were scrambling at the end of the day to fix problems. The price of oil had risen to its highest level ever and was projected to keep rising, making it difficult for most people to keep up with their bill. Our receivables were at an all-time high, and winter had just begun.

I was struggling to make sure the oil we purchased was paid for in the time allowed. If it was not paid in ten days, we could not buy more, and we would be out of business. Collecting money was becoming a huge priority, and it was not one of my strongest attributes. Kylie, on the other hand, was good at it, but I didn't think anyone could collect money from people who just didn't have it. I was scrambling at the end of every day to make sure the checks I sent out for oil were covered by the deposits we made. This time of year was always difficult. I was sure that in a few weeks the profit on the oil delivered in December would create a buffer in our account to make up for the slow payers. I knew we would be okay, we usually were, but it was an especially difficult year.

Paul was struggling to stay sane, too. He was still trying to work with James, but more and more he was turning to Sam. There was always an issue with a driver or a truck that needed his attention as well. I didn't want to bother him with finances at this time.

So, on this day before Christmas Eve, the needle found in James' coat took a back seat for the rest of the day. We would work most of tomorrow depending on calls for oil. A lot of people wait until the last minute to order before a long weekend, so it most likely would not be an early day. Sometime over the weekend, I would confront James. I knew I would also have to tell Paul, but it probably wouldn't come as a surprise. I hoped to get through Christmas first. I didn't care so much about the adults, but I was looking forward to having Renee over.

I told Kylie my plan to get through the holiday first, and she agreed. She loved Christmas and had decorated the office and her apartment in all pastel decorations. None of the typical reds and greens. She hated those colors. I loved what she had done. Kylie was not afraid to be different.

We got through Christmas Eve without too much trouble, but Christmas would not be as easy. Kylie and Lauren were barely speaking although they were trying not to let anyone know. Paul and James talked a little about work, but it was obvious things had changed between them. Renee loved her new toys and the bed I insisted we set up in the living room.

Kylie was keeping a close eye on James. At one time, she pointed out that he was in the bathroom.

"He's been in there for a long time," she said.

"So? Maybe it's taking a while." I couldn't believe she had noticed.

"I think he's doing something else," she whispered.

"What? In there? In our house?"

"It's the perfect place. You can lock the door and no one will barge in. You watch when he comes out."

She was right. He came out a short time later, and there was no doubt his eyes were different. He would pass it off as being tired, but I knew better now. After he, Lauren, and Renee left to go next door to his uncle's, Kylie took me into the bathroom and showed me remnants of powder on the counter. She looked under the sink and found a spoon. An old one from my drawer. It had the now familiar bend.

I was stunned. In my own house on Christmas Day, with his family in the other room. How could he?

Kylie was just as angry. I insisted, however, she keep her cool until tomorrow or Monday. It was Christmas after all.

Going to visit Uncle Keith on Christmas may have been the best thing James could have done. Paul's brother, Keith, and his wife, Karen, are born again Christians and attend the church that James has been going to since his marriage. His father-in-law also attends the same church. James hadn't been to church for a few weeks, so I was sure Keith was shocked to see James' weight loss, and James' eyes probably made Keith suspicious as well. Trying to help, Keith asked James to go to church with him the next day and James agreed.

When James and his family came back over to pick up their gifts and say goodbye, he told me about going to church.

"Uncle Keith wants me to go up for prayers so he can pray over me," he told me as he was leaving. He had that little sheepish grin. "He wants to save me."

"Good, because you certainly need saving right about now," I said maybe a little too harshly. Maybe church would help. He could use all the prayers he could get. Mine certainly weren't helping.

I have been a Christian for as long as I remember. There has never been any doubt about the existence of God and his son, Jesus, in my mind. However, I have not been to church, except for special occasions, since I was a teenager. I had a very happy childhood, but my parents did not agree on one thing, religion. They came from different faiths, both Christian, and they had very different ideas about how to practice one's religion. It was one of only a few things my parents ever argued about. I vowed never to let that happen in my marriage. I raised my kids to believe in God and Jesus, but we rarely went to church. Paul was raised catholic, parochial schools and all, but he rarely went to church either once he became an adult. We tried to have the children baptized when they were young, but the priest said he would not baptize them unless we promised to attend church every week. We walked out of that meeting and never went back.

I was happy when James began attending church after his marriage to Lauren. They went as a family, even having little Renee "dedicated" as they do to infants at this church. Paul and I attended the ceremony, and it was lovely. One of the few times we had gone to church as a family in years. Baptism would wait until the child was old enough to understand and make a commitment to God.

So as they drove away on that Christmas Day, I was left with mixed feelings. Obviously, James was getting worse, and everyone who saw him would know something was wrong. Stepping up for prayers in church, I hoped, would be the beginning of the healing, but his addiction would be known by everyone there, and many of them were our customers.

The questions and sympathies would come. I had failed to keep this just among us. Once again, I would have to face my extended family and good friends and explain that my child was addicted to drugs. If he didn't start to look better quickly, I was sure customers would be asking about him, too. I was being selfish right then. I was worried about how I would look, about how his addiction would affect me, Paul, Kylie, and our company. I needed to snap out of it and do what was necessary to help my son. If I only knew what that was.

As I expected, Keith came over to the house the next day after church. Although not as tall as Paul, Keith had that air of command presence. He was a wealthy man and a body builder, so he got people's attention when he entered a room. Mostly good attention, but at times people could be turned off by his eagerness to save everyone. Paul and Keith had been close, but when he became born again and tried to encourage Paul to do the same, the relationship became more difficult to maintain. They would always be there for each other, and they would always be brothers, but they no longer had much in common. However, Paul loved Keith's children and Keith loved ours. Keith came over to see how he could

71

help.

"I saw James in church," he said. "We had a nice long talk after, and he's going to be meeting with me and the pastor a few times a week. We all prayed for him. We put him in the prayer circle, too."

Prayer circle was another new term for me, but I tried to pay attention. Could these extra prayers really help? I didn't want to ask. I wanted to believe.

"Thanks. He looks up to you. Maybe you can get through to him," Paul responded kindly.

I knew he wanted to say "good luck," but he caught himself.

"We've tried talking to him and even threatened to fire him," Paul continued. "Obviously, it hasn't worked."

"I think he's going to need some kind of rehab. Just outpatient maybe, but some counseling at least," I added. I had been talking to Kylie about looking at all the options. I was beginning to think it may have to be a thirty or sixty-day program, but I hadn't mentioned that to Paul yet. One step at a time, if we had time.

"The pastor is a counselor, and Lauren's dad, Richard, has been where James is now," Keith said. "He was addicted to drugs until he joined the church and gave his life over to God when he was thirty-three. He wants to help, too. Karen and I will do anything we can to help. You know we love him."

"Thanks, Keith. He can use all the help he can get," Paul told his brother as they walked to the door.

"Do you think it will help?" I asked Paul after he left.

"It can't hurt. I don't care if he becomes one of those Bible-toting preachers, as long as he stops taking drugs."

I felt the same way. He walked over and hugged me for a long time. We would find a way to save our son, I was sure.

***

Monday started off extremely busy. It almost always happened after Christmas. The phones rang off the hook all day with orders for oil and service. I knew from experience it wouldn't let up until the end of March. We were in our busy season and every year it had gotten busier. Thankfully, I had Kylie's help. I still didn't think she was her normal self, but I could not have handled the office without her.

Our drivers were reliable and knew the area and customers well by now. Sam had proven to be dependable for the most part, and we hired a young helper for the service department. Paul had learned not to expect much from James. On this Monday, he was fine and a lot was accomplished. They did some estimates and pricing. They were going to bid on an entire new home plumbing and heating system. The job would not start until spring, but it would keep the boys busy for a good part of the summer. Paul seemed to know he had to grab James on a good day to get any real work out of him. We dared to hope maybe Keith had gotten through to him. Maybe the prayers were working.

We hoped, but we didn't stop looking for help just in case. Kylie and I had decided to see what was available to help addicts in our area. Unfortunately, there wasn't much. We figured the New Beginnings Rehab was a good place to start. If he failed again, he could detox and then do the two-week program. He could still work in the afternoons.

By Wednesday, we knew he was going to need more than prayers. He didn't show up until noon, and he was a mess. I had a no-heat call during the night, and I couldn't raise him on the phone. I called Sam, and he was able to handle it, but it was James' job. We were not happy with him and let him know. After a few attempts to explain his sorry

73

state, he backed down. He knew he needed help.

Lauren drove him to the rehab center that afternoon. In the year and a half since Kylie had been at the center, there had been a new development in the treatment of opiate addiction. Dr. Stevens explained to James and Lauren there was a new drug called Suboxone. It's used to help with the withdrawal symptoms and to cure the cravings that continue when opiates are stopped. Calling it a "miracle drug," Dr. Stevens would prescribe it to James, but he had to attend the outpatient program as well. Learning about the addiction was just as important as the medication.

When they returned and told us all about the meeting, we again dared to hope. Could it be that easy? Could this miracle drug really work?

We would soon learn for James it wasn't that easy. The first week went fairly well. Lauren took him to rehab every morning and dropped him off at the office after lunch. We all wanted to make sure he went to all the counseling sessions. He was in a good mood and talked to Kylie a lot about what he was learning. He was saying all the right things. They had a family day with Lauren and Renee going as well. He went to church and met with the pastor, too. All was looking good.

But then we started to notice the eyes. Kylie mentioned it first. I hadn't seen it, but Kylie noticed everything.

"Are you sure?" I said when she told me of her suspicion. I had learned to trust her, but I didn't want to.

"Positive. Look close next time you see him."

The next time I saw him I didn't have to look close. His eyes were rolling in the back of his head in the way that we knew was not from being tired. He quickly headed to his office, and I quickly followed. I was furious! He tried to close the door, but I was right behind him.

"This is not happening again!" I screamed as if I could somehow stop it.

"What do you mean? I went to the clinic. Everything's fine." His eyes were starting to close then as he sat down at his desk. "I'm just tired."

"Tired people don't look like this. They don't fall asleep during a conversation." His eyes were completely closed, and his head fell onto his desk. I looked at him with a mixture of emotions. Love was still right at the top, but disgust, anger, and pity were not far behind.

I left his office and closed the door. Sitting back at my desk, I told Kylie what had happened. She had been researching Suboxone on her office computer.

"He's probably not taking the Suboxone right. It can be abused either by taking too much, snorting it, or shooting it up. I've read it's a great drug if used correctly, but I think James still wants to get high. What better to use than a free prescription?"

Our hopes of an easy fix were dashed.

I called Lauren and asked her to come and get him. He wasn't fit for work, and he certainly wasn't able to drive. She was losing her patience too, and I didn't blame her.

James mumbled something as Lauren led him out to the car. No one wanted to see their child that way. We were back to square one. The prayers, counseling, and the miracle drug hadn't worked.

"What do we do now?" Kylie asked as she hugged me.

She knew I was near tears.

The phone rang. It always did at the wrong time. I let Kylie answer it as I pulled myself together. "What do we do now?" I asked myself just as a customer walked through the door.

Again, James showed up the next day looking and acting fine.

"I'm sorry, I must have had a reaction to the medication. I don't know what happened," he said, trying to look sincere.

I wasn't sure I bought it.

Kylie didn't buy it. "That happens when you shoot it up or snort it."

James glared at his sister. "Just shut up. I didn't do that."

"Okay. Sure, James. You wouldn't do that." They were both getting louder.

"Mind your own business!"

"This is my business!" Kylie shouted just as her father came out of his office.

Both kids stopped arguing. Paul looked skeptical at his son.

"Are you sober?" Paul asked in a very firm voice.

"Yes," James answered just as firm.

"Good. The furnace is out at the apartment building on Main Street again."

"Again? I was just there. They really need a new one you know. That thing's a piece of junk." James was talking to his father as if nothing had happened.

"I know, but they don't want to replace it this year, so we're just going to have to keep it running. You better get right over there. I mean now, no going for parts. If you need a part call me, and I'll get it for you. I'll send Kylie if I have to." They walked out the door together.

"What do you think?" I asked Kylie after the door closed behind them.

"I don't think it's over. I think he abused the Suboxone, and I know they won't give him more. He's probably supposed to take so many a day. They would've given him enough for a week or two, and they won't renew the prescription until then. If they find out he's out before he should be, they won't renew it at all."

"So you think he's just blown his chance with Dr. Stevens?" I asked.

"Yes, this time. They don't want to waste time with someone who's not ready."

"When will he be ready?" I asked knowing there was no answer.

"When he hits bottom," Kylie said. "When he loses everything."

"Do we have to wait until then? Can't we make him see what he's going to lose?" She seemed to have all the answers.

"On the TV show 'Intervention,' they say if you don't want to wait until he hits bottom, you can bring the bottom up to him. I'm not sure how that works, though. I think James is going to need a long-term program."

Kylie responded to my questions as best she could. We both knew there were no easy answers.

"Have you found anything in the area that will take insurance or doesn't cost a fortune?"

"Not yet. There's a lot available for teens but not much for adults. I'll keep looking."

"Thanks, Sweetie," I said just as both phones rang. It was going to be a long day.

James got the furnace going at the apartment in no time. He was on another job with the boys within an hour.

Kylie, in the meantime, was telling me between phone

calls that Tom was now out of jail and staying at the Tranquility House in the city.

"He got out yesterday and wants me to come down to see him, just as friends. He said he wants to thank me for helping him through the last four months. I don't know what I should do."

"What do you want to do?" I knew this day was coming, but was it here so soon? Was he out of jail already?

"I want to see him, but I don't want to like him. I'm afraid of what I'll feel if I see him."

"That's a tough one. If you don't see him now, you may run into him later and then what? You can't hide forever."

"Well, he can't drive anywhere for ninety days. I could avoid him for that long anyway," Kylie responded seriously, but she was smiling.

"He only has to be there at night and go to meetings, right? Do you think he could get a ride up this way?"

"I hadn't considered that. Then if he just showed up, I wouldn't be ready." She was tapping her fingers on the desk, deep in thought for a while. "That's it, I'm going to have to go down. No question about it. Tonight after work. Can I leave a little early?"

The decision was made that quick. She was just like her father. Once she made her mind up, she just wanted to do it. Thinking of her father, what would he say? He had seen the envelopes from jail, and Kylie assured him Tom was only a pen-pal. Maybe that's all it would be, but my mother's instinct told me differently.

"Sure, Sweetie, you can leave at four after you go to the bank."

"Okay, thanks. Can I go get ready before that? I'll leave the apartment door open. If it gets busy, you can just yell."

"Sure, and you'll come out in your bra and panties?"

"Good way to pick up new customers, don't you think?"

She was in a good mood. I think she always knew she would see Tom when he got out.

"As long as it's not busy, you can leave early." I gave in. She really didn't have to twist my arm too much.

She rushed around the rest of the day making sure everything was done. At three, she begged to leave and get ready. Kylie had spent a good part of the afternoon trying to decide what to wear. I think she may have narrowed it down to three different outfits.

"It's almost three, can I go get ready? Please...."

"Okay, okay. But don't forget you have to make the deposit before four." She was already in her apartment.

Thirty minutes later she showed up freshly showered with her hair all curly and done up in a half ponytail. She had put on fresh make-up and the first of the three outfits she was considering.

"What do you think?"

She had on jeans, a sweater with a scarf tied at the side of her neck, and the pair of Ugg boots I had gotten her for Christmas.

"I think you look great!" I didn't have to lie.

"I'm not sure about the sweater. I'll be right back."

She was back in a minute wearing a pretty pink shirt with the same scarf.

"I like that too," I said knowing she would show me the third option anyway.

"You're no help," she yelled back over her shoulder as she rushed into her apartment. She was having fun.

And she did show me the other outfit, but we decided on the pink shirt and scarf just when Paul entered the office.

"What's she all dressed up for?" he asked as Kylie

left to change back into option two.

I was afraid of this conversation. "She's going to see Tom."

"The convict?" he asked, his voice rising just a bit.

"Yes, and you shouldn't call him that. He's out now."

"I thought he was just a pen-pal. Don't tell me she's going to date him?" He was trying to stay calm. Kylie had made some bad choices with boyfriends over the years.

"She's just going to see him. He wants to thank her for helping him get through the last few months. It doesn't mean anything will come of it." I wasn't so sure, but I was buying time. I figured if Kylie did fall for him, it would be at least a few weeks before it got serious. We'd cross that bridge later.

"She deserves better than that, you know. Whatever happened to that guy from the fish place, the one we deliver oil to. Didn't he give her a Christmas tree? He's nice and he has a good job. He'll probably take the place over from his father."

I knew he was thinking, "anyone but a convict."

"He is a nice guy, and he did give her a Christmas tree, but that was because he was selling them and had some extras. I do think he likes Kylie, but she doesn't feel the same way. They're just friends. You can't choose who your daughter wants to be with. Anyway, I'm sure nothing will come of this."

Kylie heard the last part as she came to get the deposit.

She gave her father a hug and said to him, "Don't worry, Dad, he is just a friend."

Famous last words, I thought as I watched her walk out the door. She had that air about her of someone falling in love.

I turned to Paul and asked about James. "How was he

today?"

"Good for a while, but then he told Sam he had to go get a part, and no one's seen him since. He's not answering his phone. I don't know what we're going to do with him. This can't continue."

The phone rang, so he went back to his office as I reached for it. I hung up the phone and had to go tell Paul that the furnace at the apartment building was out again.

"That's great! Just great! And no one knows where James is or what he did to it earlier. He didn't stop in and leave you the paperwork on it by any chance."

"No, I haven't seen him since this morning," I said wishing I could help somehow. "Should I call Sam?"

"No, he's busy. I'll go. I'll see you at home."

I knew it would not be a good night. I hadn't bothered to remind him it was our twenty-fifth wedding anniversary. We never do too much to celebrate, especially since it's in January, and we're in the oil business, but I had bought a nice bottle of wine. I was hoping to have a couple of glasses in front of a fire in the living room fireplace tonight. Now I wasn't sure I should even bring it up.

As I started getting tomorrows tickets ready and in order for the drivers, I couldn't help thinking....

My daughter was falling in love. I was sure of that even if she wasn't. I wasn't sure how I felt about her being in love with Tom, but it would have to play itself out. Boyfriends come and go, and young girls fall in and out of love several times before settling down. There was nothing I could do about that. I only hoped she didn't feel she was not worthy of anyone else. If she truly fell in love with him, that was fine with me.

And....

My son was falling apart. Was there anything more I could do? I was worried for his safety as well as the safety of others. Was he driving under the influence or had he just gone home? Had he been in an accident? We often thought about that when he disappeared for hours at a time, but he always turned up safe. Would he be safe this time? There was no doubt in my mind now that he needed a live-in program before something happened. We would look again tomorrow. There must be something for adults in the area.

Chapter Seven

As I expected, Paul got home late. I heated up dinner and brought the bottle of wine over to the table. He noticed it was the kind I only bought for our anniversaries.

"Is it?" he asked looking at me with a little smile.

"Yes." I smiled back.

"How many years?"

"Twenty-five."

"That many?"

He gave me a kiss, and we toasted to twenty-five years. That was all we needed to do to celebrate. We didn't need or want fancy parties or dinners out. It wasn't that one day a year that counted, it was all the days in between. We'd had some rough patches, but for the most part, it had been a great marriage. I wouldn't trade him in. Not now anyway. It was not always easy working together, but we were doing okay.

Just as I was getting ready for bed the phone rang. My heart always jumped this time of year when the phone rang at night. It usually meant a no-heat call, and I would have to track someone down to go out. I also worried I may have let an automatic customer run out of oil, or a call-in customer didn't get a delivery on time because Kylie or I forgot to print a ticket. We were usually pretty thorough, but I always worried. For the last few months, I was worrying about James as well. Could he have been in an accident or worse? I just hated that phone to ring at night.

When I grabbed the phone, I recognized Kylie's number. Relieved, I answered.

"Hi, Sweetie. How did it go?"

"Great! I think I'm in love," she said, and I could tell she was smiling.

"I'm happy for you, Sweetie, but take it slow, okay?" What else could I say.

"Don't worry, I can't wait to tell you all about him tomorrow. See you in the morning, bye." She hung up.

Sometimes I hate to be right. Chances are it won't last, I thought as I climbed into bed.

My husband was trying so hard to run our business during this very busy time of year basically one man short. He was stressed most of the time lately, jumping from one problem to another. He could do anything that needed to be done in our company, but he couldn't do all of it, all by himself. Sometimes, I'm sure he felt like he had to.

He had asked me to come in early. Only ten or fifteen minutes, he said, but I hadn't managed to do it yet. I always pulled in the parking lot at eight. Sometimes a couple of minutes after. Most of the time Paul was there at the office or down back with the drivers or the boys, and we had an answering service, so I knew I wasn't missing any calls. I just couldn't seem to get out of the house any earlier. There was always something. A phone call. The dogs had to go out again or took too long the first time I took them out. The laundry had to be changed, the bed made. If I had a few extra minutes, I'd run the vacuum or sweep the floor. There was always something to do at home, but it was January and Paul had asked, so I should make it a priority. Maybe that would take some pressure off him. Maybe it would help, even just a little. I would try.

I pulled into the office at two minutes past eight the next morning, late again. Kylie was just entering the office as I walked through the door. I knew she wanted to tell me everything, but we needed to get things ready first, and I was worried about James.

Paul was in his office, and to my surprise, James was sitting across from him looking awful. If I didn't know better by now, I would have thought he really did have the flu. More likely it was withdrawals. I could tell Paul was losing patience, and I didn't blame him. I was upset with him too. How much longer could this go on? He was okay one day and awful the next.

"It's obvious you can't beat this thing on your own," Paul was saying.

"I'm fine, really. I just have the flu. It's going around. Lauren and Renee are sick too. I think Renee brought it home from daycare."

He was getting good with the excuses. Adding a little more detail. Maybe a little bit of truth.

"What happened yesterday?"

"I went in town for a part, and my phone died. I felt sick on the way back, so I went straight home. You can ask Lauren."

"You couldn't bother to call when you got home?" Paul asked a little sarcastically.

"I was going to but I fell asleep, and when I woke up, it was too late to call you." He had all the answers.

"I had to go back to the apartment building. The furnace went out again. What did you do to fix it yesterday morning?"

I walked out of Paul's office to continue getting ready for the day. They were talking shop and didn't need me. We would discuss the situation later. Kylie had already checked with the answering service and was printing new tickets. I knew she wanted to talk about last night, but I wanted to wait until we were alone. I didn't want her father overhearing. It may only last a week or two. Why stress him out? So I pointed to her father's office and whispered "later." She shook her head in understanding just as both phones rang. The day had begun.

I grabbed James as he tried to leave for his first appointment. "I want to talk to you."

"Later, I have to go," he said, trying to get by me.

"No, now." I was trying to be firm but it wasn't working.

"I'm okay, Mom. I'm meeting with Uncle Keith and Pastor this afternoon. I'll beat this." He pushed by me and went out the door.

Paul left shortly after that, and Kylie finally got her chance to fill me in on all the details of her first "date" with Tom. He had bought her flowers, and they sat on a couch in the common living room. She met all the other people staying there as well as the staff. Everyone was nice. When she was finally alone with Tom, they talked for hours.

"He reminds me a little of Dad," she said with a shy smile.

That took me by surprise. "How is that possible?"

"He's strong in an understated sort of way. He doesn't show it, but I know he could take care of me if I was threatened or something. I know he can fight if he had to. Does that make sense?"

I understood, but it was sad she had to think that way. What had she been through that she would be looking for someone strong enough to fight for her, to protect her?

"How does that remind you of Dad?" I asked. It did remind me of Paul, but I was surprised it reminded her of her father too.

"I know Dad's strong, but he doesn't walk around

with an attitude. He doesn't flaunt it. You just know. He's like the strong, silent type, I guess."

We both laughed at that. She was more observant than I gave her credit for.

We had to get back to work. During lulls, we searched for programs for James. We both realized he was going to need long-term help. Kylie found one program that looked promising in Bangor. We wrote down the information and phone number. I thought I'd wait a few more days. Maybe the pastor or Keith could help.

"Let's wait until Monday," I told Kylie.

"I think we should call right now and talk to them. At least to see if they have any openings. I'll call if you want."

She was pushing, but I was stalling. I'm not sure why.

"Okay, I'll call," I said. "Only to get information."

The person who answered the phone was nice but wondered why I called and not James. I was looking for information, I told him. My son was trying to beat this on his own, but I was worried. They may be able to take him in the next few weeks, but he had to be clean for seven days before he came. He could not leave for thirty days. After that, he could work in the community to help pay for the treatment. It sounded good, so I said I'd get back to him.

We finally had an option. We would see how he did for the next few days. Any slip-ups and we'd ship him off to treatment.

It ended up being a fairly good day with James leaving a little early to go to his meeting, and Kylie heading to the city after work to see Tom. They were going to a hockey game compliments of the local team. "Fun things to do sober" was their goal.

Paul and I got home at a decent hour for a change. We got in our sauna, and Paul had time to get in the hot tub

87

as well. A habit that began many years ago when Paul was the only driver. During that time, he worked extremely long hours in the winter often leaving at 4:30 in the morning, but he tried hard not to deliver oil after dark. So on some days, he rushed all day to get deliveries done before dark, then headed in to fill one truck in the evening. He would fill the other truck first thing in the morning. We had a third truck that he would use to put any leftover oil in. That way he always filled an empty truck, bringing back as much oil as possible. He was the only driver back then, but by keeping two trucks filled, he was able to handle the work alone. On really busy days, he had extra oil in our spare truck.

And he froze. His feet would freeze early in the day, but he never stopped. Most winters he would end up with frost bite at least once. His hands froze from handling the metal nozzle on the hose all day. He would shiver standing on top of the truck while he loaded the oil. It was a cold job, and all he could think about was getting warm at the end of the day. After our fifth year in business, we bought a sauna, and the following year we added a hot tub. It became routine for us to relax in the sauna at the end of the day, even in the summer. The hot tub usually followed. And so it was a usual evening for us. And the phone didn't ring.

I pinned James down the next day to ask about his meeting. He looked pretty good. Maybe the meetings would help.

"It was good. They want to help me with the stress in my life. You know, money, Lauren, and work. Mostly money and Lauren." He caught himself. We had been extremely understanding, and he knew it.

He continued, "Aunt Karen is going to talk to Lauren and maybe help her clean the house and show her how to keep it clean. Aunt Tina is going to manage my finances. I'm going to give her my paychecks, and she's going to put us on a budget. I'll have to ask her for money." He kind of laughed.

I think it made him uncomfortable, but he knew he had to do something, and if anyone could fix his finances, Tina could. She was Paul's sister, only one year older than him. They were incredibly close, and she loved the kids. She was also experienced at money management. She helped me set up our company on Quickbooks shortly after we started. I still called her with questions on how to run reports and projections. If anyone could help them, she could.

"Did you pay your mortgage this month?"

"Uncle Keith did. I'll pay him back over time."

"He offered," he continued when he saw the look on my face.

My brother-in-law had to make my son's mortgage payment for him. His wife was going to clean their house. My sister-in-law was managing his money. What kind of parents were we? How did it get to this point?

"What happened to all your money?" I was pretty sure I knew, but I had to ask.

"I don't know, just stuff, you know with Lauren and Renee. There's always something."

He was being vague again. I had heard it before. I hoped Tina could help. At least it would keep the money out of the wrong hands, both his and Lauren's.

"James, you've got to get your act together. You're going to lose everything if you don't. I don't know what you're doing or why, but it has to stop. You've got your whole life ahead of you, and I'm afraid you're going to throw it all away."

"I know, everything will be fine. I'll be in church on Sunday. They'll pray for me." He smiled. "Don't worry," he said on his way out the door.

"Easier said than done," I said out loud as Kylie came in from her apartment.

"What is?" she asked as she came around to her computer.

"James told me not to worry."

"Like that's ever going to happen. How is he today?" Kylie worried about her brother almost as much as I did.

"It looks like a good day so far. I hope it lasts. There were calls overnight, and we've got tickets to print."

The rest of the day was busy but normal. Tomorrow was Saturday and we would work in the morning for a few hours. We didn't schedule actual office hours, but we used it to catch up with deliveries and office work. Some of our customers would stop in to pay on these Saturday mornings, glad they happened to catch us there.

James seemed good the last time I saw him, and Kylie couldn't stop talking about Tom. She was headed back to the city to see him after work. It was one of those days that was actually fun, working hard but enjoying the family. It had been a while. I dared to hope it would continue.

I didn't see James on Saturday, but Kylie came out of her apartment to see if I needed help, and of course, to tell me all about her date the night before. It was nice to see her happy. I just wished she would get off the methadone. Maybe she would try now that there was no stress in her life. I wouldn't bring it up. I didn't want an argument. She was in such a good mood and heading back to the city. I was happy for her. Of course, Paul still didn't know.

Karen stopped in the office as I was getting ready to close and said she was going over to James and Lauren's house to help her clean.

"Have you been there lately?" she asked me.

"I haven't been inside since they moved in. I went over to pick up Renee, but James met me outside. Knowing how the apartment was, I can only imagine what the house looks like." I was embarrassed to be having this conversation with my sister-in-law about my own son and his wife.

"It's really, really bad. It actually smells and you can't walk anywhere. I think she's a hoarder. There's so much junk. And I don't know what they use to eat with because the counters are piled so high with dirty dishes. I was there for a while yesterday, and I'm headed back now. Since Lauren won't be home until later, do you want to come with me?"

I think she wanted me to see how bad it was, and I didn't have a good reason to get out of it, so I reluctantly said I'd meet her there when I finished up at the office. The last thing I wanted to do was clean my adult son's home. I did not want to do Lauren's job, after all they were grown-ups. They should be able to keep a house fairly clean. Maybe not eat-off-the-floor clean, but clean enough to not be a fire hazard or mistaken for the town dump. If not for themselves, then at least for Renee. She deserved a decent, safe, reasonably clean home. Why couldn't they see that?

I arrived there shortly after lunch. It was way worse than I had imagined. Karen was already filling bags with stuff to be thrown out.

"Should you ask her before throwing things away?" I asked even though I didn't want to question what Karen was doing, after all she was trying to help. I just didn't want Lauren to be angry and blame James.

"No, if I ask she'll want to keep it all, and it's just junk. There's another bag over there you can start filling. Don't worry I'll take the blame. I don't want your daughter-in-law hating you. I don't care if she hates me. It has to be done."

We spent the next four hours filling bags to go to the dump, while running loads of clothes, sheets, and blankets through the washer and dryer, and cleaning off counters, washing dishes, cleaning the fridge, and cleaning the stove. We had barely made a dent, but it was getting dark, and Lauren would be home soon. We didn't want to be there when she came in, so the rest would have to wait. Karen said she would come back next week, but I'd be working. Maybe I could help next weekend, I told her as we left together.

"I'll keep in touch," Karen said. "I'll see Lauren tomorrow at church and let you know how it goes. It's no wonder James turned to drugs. No one should live like this. They both have to change their lives. I think Lauren is as much at fault as James."

Karen was a really good person, I thought as I got into my car. Not many people would give up a Saturday afternoon to clean a disgusting house for someone who was perfectly capable of cleaning it herself.

Karen called on Sunday to tell me Lauren was furious with her. She never thanked her for cleaning, but evidently we had thrown away some things she was saving. That was all she noticed.

"There is a woman's group at the church. We've asked Lauren to join," she told me. "Maybe she'll learn some things, but I don't think she'll ever let me back in her house, and there is so much more to do."

"Thanks for trying, you helped a lot. I'm sure she'll see that when she calms down. Was James at church?" I asked before I hung up.

"No, Lauren said he didn't feel good," she said hesitantly.

I knew she felt sorry for me. We both knew why he didn't feel well. "Maybe he has the flu. I hope he stays away from Renee. I would hate for her to get sick," I lied, and Karen knew I was lying. So why bother to keep up the charade?

Monday morning came before I knew it. Weekends go so fast this time of year. I pulled into the parking lot at one minute before eight, still not early like Paul had asked. He had been at the office since before seven.

"Right on time as usual. Have you heard from James?" he asked as soon as I opened the door. "We're supposed to be at the installation job at eight, and he was going to help me load up."

"No, I haven't talked to him all weekend. I told you Karen said he was sick yesterday. I'll try to call him," I said as I made my way to the phone to take the calls from the answering service.

"Don't bother, I already tried. He's not answering. If he shows up, tell him I'm looking for him."

He headed down back to load the older van, but I knew he needed the larger one James used. I was trying to come to terms with the fact we may have to fire him and hire someone dependable. How would James survive without his paycheck or insurance? How would he take care of Renee? Lauren I didn't care so much about. I was still angry with her for the way she treated Karen.

Kylie walked in just then. She was never early either. I guess she got something from me.

"Please check the answering service. I have to try to find James," I said to Kylie. The day was not starting out well.

I picked up the phone and called Lauren. "Is James

there?" I asked. "He's not answering his phone."

"He's in bed. I can't wake him up. He was out pretty late."

"Where was he?"

"I don't know. He took off after dinner to go to the store and didn't come back until after one."

"Please tell him to call me as soon as he wakes up."

Kylie was waiting for an explanation when I hung up the phone, but I think she could have figured it out on her own.

"James is still in bed and won't wake up. Lauren said he was out until one in the morning. She doesn't know where. He didn't go to church yesterday either. Dad's furious with him. I don't know what to do," I blurted out in almost one breath.

"Fire him!" she yelled. "You can't let him get away with this. He was out doing drugs and can't show up for work. If you let him keep getting away with it, he'll keep doing it."

"I know, but what about his family? What about Renee? He'll lose his house. How can we do that to our own son?" I knew she was right, but I wasn't there yet. I still held out hope. Then Kylie said something that stated it all so simply.

"You're going to love him to death." A phrase that put it all in perspective. "Don't love him to death," she said again quietly.

I sat down at my computer. We had work to do, but I couldn't get that phrase out of my mind. If I continued to allow him to do drugs by covering for him and paying him for working when he wasn't, I was allowing him to kill himself with these drugs. I was beginning to realize the only way to help him was to not help him at all. A very hard thing for a mother to grasp.

And then it happened, something I never imagined possible. I was signing into our company checking account online like I do almost every day. We were starting to build a cushion, but funds were still tight. The price of oil was skyrocketing. Covering the almost $25,000 in checks I was sending out daily to pay for our oil was still a challenge. I was always adding and subtracting in my head as money came in and went out of the account, but I verified it daily online. I knew immediately something was wrong. Had I forgotten a check I wrote? Did we add up the deposit wrong? Those things do happen but not this time.

I scanned down the page looking at the cleared checks. And there it was. Five separate checks had cleared over the weekend. Each one was for $250. I was confused. I hadn't written or printed any checks for that amount, let alone five. I clicked on the little camera beside the check amount to see a copy of the check. I didn't want to. I think I knew what I was going to see.

There, right in front of me, was a copy of one of our company checks written to James and signed by me. I recognized James' handwriting. I felt sick.

I'd been trying to help him. Paul had been so patient. We'd been paying him for work even when he wasn't showing up. I'd paid his mortgage and had given him money back in October. How could he do this to us? I viewed the other four checks just to be sure, but I knew. They were all the same. All written to James and cashed at the local supermarket. All in the last few days. No wonder he was sick. He deserved it.

Reality began to sink in. He must have come in when we were closed and stolen the checks. Did he think I wouldn't find out? I trusted him and Kylie with everything we had, never imagining one of my children would steal from us. Usually, they only had to ask. I was pretty easy to get money out of, for a good reason, of course. I felt violated. I looked at the box of checks sitting under the printer. They were all ready to load when I had to print the daily checks for oil and other expenses. I never thought to lock them up.

Then I began to panic. How many did he take? Had he cashed more? Did he have some hidden for another time? Did he take anything else? I had my personal checks here too. I needed to check that account. I was really panicking now. I had let this happen. I shouldn't have left checks out like that. They were not in the customers view, but James came behind the desk all the time. What an idiot I was! I knew he was doing drugs. I should have locked everything up. My head was spinning.

I snapped out of it for a few minutes to take a call and talk to a customer. I was in a daze when Kylie asked what was wrong.

"Nothing, Sweetie. I was lost in thought. Have you entered yesterday's tickets yet?" I tried to change the subject. I couldn't tell her James had stolen from us. She didn't need to think any worse of him than she already did. They were close once, and I hoped they would be again.

I would handle this myself. But how? I can't very well close the account, and I don't know the check numbers or amounts to put stop payments on them. The last thing I wanted to do was tell our banker my son had stolen checks, and I didn't know how many or what he was going to do with them. Our banker is also an oil customer. It's a small town, and I didn't want anyone to know, not even Paul.

What would Paul say? What would he do? He'd been trying so hard to help James and get through to him somehow. James had already let him down so much. Paul would not only fire him, he would disown him. James had crossed the line. After everything we had done, Paul would never forgive him.

I decided I would confront James myself this time. If it happened again, I would have to tell Paul. We would have to fire him and change the locks on the office door. But what could I do with the checks in the meantime? It was a large, heavy box since I had just ordered new ones about a month ago. It was still nearly full. I couldn't take them back and forth to work with me. Then I realized one of our filing cabinets had a locked drawer. If only I knew where the key was. I would find it later. I needed to get back to work. It was going to be a long day.

I called Lauren again later that morning, and James was still not up. I didn't think he'd be in at all. Paul called to check, but I had no good news. Sam was helping, but they needed James, or they were going to have to hire another master heat technician.

That long-term program was looking like our only choice. Would he go? I could hold those forged checks over his head. Maybe that would work.

He never made it into the office that day. I was sure he was avoiding me. He must have known I would find out. At the end of the day, I called Lauren again. This time, she didn't answer. I found the key to the file cabinet. After Kylie left for the day, I locked all the checks in the bottom drawer. When I did, I was able to see he had taken the checks from the bottom of the box, but there were no more pages missing. Hopefully, he would not get any more, but what if he had taken some from the middle? I left for home feeling sick to my stomach.

Paul arrived home shortly after I did. He was not in a good mood. The tension was building in our relationship. He was snappy and sarcastic. He wanted to blame someone for

James' issues, and I was the only one he could think of. Couldn't I talk to him? Couldn't I make him see what he was doing to himself, his family, and our business?

"Don't you think I've tried?" I responded to his questions trying not to raise my voice.

"Just like you tried with Kylie." He left the room before I could answer.

He was right, I hadn't helped Kylie soon enough. If I hadn't let her go out so soon after the first incident, she may not be on methadone today. I lived with that guilt every day.

Paul came back to the kitchen in a towel ready to get in the sauna. "I'm sorry, that wasn't called for. I know you did all you could. Go get ready for the sauna. Why don't you get a couple of beers and we'll talk."

I got in the sauna a few minutes later, and we did talk. I told him about the long-term program Kylie had found. We talked about hiring another technician. We talked about how to help Lauren if James went away. We talked about sending Sam to classes to get his license. We didn't talk about the forged and missing checks. Paul had enough to worry about.

Chapter Eight

James practically crawled into the office the next day. I was so angry I could barely look at him, let alone speak to him. Three more checks had cleared overnight. He must have had quite the weekend.

"I know you're upset. Let me explain. I'm going to sell my snowmobile, and I will pay you back everything. I promise."

"You're right, you will pay me back every penny! How could you? How could you come in here and violate our trust in you? I trusted you with everything. Now, do I need to change the locks? Lock up all our things? What else have you taken?" My voice was raised, but I wasn't yelling. I didn't want anyone else to hear.

James sat on the small couch in the office. Kylie hadn't come in yet, and Paul was down back with the boys. He put his head in his hands.

"I haven't taken anything else, I swear."

"Why, James, why?" I had calmed down a little. I looked at him and realized he looked thinner, much thinner. He looked like he lost ten pounds since Friday. "What's happening to you?"

"I don't know. I just can't stop. I don't know what to do."

I noticed he was shaking. I sat down beside him and put my arms around him. "You need serious help. You can't beat this alone. You are addicted."

"I know."

"What about Dr. Stevens? Can you go back to see him? Get back on Suboxone? If you take it right, it might work." My anger had turned to pity. Instead of yelling, I was consoling.

"They didn't work for me. Uncle Keith, Pastor, and Richard think I shouldn't take them either. I just need to stop. Suboxone is just another drug. Look at Kylie, she's still on the methadone."

"I know and part of me agrees with you, but look at you. You're a mess. Kylie found a program in Bangor. It's a ninety-day residential program where you work in the community after thirty days to help pay for it. I talked to them a few days ago, and they sound nice."

"How can I leave my family? What about my job?"

"We'll all help, and Lauren and Renee can visit. You have to get better for them. We'll deal with the job later, but I'm sure it will still be here for you. Dad's angry but he still loves you."

"Does he know about the checks?" he asked.

"Not yet."

"Are you going to tell him?"

"I guess that depends on you. Are you going to get treatment?"

"I guess I don't have a choice, do I?" He was still sitting with his head in his hands when his father entered the building.

"What's your excuse this time?" Paul grumbled as he walked by James.

"I don't have an excuse. I messed up." James looked up at his father but didn't get off the couch.

Kylie was in the office now, and thankfully no customers had come in yet, so it was a good time for a family meeting.

100

"We were talking about the residential treatment place," I began the conversation. "But James is worried about his family and his job."

"If he doesn't get help, he can stop worrying about his job because he won't have one." Paul had stopped by his office door. Now he came back to join the conversation.

"How can I leave my family?" James looked up at all of us, but Kylie said it best.

"How can you not?"

Kylie continued, "You're not here for them now. You can't support them. You're high most of the time, and when you're not high, you're trying to figure out how to get high again or you're sick. It's only a matter of time before Lauren leaves and takes Renee with her."

"That's no way to live," Paul said to James. "You need to do this for them and for us. We'd like to have you work here, but I'll be clear, we can hire someone else. You are not irreplaceable." After a moment of silence, he added, "You look awful. You're so thin. Doesn't Lauren feed you?"

"I haven't been feeling good." James tried to brush it off, but Kylie wouldn't have any of it.

"People don't eat much when they're high," she said.

I knew that, but this weight loss was extreme, worse than Kylie's during her episode. To make matters worse he had shaved his head and had cuts on his face from shaving that morning as well. I was starting to think he needed to be hospitalized, but I knew he mostly needed to stop getting high and to start eating.

"Okay. Can you set it up for me?" He was looking at me and trying to avoid Kylie. To him, she was trouble. He couldn't lie in front of her because she had been where he is now.

"I'll call them. The one stipulation is you have to be clean for seven days before you go," I said, wondering how he was going to manage that.

"Set it up for Friday. Tell them I haven't done anything since last Friday," he said with a sigh, his head back in his hands.

I wanted to hold him like a baby and tell him everything would be all right, but he was an adult, and I wasn't so sure everything would be all right.

Paul asked James to come into the office so they could go over some things. They would have to figure out how to manage without him. If he could stay clean for the rest of the week, they could get a lot done, but again I wondered how he'd stay away from drugs for any length of time.

I looked at Kylie and said, "Thanks for your help. He doesn't like to hear it, but he needs to. We need to get busy now. There are some tickets on the desk that need to be printed." After she was behind the desk, I grabbed James' coat and got his key ring from the pocket, trying to be discrete.

Kylie noticed. "What are you doing?"

Now what? I really didn't want to tell her about the checks, especially if James was going to get better, but I could use her help before James came out of his dad's office. It was one of the biggest key rings I had ever seen.

I took the keys over to my desk and grabbed my keys from my pocketbook.

"I want to take his office keys back until he gets better. He can keep the garage and basement keys, but there's no need for him to be in the office alone, at least for now."

"I agree. You don't want him in here shooting up in his office at night. If he's high, he would probably leave the door unlocked. And my apartment's right here too. Let me see those, I'll find them."

She took his key ring, and I held up mine so we could

match up the office keys. We found the deadbolt and lock keys quickly, and Kylie took them off the ring.

"You know he has your house key too. Should I take that off?" she asked.

I didn't remember giving him one of our house keys since he wasn't living at home when we bought the house. Maybe Paul had given him one. Kylie or Paul tried to go home every day around lunchtime to let our dogs out. Paul could have asked James to do it and had given him a key, but I didn't think so.

"Yes, I don't think he should have it right now. I can give it back to him later when he's better."

She took that key off too and replaced the key ring in James' coat pocket. "Are you going to tell him?"

"Not now. There's no reason he should even know they're missing."

I found the phone number for the facility and called. We went over some details as they assured me again they could help him. They would be expecting him on Friday. I let James know everything was arranged, and we all got back to work. We could work out the other details later.

Keith stopped in later that afternoon. "I saw the van and wanted to see how James is doing. He wasn't in church," he said, genuinely concerned.

"Not good, but we've got him into a ninety-day program. I'm hopeful. He's down back if you want to talk to him, but I'll warn you he looks awful."

"Yeah, I'll go say hi," he said. "I'm worried about him. Where's the program?"

"Bangor. I know it's far, but at least he won't be able to walk home."

"Who's taking him?"

"I assumed Lauren would."

"Why don't I take him? Karen can come too. That way if he tries to change his mind, we can persuade him to stay. Lauren couldn't do that. We'd have three or four hours to build him up, encourage him."

"That's a long ride, there and back. Are you sure you want to do that?" I was a little shocked he would offer. It would take most of the day, and James wasn't even his child. But he had a point about Lauren, and none of us could leave for that long.

"Yes, it'll be good. I love the kid. I'll go tell him."

"Thanks." So it was all planned, as long as he stayed clean.

Kieth left to go down back just as Lauren pulled into the parking lot with Renee. Sometimes, the office felt like the local gathering spot. Sometimes, I loved it. This wasn't one of those times.

Lauren came in with Renee who ran around our desk for big hugs and kisses. My favorite part. But then I had to deal with Lauren who I knew wasn't happy with any of us right now.

I decided to let Kylie explain what was going on while I played hide-n-seek with my granddaughter. I listened, ready to rescue Kylie if she needed me to, but it wasn't necessary this time. They were getting along a little better. Lauren had confided in Kylie about some of the things James had done over the weekend. Kylie was the expert in all things drug related, after all.

I suddenly felt sorry for Lauren. She could lose the life she had, good or bad, if James didn't get better. I still felt if she could be a better housekeeper and partner, maybe James would enjoy his life more and not turn to drugs. But James, and only James, was the one who took the drugs. Lauren didn't force them down his throat, up his nose, or in his arm, whichever he was doing now, and James was the only one who could stop.

Lauren had been listening to Kylie with the appropriate responses, but I could tell she stopped listening when Kylie told her Keith was going to drive her husband to Bangor. By now I knew Lauren well enough to know she would not say anything to us if she disagreed. She would go tell James.

That's exactly what she did. She headed down back to where Keith, Paul, and James were making arrangements for the drive to Bangor and the work that needed to be done first.

Afraid she was about to make trouble, I asked Kylie to go with her while I kept Renee.

Fifteen minutes later, Lauren and Kylie came back. Lauren took Renee and left without a word. Then Kylie filled me in.

"Lauren is such a bitch!" she said as soon as the door closed. "All she cares about is driving him there. It's like she wants to be the hero or something. Keith tried to explain he thought it would be better for James to say goodbye to her and Renee here and not in Bangor. James would worry about them on the long drive home. Keith's afraid James might change his mind, but Lauren didn't care. It's all about me, me, me, with her!"

"So what did they decide?" I asked trying to get Kylie to the point. It was always a yo-yo relationship between her and Lauren. Kylie could go on forever once she got started.

"Keith is really good with this stuff. He put her in her place saying this wasn't about her but about James and what was best for him, and it was best for James if she didn't drive him. Then she turned and stomped off. I think James is going to get an earful when he gets home. I hope it doesn't put him over the edge."

"I hope he can handle it. We have to get him up there." I realized I didn't feel quite as sorry for her anymore.

Somehow James managed to stay clean until Friday, or at least we thought so. He helped Paul tie up some loose ends, and he cleaned up his van. Sam was going to use it while he was gone.

Friday morning, James showed up looking very thin and very depressed but not high. Once again I allowed a glimmer of hope to enter my thoughts. I would miss him terribly, but I told him we would write often knowing no calls or visitors were allowed for the first thirty days.

"As soon as you can have visitors, Kylie and I will come to see you," I said, trying to cheer him up. "I'm sure Lauren will drive up too, with Renee. It won't be so bad. You won't have to think about anything except getting better. This is a good thing. You'll come back a new, healthy person with a fresh start. Karen and the girls at church are going to help Lauren learn to clean and cook while you're away, so you'll both be better." I knew I was rambling, but I had to get the words out. I wanted so much for this to work. Just get him there, I thought, and they'll fix him. And I will have my son back. I was afraid if this didn't work, James would die.

As I sat there with him on the small couch in the office, it was the first time I really felt he may not survive. I fought back tears as the realization hit me. Where were Keith and Karen? If they didn't get here soon, I was going to get emotional, and that was not how I wanted to send my son to rehab.

Paul was in his office, and Kylie was on the phone. The second phone rang, so I left James on the couch to answer it. Kylie took my place next to him as soon as she got off her call.

She hugged him and said only one word. "Stay."

Keith and Karen pulled into the parking lot just then, and James stood up to leave. I went to Paul's office to tell him they were here. I knew Paul and James were not on the best of terms lately as much as Paul tried to hide it, but I thought he would want to say goodbye.

He followed me out to the parking lot as Keith was putting James' bags in the trunk. We all hugged James, even Paul, and tried to give him some final words of encouragement. We thanked Keith and Karen for taking him and then watched them drive away.

Paul put his arm around my shoulder and that was it. I broke down and cried. I'm not sure why. He was on his way to get help, but I couldn't stop. We walked back into the office, and Paul held me until the sobs subsided.

When I pulled myself together, Paul said he was worried about him too, but there was nothing more we could do for him.

"You've done all you can do, now it's up to him."

"I'm afraid he's going to die," I told him as the tears flowed again.

"So am I," he quietly said as he pulled me closer. It was the first time either of us had said it out loud.

Just then, Kylie came over with that sense of humor of hers and said in a little girl voice, "Can I get in on this hug too?" So we pulled her in close, and we all held each other.

Paul was the first to speak. "That's it, back to work!" he commanded in his fake, bossy voice.

"Yes, sir," Kylie said and gave a salute. I noticed her wipe away a tear as we all went back to work.

Four hours later, Keith called.

"We just left him. We stopped and got some lunch first. It's a nice place, old but clean. The people who run it are really great. So are the people staying there. There are some older guys, but most look to be around James' age."

"Do you think he was okay when you left him?" I asked.

"Yes, he seemed good. We talked to him all the way up, and we prayed with him. We told him he had to do this for his family, and he knows that. It's going to be hard, but I think he can do it."

They were on speaker phone, so Karen jumped in, "He looked okay, Jess. He'll be fine. You know the guy in charge said something that shocked us. He said, 'Why is he here? He has family who will drive him all this way. He still has a wife and a child he sees every day. He has a home and a job. His parents haven't disowned him. He hasn't been arrested. Usually, people come here crawling to the door and begging us to take them in because they have nothing left. I'm not sure he belongs here.' That's what he told us."

"We're hoping it won't get that bad," I said to them, realizing we were all getting educated on this road to recovery.

"That's what we told him." It was Keith this time. "But he said he wasn't sure he was ready. I thought for a minute he wasn't going to keep him. I practically had to beg him to let James stay."

I knew Keith had a way with words, and I was so glad he was the one up there with James. I thanked them again for taking my son to rehab. Things you never think you'll have to say when you have kids.

After I hung up the phone, I filled Kylie in on the conversation.

"He'll be fine," she said. "He's there and that was the hardest part, just getting him there."

As the day wore on, I let myself continue to hope this was the beginning of the end of my son's drug addiction.

Chapter Nine

The weekend flew by with a few no-heat calls but nothing serious. It was Monday morning before I knew it. Mondays are always busy, and of course, I pulled in at three minutes after eight. Paul was still in the office.

"Right on time as usual," he said.

I tried to ignore the cynicism in his voice as I ran to take the phones off the call forwarding that sends them to the answering service.

"I know, I know, I'm sorry," I said as I dialed the phone to check in with the service for any new calls that may have come in since they faxed over their list an hour ago.

I turned on both computers to let them warm up. Paul had already sent the drivers off, but a couple of new deliveries couldn't wait until tomorrow, so they would have to be called in over the radio. Paul said he'd take care of that and left to go to his office.

"He doesn't look happy," Kylie said. I hadn't heard her come in.

"No, he's not. I've got to get here earlier especially on Mondays. Can you come in earlier too? Just ten or fifteen minutes." She had to do the round trip to the methadone clinic on Mondays, so I knew why she was late today, but we both needed to change.

"Yes, I can do that, no problem."

"Thanks," I said. Knowing she would want to talk, I added, "Can you print these tickets? Then you can tell me all about your weekend."

I signed on to the online banking site to check our balance as usual. And there it was again. Two more checks I didn't recognize. How long would this last? I thought it was over. I made sure Kylie was distracted and clicked the camera to view the checks. Sure enough, they were written in James' handwriting to himself and signed by me. They were cashed on Wednesday. The day after he assured me it would never happen again, and two days before he went to rehab. He was supposed to be clean for seven days. What would happen now? We hadn't heard from him at all, a good sign. My stomach couldn't take much more of this. I was carrying around a bottle of tums in my pocketbook now.

We were never going to get ahead this way. Not only was James stealing, but our regular customers were struggling to pay their oil bills, and new customers were bouncing checks. I was thinking we were going to have to stop taking checks from all the new customers. Another one was returned over the weekend. This was the third bounced check in two weeks. When people couldn't pay their regular oil company, they would go to a different one. I'd have to talk to Paul about it. The price of oil was even higher than last week, and a cold snap was forecast.

I closed the banking site before anyone noticed and finally turned to Kylie to let her know she could talk to me. This was routine after she had seen Tom. She always filled me in on all the details. Well, probably not all of them, I was her mother after all. Kylie had never had a lot of girlfriends, and I couldn't think of anyone she was close to right now. So I filled in as best I could.

"It was a great weekend. He got a job, but he can't start for another week. It's for a cement company, pouring foundations. He's excited about it." Then she hesitated and looked down.

I hate this part. "What's wrong, Sweetie?" Was he going to break her heart?

"Nothing's wrong. It's just he hates that I'm on methadone. He doesn't mean to, but he makes me feel like such a loser. He did drugs too. I told you that, remember?" I shook my head, I did. "But he was able to stop without any help, and now he's been clean for well over a year and going to all these meetings, and he thinks he knows it all. He thinks being on methadone is the same as being on drugs." By the time she stopped talking she was near tears.

Was this the opening I was waiting for? I wanted her off methadone too, and maybe he could help. But I didn't want her to do it for him. I didn't want a new boyfriend telling her what to do. But there was nothing wrong with him supporting her while she weaned off. As long as it was her decision. I was over thinking.

"What do you want to do?" I finally said to Kylie. "It's been a year and a half," I added, figuring as her mother I had a right and an obligation to nudge her a little in the direction I wanted her to go in. A new boyfriend did not.

"I know I should, but I'm scared. I never want to go back to that life, and so many people fail when they try to get off. I don't want to have the cravings or the withdrawals. I want to sleep and be normal."

I understood. I had gone through it all with her.

"What's the worst that can happen?"

"I fail and become a drug addict again."

"If that happens, you go back on methadone. That's the worst case, but you won't let that happen. If you wean down slowly, you'll know how you feel each step of the way. If you get to a level that's too difficult, you go back up and try again after you stabilize, right?" I had been rehearsing this conversation in my head.

"I guess you're right," she said, sounding a little

unsure.

"Tom and I will help you get through it. How do you start? Do you have to get an okay from your counselor?" I wanted to pin down the details before she could change her mind.

"Yes. She'll probably try to talk me out of it as she always has. I have an appointment on Thursday. I can probably start next week."

"She won't talk you out of it this time as long as you're firm. You have to let her know you're ready. I know you can do it. More importantly, I think you know you can do it. It's time." I gave her a hug as the phone rang reminding us we had to work.

As I hung up the phone and went to print another ticket, I dared to think maybe in ninety days when James came home, both of my children would be drug-free, and we could put this mess behind us forever.

Two days later that dream was crushed.

Chapter Ten

I received a call from James on Wednesday. I was surprised to hear his voice when he said, "Hi, Mom."

"I thought you couldn't call for thirty days?" I asked.

"I'm not supposed to."

"Then why are you? What's going on? How are you doing?" I said, hoping he only wanted a pep talk and had asked for a phone call.

"I'm fine. How are you? How's Dad making out?"

Did he just need to check in? Make sure we were doing okay without him?

"Good, we're all good. We miss you but we'll be fine. We're getting by. Don't you worry about us, you only need to get better." I was trying to say all the right things to keep him there, and then I heard it. "Was that Renee? Did Lauren go to visit you?" He didn't have to tell me. I knew.

"No, I'm home," he said. Then added, "It wasn't for me. I couldn't leave my family. I have to support them. I'm better. I've even gained some weight. I'm going back to the outpatient clinic. I think my health insurance will pay for counseling with a substance abuse counselor too. It'll be okay, Mom. I just have to do it my way."

He was rambling on waiting for me to say something, but I didn't have anything to say. When he finally stopped talking, the phone was silent. I felt tears begin to form in my eyes. Not now, I told myself. My dream of having my son back to his old self was over. There was nothing I could do about it. There was still silence on the phone.

"How long have you been home?" I finally asked, wondering if he even made it through the weekend. "How did you get home?"

"Lauren picked me up on Sunday."

He had lasted two days.

"Were you going to hide out at home for ninety days?"

"No, I just didn't know how to tell you. I don't want you to be upset."

"Well, I'm disappointed as I'm sure everyone will be when they find out. We worked hard to get you there. You could have at least stayed longer than two days."

"You don't understand. I couldn't stay there."

I could hear his voice crack, so I dropped it.

"What are you going to do now? We can't have you back unless you can convince your father you're past all this."

"I'll come in tomorrow to talk to him. Can you tell him I'm home?"

"Thanks, let me break the bad news to him. By the way, there were more checks that came through. You said you didn't have any more." My disappointment suddenly turned to anger.

"That must have been the same time," he lied.

"No, they were cashed the Wednesday before you left. Were you high when you went up there? Is that why you couldn't stay?" It made sense now. He was probably having withdrawals. They weren't a medical facility and couldn't help him detox.

"No, I was clean, and I'm clean now."

I knew he was lying about last week, but I didn't know about now. There was no need to go on. He wouldn't tell me, and what could I do if he did confess? It was too

115

late.

We were back to square one, and someone had to tell Paul.

Paul took the news of James' return better than I expected. He wasn't surprised.

"I wouldn't have been able to live with a bunch of people I didn't know either," he said. "What's his plan now?"

"I think he wants to work. Kylie checked with the health insurance, and they'll cover individual substance abuse counseling for a limited time. That might help. He said he'll continue meeting with the pastor from his church, too."

"I don't want him anywhere near the company if he's screwed up. I mean it, Jess," he told me in no uncertain terms. "We've worked too hard to have him mess it up now."

"I know, I feel the same way."

"Don't misunderstand me. I want him to be part of this company, and we could really use his help but not the way he was. Do you know he spilled my entire tool box in Brad's driveway? Tools rolling everywhere and he just walked by them like he didn't notice. And don't get me started on the condition he left the van in. It's only a year old, and he's turned it into a piece of junk. The same with the tools. He doesn't take care of anything anymore. When he started here, he wasn't like that. I could go on about the things he's done, but it won't do any good. He just needs to change. That's all I'm trying to say."

He was having the same mixed feelings I had. I understood.

"You know," he continued, "he's always been a little different, I guess, but he is so smart. I keep thinking I can work with him. Show him how to do things the right way. Now I'm not so sure."

"He's going to come into the office tomorrow morning. Do you want to talk to him?" I waited not sure what to do if he said he didn't.

After a heavy sigh, he said, "Yes, I'll talk to him, but I'm warning you he has to change."

Things were almost back to normal for a few days. James promised to sell his snowmobile to pay the company back for the stolen and forged checks no one but me knew about. All together they totaled over three thousand dollars. He had an appointment with a counselor in the city the next week. Kylie talked to her counselor, and they agreed to drop her dose by five milligrams a week. She wanted to do ten but agreed to start at five. Once she had made up her mind, she wanted it done.

It was bitterly cold and forecast to stay that way through the weekend. Our first no-heat call came in just after midnight on Friday. I was relieved when James answered my call and was eager to go out to service the customer's burner.

The next call came in a couple of hours later. This time, James did not answer his phone. When he didn't return the call in a half hour, I called Sam. Fortunately, he answered and said he would see what he could do. He doesn't always answer his phone, so I considered it a good night. We were working in the morning because of the cold. I'd catch up with James then.

James never showed up at the office or answered his phone the next morning. I finally called Lauren. She said he was sleeping because I had him out all night. I listened as she told me I should not have given James all three no-heat calls. Sam should have taken at least one. James was exhausted, she said, and he needed to sleep.

Kylie was sitting next to me as I listened to Lauren.

When I hung up the phone, she said, "He was out all night, right?"

I shook my head, yes, and she continued, "It was Friday night. He probably had no problem finding drugs and the perfect excuse to be out."

"That's just great! He was in our van, with our name on it!"

"I don't know for sure, but I'm just saying…."

"I know. How much does this stuff cost anyway? Tina's taking his paychecks, so how would he pay for it? I don't want him owing some drug dealer money."

"Mom, you never owe drug dealers money. They don't give out drugs on credit. Either you have cash or you don't get drugs." She was being the teacher again.

"If James came in and asked you for money to pay a drug dealer, it would not be for money owed, it would be to buy more drugs," she continued her lecture. "Don't ever let him tell you he owes some really bad guy money. Okay?"

"Okay," I answered like a good little student. It was a little too late but nice to know for future reference. I had never told anyone about the incident in October when James first borrowed money for that same reason. I had given my son money to buy drugs.

"So how does he buy drugs in the middle of the night with no money?" I asked Kylie.

"I don't know. Steals it, maybe. Who was the service call for? Did they pay him with cash?"

"I don't know how they paid. I haven't seen the bill. You don't think he would do that, do you?" Had James found another way to steal from us?

"I don't think 'sober' James would do it. But 'wants desperately to get high' James would. If you get those

118

cravings or you're having withdrawals, you will do almost anything to get drugs. Eventually, most people learn the consequences afterward are just not worth it."

She had been there but had never stolen from anybody, at least I didn't think so. I'm sure she doesn't tell me everything.

"Thanks for the education. You don't have to stay here today. It's your day off. Go ahead, I know you're heading in town. I'll deal with your brother when I catch up with him."

"Are you sure? I know it breaks your heart but you have to get mad, so remember 'don't love him to death,' okay?"

"I'll remember. I'll just wring his neck instead. You go on, I'll be fine."

We laughed as she headed out the door. It was nice to see her happy. I was worried about how she would feel next week when they changed her dose, but I was more worried about her brother.

I had another no-heat call Saturday night, but the customer was only out of oil. I explained how he could use five gallons of K-1 kerosene to get by until Monday and save the after-hours charge. Then I talked him through bleeding the air out of the lines to restart the furnace. Paul had shown me how to do this many years ago, and it came in handy. Some people wanted us to take care of everything, but many people welcomed the chance to do it themselves and save money. Paul believed it was better to educate them and save us the late night trip. We kept a number of five-gallon pails of K-1 kerosene in the pick-up truck and each van for those emergencies. That way we wouldn't have to take an oil truck out in the middle of the night for one delivery.

Thankfully, I didn't have to try to reach one of the boys.

James checked in on Sunday and apologized for not getting back to me. Paul was with me so I simply said I would talk to him on Monday.

"You better be on time and ready to work," I said for Paul's benefit.

When I saw James on Monday, he looked fine, still thin, but no worse.

"What happened Friday night?" I asked. "Do you have the invoice for the job?"

"It was a clogged oil filter," he said as he handed me the invoice marked paid.

"Where's the check?"

"It was cash. I'll get it to you later." When he saw the look on my face, he continued, "Lauren saw the cash in my wallet while I was sleeping and took it to buy groceries. She didn't know it wasn't our money. I'll get it from Tina as soon as I see her."

"Lauren said you were out all night on three different calls. What's that all about?" I still wasn't sure I believed him about the money.

"I was wide awake and didn't want to go home. I sat in the parking lot at the lake for a long time and prayed for help. I'm trying to make things work with Lauren, but sometimes it's so hard."

I thought he was near tears. He was believable, but I wasn't sure. I certainly would understand him not wanting to go home. From what Karen had told me over the weekend, the house was no better, and Lauren was refusing help.

Maybe I had jumped to conclusions. "Okay, get me that money as soon as possible," I said to James. I would give him the benefit of the doubt this time.

***

A couple of days later, I was blindsided again. I received a call from the grocery store in the next town over. It was one of the larger chain stores, so I didn't know anyone who worked there. Kylie answered the call and handed the phone to me. The nice man on the phone explained that he had two returned checks with my name on them written to James and signed by me. However, the account that the checks were drawn on was closed. I recognized the bank name. The checks were from an old account I had closed quite a few years ago.

"I didn't write those checks. They must have been stolen," I said. I knew they might go after James, but I couldn't cover for him this time.

"It's okay, Ma'am. I didn't think so. Thank you," he said and hung up the phone.

That was it. I waited for James to say something, for an arrest warrant, a police officer to show up for a report, or something, but nothing happened.

I did confront James, but he had some kind of excuse and a promise to pay me back. This time, I told him he was not allowed in the office alone. I would tell Paul to change the locks.

I told Paul at dinner that night. I never told him about the company checks James took, but I told him about the ones on the closed account.

"I think we need to change the locks to the front door," I said not mentioning I had already taken the keys from James' key ring. He obviously had others.

"I can't believe he would do that," Paul said as he tried to understand how his own son could steal from us.

I remembered how sick I felt when I first realized he had stolen from us a few weeks before. Now I was sure Paul was going through the same emotions.

***

So the next day, Paul changed the locks never mentioning anything to James.

Unlike her father, Kylie was not surprised about the checks, but she stopped short of saying "I told you so." She was doing well on her lower dose of methadone this first week. So well, in fact, she asked to drop down another ten milligrams the next week.

The next week was extremely difficult for all of us.

Kylie was feeling the withdrawals from the next drop in her methadone dose. She was determined to stick with it, but she was not feeling well and left the office often. I began to wonder if I should have asked her to wait until spring, but she was committed now, so I wanted her to continue.

I was pretty sure James was having withdrawals too. He called in sick on Monday and Tuesday and when he showed up on Wednesday he still looked awful.

"I know what you're thinking, but it's just the flu," James said as he entered the office.

He was right. He knew what I was thinking.

Paul thought the same thing. "This is ridiculous, we can't run a company this way!" We were behind with scheduled jobs while emergency calls were still pouring in. "I thought he was supposed to be getting help."

"He met with a counselor last week, and I think he has another appointment in a few days. Maybe he really did have the flu."

"Well, he better turn this around fast. I didn't plan on doing his job all winter." His tone revealed the anger, frustration, and disappointment we both felt.

Later that day I got a call from Paul on his cell phone.

"Did you call James off this job and send him on an

122

emergency call?" They were on an installation that Paul had been putting off until James could help.

"No, I haven't talked to him since he left with you this morning."

"I knew it. He's been gone for two hours. He said you needed him and took off. I should have checked with you before he left." The despair and frustration were even more apparent in his voice.

"I don't know what to say. I thought he was past that."

"Obviously he isn't!" he shouted into the phone as he ended the call.

I tried to call James but got no answer. I still hadn't heard from him by closing time. Was he in an accident? Jail? Probably not. My son probably went somewhere to get high.

Needless to say, Paul was not in a good mood when he got home very late. He had stayed to finish the install and get the furnace running. Sam was able to help after the emergency calls were done.

We barely spoke that night. The stress was taking a toll on our marriage. I could see the signs. I was afraid our marriage was about to collapse, and I didn't know how to stop it. It had happened only once before, about seven years ago.

Back in 1998 when our kids were teenagers, we hit a rough patch. They were typical kids, but they had their issues. We were always stressed with company problems, especially in the cold months. It's hard to leave problems at work when you work together. So, because of our work stress, the kids, the cold, and the long days, we were a walking time bomb ready to explode. It had been a particularly long few weeks. The arguments usually started at the dinner table. We had been having these arguments regularly with someone leaving the table in tears almost every night.

I wasn't sure what made that night different, but it was particularly bad. Paul slammed his fist on the table and went off on a profanity-laced tirade about something. I'm sure he was justified. We were all making mistakes. Typical, human, and adolescent mistakes, I tried to tell him. I stood up to walk away, our dinner uneaten as usual, when he grabbed my hair. I have always had long hair, and he grabbed it by the ends. He didn't pull it but just held it enough to stop me. I froze. So did the kids. So did Paul. We stood there for just a second. Paul dropped my hair and stomped away. I told Kylie to get a few things, we were going to Grammy's. James said he would stay with Dad, so Kylie and I quickly and quietly left.

My mother's house was five miles away. I tried to hold it together for Kylie's sake. I had never left my husband before, and we had been married eighteen years at that time. I had always said if I left it would be for real. I wasn't going to run home to my mom every time we had an argument, and we did argue a lot at times. We had always managed to work things out as ours was mostly a happy marriage, but this time it was different.

My mom welcomed me with open arms. "You can stay as long as you need," she said. My dad had passed away a few years before, and I think she would have loved for me to stay forever. After Kylie went to bed, I cried in my mother's arms for what seemed like hours. I had failed, I told her. I failed my husband, my kids, and my marriage. I cried myself to sleep.

I had left my husband, but I had not left my job. That was our other baby. We had started it from its infancy, and I would not let it down. So I went to work. Paul and I spoke very little that day, but the job got done. Then I spent another night at my mother's.

The next day would be the same, but as we locked the office door to leave, Paul asked if I was coming home.

"Do you want me to?" I asked, my voice quivering a little.

"Yes."

"Okay," I whispered. That was it. No discussions, no "I'm sorry," no "I'll never do it again." We were both hurt and needed to heal. But a line had been drawn in the sand.

That was a long time ago. While we worked hard not to ever cross that line again, I could see it inching closer.

We would somehow get through the next few weeks. James was barely showing up for work but assured us he was getting better. For some reason, we kept feeling sorry for him and let him remain "employed."

Paul was getting more and more frustrated with both kids. And with me since I always tried to stand up for them, especially Kylie. I wanted her off the methadone. I had convinced her to do this and would stand behind her.

Kylie was in the throws of withdrawal. Determined to make it on her schedule, she would not adjust the dose up or even maintain the lower dose for a few weeks. The dose would be lowered by ten milligrams each week no matter how she felt.

Her hands shook again, and she felt sick most of the time. She would often run into her apartment to vomit or lie down until the waves of nausea passed. It was heartbreaking to watch, but I hoped it would be over soon. Needless to say, there were times when she wasn't much help in the office.

I wasn't as forgiving with James. He had somehow managed to get a hold of one of my credit cards, and I had just gotten a bill with three large cash withdrawals. I was furious. I called the card company to say the charges weren't mine and was told they would investigate. When asked point blank if a family member could have used the card, I said I wasn't sure.

"It could have been my son, but if he used it, he didn't have my permission." I gave them his full name and address. Then I worried about what would happen to James. I didn't really know for sure it was him, and of course, he denied it.

When she was feeling up to it, Kylie was trying to collect from some of our slow paying customers. Money was tight. When we should have been saving for the summer, we were still barely getting by. Our receivables had never been so high. James was not helping either.

Kylie hung up the phone from a customer who owed several hundred dollars for service work James had done.

"Mom, Mr. Miller said he paid James in cash when he finished the work a few weeks ago."

Not again, I cringed. James had never paid for the money Lauren had used to buy groceries. Now another customer's cash payment was gone.

"Show it as paid in the computer. I'll deal with your brother." I knew Kylie was getting more disgusted with James, and it broke my heart. They had been very close growing up. I wanted to say I was sure James would pay it back, but I knew she wouldn't buy it.

Just then Mark from the convenience store down the road came in. I knew who he was, but he was not a customer, and he didn't look happy.

"Is James your son?" In fact, he was angry.

"Yes, is something wrong?" I asked dreading the

answer.

"I'll say there's something wrong. I let him cash two checks at my store last week for $400 each. He said it was for parts for you guys and the banks were closed, so I agreed. I know he's a nice kid but both checks bounced. I only agreed to cash them because you guys have been in business a long time, and you have a good reputation around town."

"I'm so sorry. I'll cover the checks. Do you have them with you?" I was so humiliated. I wanted to crawl into a hole.

He gave me James' checks, and I gave him a company check for $870 as I quickly calculated in my head how much our checking account balance was.

"Thank you. I knew you'd make good on them." His tone had changed.

"Again, I'm so sorry," I said as he walked out the door.

Kylie heard everything. "Why did you cover his checks?"

"I had to, it's our company reputation. Right here in town." I sat down and put my head in my hands trying to recover.

"You can't let him get away with that. You've got to do something."

"I know, I know. I'll do something. I can't talk about it right now." I got up and went to the small bathroom in the office. I managed to pull myself together without breaking down in tears, but I didn't know what I was going to do. Again, I thought we couldn't go on like this.

I confronted James as soon as I saw him. He had the same excuses. When he realized I wasn't buying them this time, he told me he was thinking of going to the methadone clinic.

"I thought you hated that. You told me once you'd never take methadone," I said to James.

He looked at Kylie who was now next to us.

"Do you think you can get me in? I need help." All talk about the $800 was brushed aside. He was good.

"I can't 'get you in.' It's not like that. You have to go to an interview, and they decide if you're a good candidate."

"Can you get me an interview? I need to do something. I can't stop." He was shaking. Probably in withdrawals again.

I knew Kylie felt sorry for him then. "I'll call my counselor."

"Thanks, I need to go home. Let me know when I have to be there," he said as he walked out the door.

He left without any talk of repayment. I knew that money was gone as well as the cash payment for the service call. He was slowly but surely breaking our company. And I was covering for him. The credit card company would issue me a new card. While I wouldn't be responsible for those charges, the other money we would never see, and I was afraid there was more missing.

Kylie made an appointment for James at the methadone clinic for the next day. He took his own vehicle since we didn't want our company van in the parking lot. I was certainly not happy another child of mine was going to be on methadone. I must be a really bad mother to let this happen, I berated myself. But what other choice did we have? It had helped Kylie. She had never gone back to doing drugs. Although she wasn't completely normal, it was better than the alternative.

I assumed the intake interview went well because

they gave James his first dose of methadone before he left the clinic.

He proceeded to crash his car on the way back to town. Fortunately, he only ran off the road and into a field. He called Sam to come help him get the car back on the road, and no police were involved. James claimed he fell asleep, but Kylie was convinced he lied about how much heroin he was taking to make sure he got a large dose of methadone.

He never went back to the methadone clinic.

So again we were back to square one. The outpatient clinic with the miracle drug didn't work, the prayers and counseling didn't work, the ninety-day recovery center didn't work. Now we could add the methadone clinic to the growing list of treatment options that did not work for James. What was next?

Chapter Eleven

We continued as best we could. The stress on all of us was building. Paul grabbed James whenever he showed up looking fairly normal, and the rest of the time, he figured things out for himself. I was handling the office mostly by myself now as Kylie's withdrawals were getting worse. Paul really didn't understand what was going on with her, and when I tried to explain, he would simply say never mind, he didn't want to know.

Tina had given up on doing James' bills. She showed up at the office with all his paperwork and dropped it on my desk.

"I really thought I could help," she explained, "but I can't do it anymore."

"It's okay. Thanks for trying," I said not knowing what I would do now.

"You can't do this either. They just don't get it. Both of them want all their bills paid, while at the same time, they want me to give them all their money back to spend on other things. I've tried explaining finances and putting them on a budget. James, and Lauren too, still come to me constantly asking for more money. I told them if they take more money out of the account, their bills won't get paid. Then they blame me for not paying their bills. I paid his last mortgage payment out of my pocket thinking I would get it back next month, but that's not going to happen."

"I'm so sorry." Again, I was ashamed of my own son.

"It's not your fault. They're adults. I realize now we're going to have to let them fail, or they'll never learn. Give this paperwork back to them. They'll either sink or swim. Whatever you do, don't pay their bills. We're prolonging the inevitable. Let them fail!"

Tina said the last part pretty loudly. I had always been just a little intimidated by Paul's sister. She's very smart and firm in her convictions. I admire her strength and independence. She's taught me so much over the years, so when she said to let them fail, I knew I had to do just that.

But how do you let them fail when there is a two-year-old involved? And not just any two-year-old. We're talking about the cutest, sweetest, most adorable two-year-old ever. We're talking about my only grandchild. At this point, I was caring less and less about the adults, but I loved my granddaughter so much. What would happen to her if her parents couldn't get their act together?

I told Tina I would stay out of it. I thanked her again and apologized over and over for my son's treatment of his aunt. I knew she loved him, however, love was not what he needed. She had the strength and conviction to stop helping him. I hoped I could do the same.

When I saw James later that day, I gave him the paperwork and told him he was on his own. I let him know Tina had made the last month's mortgage payment. He needed to pay her back somehow, and there would be no one else to make the next payment. The last three months payments had been made for him. First by me, then Keith, and now Tina. That was it, no more I told him, don't even think of asking.

In the meantime when Kylie was in the office, she spent a lot of time researching drug abuse and addiction. We

131

were both hoping there was some miracle way of helping James.

"He should get arrested and go to jail," she said one day.

"That's what I'm trying to prevent," I replied, a little shocked at what she had said.

"It may be the best thing. He probably wouldn't serve too much time but long enough for him to get clean. They have addiction counselors in jail, you know. Then he would be on probation for probably a year or two, and they would do random drug testing. If he got caught with anything in his system, they would put him back in jail for a while. It may be the best thing."

"It's a thought. I wish there was a place that would lock him up to keep him in treatment long enough to get help, but I'd rather not see him go to jail. That could ruin his whole future."

I realized I shouldn't have said the last part since Tom had just gotten out of jail. I had finally met him when she brought him to the office on a Saturday morning a few weeks earlier. He was a nice looking young man, tall and thin with brown hair and eyes. He was also extremely nice and well mannered. I could tell right away he adored Kylie. We laughed over some of the letters he had written to her while he was in jail. He was easy to talk to and was not uncomfortable being around Kylie's "Mom" like some boyfriends are. I liked him and was happy for her. I hoped he would not break her heart.

I also hoped if they were together forever, his criminal record would not come back to haunt them. That's why I didn't want James to get arrested. I wanted to get him the help he needed to get better before that happened, but we were running out of options.

"I'm sorry, I didn't mean anything by that," I told

Kylie.

"I know, Mom," she said. "I think about Tom's record too. But I love him sooo much!"

I knew that, but would it be enough? I hoped so.

I found myself barely getting through the days. We were all on edge. I was trying to keep my family together as well as run the day to day oil delivery end of the business. Paul was upset with pretty much everyone by now. Kylie and James were barely speaking, and when they did it usually ended up in an argument. I knew I couldn't really depend on either of the kids. Paul felt the same way too. Not only James, but Sam was acting up now as well. We had come to depend on him more and more, and I think he was starting to resent it.

When I wasn't dealing with a family crisis, I was trying to get invoices posted in the computer, tickets printed, and deposits to the bank. Making sure we had enough money in the company checking account to cover the oil payments was one of the biggest issues, and I was sure there was more money missing.

Things weren't much better at home. The phone rang most nights now, and I cringed every time I heard it. A few nights ago, I couldn't reach either one of the boys and had to wake Paul. There was a no-heat call at the apartment building on Main street that had been giving us so much trouble.

Having no other choice, Paul had to go himself. It was one o'clock in the morning. He didn't get home until six, just in time to shower, shave, and head back to the office to get the drivers off on their delivery routes. He explained to me he had to stay there and hit the restart switch about every fifteen minutes to keep it running. He said he finally realized

James had used the wrong size pipe when he was there last. The furnace was not getting enough oil. He would go back to fix it as soon as the drivers were on their way. He wouldn't ask either of the boys.

James had been calling me at night lately as well. He would sometimes go on about his problems with Lauren or Paul. He would talk about his addiction and his trouble beating it. My son told me he asked God to help him, but James didn't think God was listening. I knew at these times he wasn't home, and I'd ask where he was. Sometimes, he was at the beach sitting in the van. That wasn't too far from his home, but I worried the police would stop and ask questions. At times I thought he was clean, but at other times I was sure he was high. Those were the times my son wouldn't tell me where he was.

During one of these conversations, I began to worry about suicide. He sounded so depressed. Could that be what had caused all this? I talked to him about antidepressants and asked him to make an appointment with his doctor. I would remind him the next day.

He did see his doctor the next week and was given a prescription for the drug Paxil. It would take three to six weeks to notice a difference. I prayed he would make it that long.

Paul and I continued to argue constantly as we watched everything we worked for fall apart. He was trying to hold up his end of the business while I was trying to hold up mine. We were never on the same page. I worried about the kids and bills. He worried about the quality of work and our reputation. At a time when we should have been supporting each other, we were unable to connect. Wallowing in our own problems with anger right under the surface, waiting to boil over.

Many dinners went untouched. If something indicated an argument coming, I started wondering if I should even bother to cook. I knew it wouldn't get eaten.

This particular evening started out pretty typical, but there was definitely more stress in the air. By the time we sat down to dinner, Paul was angry, frustrated, and sarcastic. James had not shown up for work again.

"Why are we still paying him?" he yelled and glared at me as he slammed his fist on the table.

There was no talking to him when he got this way, so I stopped eating. That made him angrier.

"Go on, don't eat! It's all my fault, isn't it!" he screamed.

I got up to leave the table, knowing dinner was over, again. As I walked into the kitchen with my uneaten plate, Paul picked up a small bowl filled with melted butter and threw it. I had made haddock, one of our favorite meals. Paul liked to dip his in butter, so I had melted some in a small glass bowl to go with his dinner. Now that bowl, butter and all, flew by my head. It didn't hit me. I'm not sure if he intended it to or not, but I ran out of the kitchen. He followed me and grabbed my shoulder. As I turned around, he had his hand raised to hit me. I froze. Paul had never been violent. He screamed, yelled, swore, and pounded his fist, but he had never laid a hand on me or the kids. What was happening to us?

We stood still for a few seconds as Paul stared at me. Did he hate me? I wasn't sure. At that moment, I think he did. But he lowered his hand and slammed the bedroom door as he stormed back into the kitchen.

I grabbed my pocketbook and keys and left. It had happened again. The stress of the business and the kids had come between us. That line in the sand had been crossed.

135

I drove to the office, not knowing where else to go and not wanting anyone to know. I sat there for a couple of hours crying and wondering if I could find something to sleep on. I didn't blame Paul. It wasn't his fault. We were all stressed. We were scared for our son and our business, both feeling helpless and wanting to blame someone. I was messing up and forgetting stupid things as my mind was constantly on James. He was the first thing I thought of when I woke up in the morning and the last thing on my mind when I fell asleep, if I fell asleep.

Paul was fighting a losing battle. We all were. Would we lose our marriage as well? We had been married for twenty-five years, would we see twenty-six?

Three hours after I left, my phone rang. It was Paul. I was afraid to answer. Was he still angry? Would he be even more angry at me for leaving? Was he calling to tell me never to come home again?

"Where are you?" he said quietly when I answered the phone

"At the office," I answered just as quietly.

"Are you coming home?"

I paused, starting to cry again. "I don't want to live like this anymore?" I choked out through sobs.

"Neither do I," his voice trembling too.

I cried harder.

I went home, and we held each other all night. We would get through this together somehow, we vowed.

The unthinkable happened a couple nights later.

Lauren called me at ten o'clock in the evening. I was surprised to see her number on the phone. She never called me, so I immediately thought something had happened to James. My heart was pounding in my chest when I answered. I had been on the verge of sleep.

"Have you seen James?" she asked in a panic.

"No. I haven't seen or heard from him since this afternoon." I wondered why she was in such a state when he was now known for disappearing for hours at a time. "What's wrong, Lauren?"

"He left at seven to go to the store, and he hasn't come back. He's not answering his phone."

Again, I was thinking that was normal behavior for him nowadays.

"He has Renee," she cried.

Now I understood.

"Why does he have Renee?" I asked her although at this point it didn't really matter why. He just does.

"He was only going to the store, he said, so I told him to take her. I figured if he had Renee he would come right back. I'm worried sick."

I was worried sick too, by now.

"I don't know what to say. He sometimes stops by the beach," I said to my distraught daughter-in-law.

"I've looked there. I've been driving around for an hour. I don't know where else to look. If you hear from him, will you let me know?" she said through tears and hung up the phone.

My heart broke for her. I have criticized her and even put some of the blame on her for James' problems, but she loved Renee. Now Renee was out in a vehicle driven by my son who quite possibly was high. Would he put his two-year-old daughter in danger to do drugs? I didn't know anymore. I was sick with worry, and there wasn't anything I could do.

The call woke Paul up. I told him what was going on, and we sat there in bed hoping the worst wouldn't happen. I

137

prayed James would not do anything to risk his daughter's safety. I knew he loved her. There had to be a good explanation.

Then I thought back to Lauren. As bad as I felt for her, I was now filled with mixed emotions. I was angry with her for sending Renee with James, even if he was her father, but I knew how easy it was to trust him and believe everything he said.

It was a long night. I never heard a word from anyone.

At seven o'clock, I called James. When he didn't answer, I called Lauren. I could tell I woke her up.

"Is everything okay?" I asked.

"Yes, James came home about an hour later. I guess he stopped at a friend's house and left the phone in the van. Renee slept on his lap for a while. James is in the shower now. Do you want to talk to him?"

"No, I'll see him at work," I said, trying to stay calm. She could have called to let me know they were home. Paul and I hadn't slept all night.

When James showed up at work, I asked him about last night. I thought he looked okay, maybe tired. I never could tell for sure.

"Lauren overreacted," he said and then told me the same thing Lauren had.

I wondered if she was covering for him. I would never know, but Kylie had once said to me that a drug addict would sell his own child for drugs. I knew he wouldn't sell his child, but would he endanger her life?

Keith came over to the house the following weekend

with some information he wanted to share with us.

"Richard heard of a program called *Teen Challenge*."

James was twenty-three, no longer a teen but I kept listening. I'd listen to anything at this point.

"Don't worry about the name, they have programs for all ages," Keith continued. "It's a Christian-based program for addicts. It has one of the best success rates of any program out there. They have a couple here in New England, and it's not too expensive. The people stay at a house and do all the work to run the home themselves. The residents all chip in to do chores, like cooking, cleaning, mowing the lawn, doing laundry, and other stuff. They have Bible classes and classes on addiction. They offer job training too. They go around to the different churches and give their testimony."

"I'm sorry," I interrupted. "What did you mean when you said 'they give their testimony'?" I had never heard of that phrase except in a legal sense.

"They tell their story of addiction and finding help usually through the Lord. They're Christian, but all denominations are welcome."

"Has anyone mentioned this to James?" Paul asked.

"That's why I'm here. We talked to him about it the other day when he met with Pastor. He doesn't want anything to do with it." He paused, "I was thinking you guys could talk to him."

"You know what happened the last time we tried to send him to a residential program. I don't think he'll go," Paul responded.

"It would be a great opportunity for him."

"Not if he won't stay," I added. "Any way they can lock him in?" It was meant entirely as a joke.

"They have had some people sentenced to prison and the judge sends there instead. I think it has to be worked out with the courts."

"So now we just have to get him arrested," Paul said with a little laugh.

We hadn't had much sleep and were pretty sure this would not work for James. We didn't want to sound like we weren't grateful for Keith's efforts, but he laughed too.

"How long is the program for?" I was thinking maybe James was beginning to realize he needed to be away for a while.

"Fifteen months."

I was sure there was no way he would commit to that.

"After thirty days, his family can visit. With married people, they can earn weekend passes after so many months," Keith continued. He could tell he was losing us.

"You know he couldn't do that," Paul replied. "He wouldn't last the first thirty days. Don't get me wrong, I think it's great. I would love to have him do it. If you can talk him into it, we'll be supportive. We'll talk to him too. I just don't think he'll go for it."

"Well, keep it in mind. It's a great program. Some of the guys from the program are coming to our church in a few weeks. I'm going to make sure James is there that day." He headed for the door.

"Thank you. We'll try talking with him too, but I just don't want you to get your hopes up," Paul said to Keith as he left.

After he was gone, Paul looked at me and shook his head.

"He's crazy if he thinks James would ever go for that."

Chapter Twelve

Again we struggled through a few more weeks. James had his good days and bad days. He continued with his counseling and meetings with the pastor at church. He stayed on the antidepressants too. We hoped he was getting better, but then he would call in sick or just not show up. He knew now that we could tell if he was using drugs, so we figured that was the reason for all the absences from work. If he was high, he stayed away.

There was no mention of paying me back for the money he stole, and I didn't want to ask about his bills. I had a feeling his last mortgage payment hadn't been made. It broke my heart to see all the work to get him to manage his money and have good credit had been wasted. I had finally come to realize I couldn't keep paying his bills. He would have to learn the hard way. I told myself that at twenty-three, he still had time to recover and have a normal life if he could just stop. Now.

Kylie was trying to manage her methadone reduction. Eager to be done, she was increasing the amount the dose was lowered every week. I worried as each week became harder and harder for her. My daughter was getting thin and more emotional, running to her apartment in tears two or three times a day. The obsessiveness was worse now with her constantly counting, organizing, and redoing mundane tasks. Her movements were jerky, her body jittery, her hands trembled.

Paul again asked what was wrong with her. I simply said she's trying to get better. Please give her time.

"What is it with my kids?" he asked. "No, I mean, what is it with your kids?"

They were always my kids when they weren't acting up to his standards which seemed to be all the time lately.

At the end of March, I took a hard look at our finances. After the long cold winter, we had plenty of cash on hand, even after James had helped himself to a good chunk of it. However, the amount of cash was not anywhere near enough to get us through the slow times that were just ahead. Our receivables were double what they usually were at this time of year. Kylie and I were doing what we could to collect money from customers, but more often than not these people just didn't have it, and to make matters worse, they needed more oil.

These were people we'd known for years, some from when we started the business almost seventeen years ago. Now they were asking for more credit. How could we say no? Paul didn't want me to deny any of our long-term customers the oil they needed. They promised to pay over the summer, but I knew that most couldn't pay more than they already owed. Some were on fixed incomes, many elderly, all good people.

So we continued to provide them with oil. We offered fifty gallon deliveries at the same price per gallon as one hundred gallon deliveries just to get them through until spring, hoping the price of oil would go down at that time. It didn't.

I knew I had to talk to Paul. He'd been letting me handle the finances alone for many years, but this was different. I hadn't been this nervous about our financial situation for a long time.

"Paul, when you get a second, we should talk about the receivables," I told him, knowing that it was going to be a difficult conversation.

But Paul was good at making things work. In the beginning, we struggled to get the company off the ground and found ourselves drowning in debt. Paul said we would pay one bill at a time. Every time he brought in a check it went for a specific bill, and sure enough, we slowly climbed out of that mountain of debt.

This wasn't exactly the same. We weren't in debt now, but I could see it coming. Was there a way to stop it? Did we have to change the way we did business? Cash only maybe? That's what a lot of companies were doing. I just knew we needed to figure it out before it was too late.

Later that day, I had Kylie handle the phones, and I joined Paul in his office. I brought our list of receivables and projections for the coming months along with our current financial situation.

At first glance, it didn't look so bad because we had money in the bank. But when I explained to Paul we usually had much more than that at this time of year, he understood.

"Where's all the money?" he asked.

I handed him the very long list of receivables.

"It's all right there. If everyone paid everything they owed, we'd be fine, but I sincerely doubt that's going to happen."

I hadn't mentioned the money that was missing because of James, and I still feared there was more I was overlooking. He had his snowmobile up for sale, but no one buys snowmobiles at the end of March.

As he looked over the list, he knew as well as I did we would never get paid for a lot of the oil we delivered that winter. Sometimes, I get the impression people think we get

143

the oil for free.

"I knew it was high, but I didn't realize it had gotten that bad. You're right, you can't count on a lot of this money," Paul said with a sigh.

"Kylie and I will keep trying to collect, but some of these people just don't have it. Any ideas?"

He was always thinking of ways to survive. We had been buying foreclosed homes and putting the drivers to work painting and fixing them up during the slow times. The boys fixed all the plumbing and heating issues. Then we would sell them for a profit in the fall. We had averaged about one or two a year and it certainly helped to get through the off season. I didn't think it would be enough this year.

I was right. Paul did have an idea.

"I was thinking we should get into the propane delivery business. We're installing propane furnaces, and the boys are trained to service them. We would have to send one of the drivers to a class to get certified."

"And we'd have to buy a propane truck," I responded. I was not quite as excited about the idea as Paul was.

"I know, but we can get one from the same company we bought our last two oil trucks from. Our credit's good."

He pulled out some brochures from his desk drawer and proceeded to show me the different styles and the one he thought would work best for us. I could tell he had been thinking about this for a while.

"Don't you have to buy the propane tanks too?" I asked as the dollar signs added up in my head.

"Yes, but I've talked to a couple of suppliers. We don't have to buy too many to start. Eventually, we would buy in bulk to save money, and we have plenty of room down back to store them. There's more profit in propane because of the added expense of the tanks, and it's becoming more common especially in commercial properties and apartment buildings."

He'd done his homework.

"Propane is more of a year-round product," Paul continued, "it's used in cooking, clothes dryers, and pool heaters. I know it's still used mostly for heat, but it should help during the off season. We can get quite a few accounts right away because we installed a bunch of furnaces."

He was ready to expand our business again. It made sense. It was the next step to being a full-service plumbing and heating company.

"What about James? Can we do this without him if we have to?" I was not entirely convinced it was the right move for us, but I listened.

"Yes. If he doesn't come around pretty soon, we'll hire someone else. I'm not saying we should jump right into this. Just give it some thought, okay?"

"Okay. I have to get back to Kylie. She's not having a good day." As I got up to leave, he stopped me.

"Is she all right?" he asked, his face showing the concern he felt for his daughter.

"She's struggling, but I think she'll make it. She's determined, and Tom's been a big help."

Kylie was with Tom as much as possible lately. She told me she couldn't do this without him. I was wondering what was going to happen when he was able to leave the Tranquility House. I was sure it was coming right up. Was he planning on moving in with Kylie? Paul would not be happy about that.

"Is she still seeing that guy?"

"Yes. She really likes him. Kylie says he reminds her of you. I don't see it, but he makes her happy."

"He's a convict. There's no future for him. He'll never get a decent job. Where does she find these guys?"

Paul was whispering now so there was no chance his daughter could overhear.

"It's her life. She has to decide what's important to her. I told her the same thing you just said. She knows the potential problems ahead if they stay together." I was whispering now, too.

"I just don't like it."

"I know." What else could I say? He had made that very clear.

I left Paul's office not knowing what to think. I went in there knowing we needed to cut spending somehow and left wondering if we needed to spend money instead. Should we get in the propane business? It wasn't a bad idea, but it had been an extremely long winter, and it wasn't over. I would let the idea sit there in the back of my mind for a while. I had tickets to organize for the next day.

James' drug issue came to the forefront again a couple of days later. It was a Saturday morning, the first one I had not worked in a very long time. It was mild, and the drivers were caught up with their deliveries. Paul and I decided we didn't need to open the office on Saturdays anymore for a while, probably not again until next winter.

It was just before noon when my phone rang. I recognized the number. The call was from our bank. This can't be good since banks don't call when everything is fine. I was pretty sure we weren't overdrawn. That really wasn't an issue this time of year. So my thoughts went immediately to James. I took a deep breath and answered the phone.

"Hi, Jess. It's Amy from the bank."

"Hi, Amy. Is everything all right? I didn't bounce a check, did I?" I said with a chuckle. She has been at the bank since we were just starting out in business.

146

"No, of course not. I hate to bother you, but I thought I should check with you. James is here with a company check, hand written to him and signed by you. It doesn't look like your signature. It's for $600. Should I cash it?"

I could tell by her voice she was uncomfortable asking. I knew if I admitted I didn't write the check, I was admitting my son was trying to steal from us. I could easily say he needed the funds for a part or something, and I gave him permission. I quickly deduced that if he got away with it once, he would try this stunt again.

"No, Amy, I didn't authorize that." I felt awful. Not only did my banker know we had a problem with our son, I also felt bad for James. I knew he would be embarrassed when Amy told him she couldn't cash the check. I could see him trying to cover himself with a flimsy lie. He was trying to steal from me, and I was the one feeling terrible.

"I'm sure he has a reason for needing the money, but until I talk to him, I'm not sure what it is," I said. "Can you ask him to step outside and give me a call?" I was trying to cover his butt while he was trying to get money for drugs. I was sure he wouldn't call me.

"Sure, I'll tell him," Amy said.

She's a little older than I am with kids about the same age as ours. We talk about our children whenever I see her at the bank. Now it would be difficult, embarrassing, and awkward.

I thanked her for calling and hung up. Not again, I thought as the knot in my stomach tightened. Where did he get another check, and did he have any more? Were we about to be bombarded with forged checks again? Was I financing another drug binge? As much as I didn't want to, I knew I had to call Amy back.

"Hi, Amy, do you have a second to talk?" It was noon, closing time on Saturday.

147

"Sure, Jess. Hold on, I'll go in my office."

She picked up the extension in her office and said, "Okay, what can I help you with?"

"It's about James. Something's going on with him that I'd rather not talk about, but I'm worried he may have more checks and may cash them somewhere else. I don't know what to do until I can get a hold of him." I knew my voice was starting to crack even as I was telling myself to hold it together. It was so hard to admit James was out of control, especially to someone we did business with and respected, but I knew I had no choice.

"Okay, do you know what check numbers he has?"

"No. I don't know where he got them. I was sure I had them locked up."

"That's okay. Can you come in Monday with a list of all your legitimate outstanding checks? We'll put stop payments on everything else. I'll put a hold on everything that comes in over the weekend. We'll figure out how to move forward with the account after that. You have options, but we can talk on Monday."

"Thank you so much," was all I could get out before I started to cry. I held my hand over the phone.

"Don't worry, Jess. I'll see you Monday, and we'll figure it out."

Thankfully, she didn't wait for a reply from me before hanging up the phone. I think she knew I couldn't talk.

When would this stop? Would James survive another binge? Would I survive another of James' binges? I quickly ran to the bedroom to pull myself together before Paul came in for lunch. I would tell him everything on Monday I vowed, but I didn't want to ruin our weekend.

***

148

James called me that night after ten. I couldn't understand what he was saying. He was high and he was crying, saying he was sorry, I think. I didn't know if he was home or out driving somewhere. I hoped he wouldn't drive in his condition, but he just mumbled into the phone and hung up. I never slept after that.

I tried to reach him on Sunday, but he didn't answer. I told myself again if something happened I would hear. He was probably sleeping it off, if that's what they do. Our first weekend off in months was not as nice as I had hoped. All I did was worry. I worried about James, about telling Paul, and about facing Amy on Monday.

Monday morning was busy as usual. I couldn't find time to get to the bank, so I called and talked with Amy. Nothing had come in, she said. She'd watch the account and let me know of any suspicious activity. I finally told Paul, just about the one check. I was sure James had a good reason, I told him, but we can't trust him until he beats this thing. Paul was once again disappointed and angry.

Keith stopped in later that morning.

"James hasn't been to church in a while," he said.

"I'm not surprised." I must have been overly abrupt because I knew Keith could sense a change in my attitude. "I'm sorry, I haven't seen him since Friday, but I'm not happy with him."

"Is everything okay?"

"No, but I don't want to talk about it," I replied a little too harshly. "It was a long weekend," I added. It was my problem, not his. I knew he only wanted to help.

"Richard and I were thinking we should all get together with James and see if we can persuade him to go to *Teen Challenge*."

149

I didn't say anything. I was losing confidence in my ability to help James at all. I didn't like the way I was feeling.

He went on, "You know, like an 'intervention.' If all of us talked to him. I mean you, Paul, Karen, me, Richard, Lauren, and Kylie, maybe Tina. We could force him to listen. Confront him with where this life is leading him. Richard said Lauren's ready to leave him if he doesn't get help. If James thinks he's going to lose her and Renee, his job, his home, and all of our support, maybe that would convince him to go."

It all sounded good. Like on the television show Kylie talked about.

"If you don't want to wait until he hits bottom, you bring the bottom to him." I was quoting Kylie from one of my "lessons."

"Yes, that's it. Where did you hear that?"

"Kylie heard it somewhere. On TV, I think. I'll talk to Paul. When did you want to do this?" It was nice to know so many people cared about James. I wish James cared enough about all of them to stop what he was doing.

"How about tomorrow after work. Can we do it at your house? I'll have Lauren bring him over."

"Sure. We close at five so make it five-thirty," I told Keith, and he left the office.

Was I supposed to provide refreshments? I had never hosted an "intervention" before. I couldn't very well offer wine and beer. When James wasn't doing drugs, he was drinking more than he should, and Keith and Karen had given up drinking when they joined their church. What did it matter? I knew they were not going to persuade him to go away for fifteen months. But we had to try. I couldn't just give up.

***

150

So the next night, we held an intervention at our home. No refreshments. Lauren made sure James was there. He thought he was going to Keith's house next door. When Keith walked him into our living room where we were all seated, he figured out quickly what was going on.

Keith was the designated speaker.

"James, we brought you here because we all love you. We want you to beat this addiction that is ruining your life and your family. We know you've tried to get help but nothing has worked so far. Is that right?"

"That's right," James admitted.

"You know you need help, right?" Keith continued.

"I know."

"You know you have to get help for Lauren and Renee as well as for yourself. You're tearing their lives apart. You can't take care of them like this. They need you. You made a commitment to take care of them when you got married. You made an oath to God that you would do that. You're not doing that now. Are you?"

"No." James' voice started to crack.

Keith was good.

"Everyone here loves you. We'll all do whatever it takes to get you the help you need. Your parents will keep your job open. Karen will help Lauren with the house. We'll all pitch in to keep your bills paid and make sure Lauren and Renee are safe while you're gone. Isn't that right?" he said, looking around the room as everybody said "yes" and shook their heads.

"We think *Teen Challenge* is the best place to go," Kieth continued. "They have one in Augusta."

"Isn't that a year and a half commitment?" James asked.

"Fifteen months," Richard jumped in. "But they have an unbelievable success rate." He was the expert on the program.

James met his father-in-law's eyes and said, "I can't leave my family for that long."

Richard pressed on, "It's a great program, and they have people who are married with children. After thirty days, Lauren and Renee can visit every Sunday, and after six months, since you're married you can leave for one weekend a month."

"James, you won't have to worry about anything. You only have to think about getting better." Keith was speaking again.

I figured it was my turn next, but Paul beat me to it.

"Your mother and I love you, but we can't go on like this. We'll keep your job open and help your family while you're gone, but you have to get help."

"I'll support you and come visit with Renee whenever we can," said Lauren.

I noticed a little something in the way she said it, like she wasn't sincere, just saying the words. Maybe rehearsed. I could tell the drugs were taking a toll on their marriage.

"I'll visit you too. I know what you're going through, and I want my brother back. I miss him." Kylie choked back tears. She's been emotional lately anyway, and she truly did love her brother but not the person he's become.

Karen said she and the woman's group from the church would help Lauren and Renee while he was gone.

After everyone said their piece, we waited. James looked around the room as if he were looking for a way out. We had cornered him, but we felt it was necessary.

Keith was the first to speak again. "What do you think, James?"

He sighed and said, "I don't think I have a choice."

"So you'll go?" Keith asked, pinning him down for an answer.

"I'll have to think about it. Make some arrangements."

"We'll make all the arrangements, you only have to agree to go," Richard jumped in again.

They were sounding a little like car salesmen, but I understood they wanted a commitment out of him. A commitment for fifteen months of his life. They made it sound so simple. Just say yes, and we'll all clap, and life will be good again.

But they weren't the ones committing to be locked away from the world for over a year. He hadn't lasted two days at the ninety-day program. Don't get me wrong, I wanted him to go and come back all better. I was ready to "not" worry about him for a while. It would be nice to know he was safe and so was everyone else. I was already planning the visits. I'd ride up with Kylie. We'd bring him anything he needed. Snacks, clothes, blankets, or whatever he asked for. We'd make a day of it, maybe once a month. I desperately wanted him to go. But I didn't think he'd stay. There were no locked doors, and he was an adult. He wouldn't last a week.

James refused to just say yes. He only agreed to think about it and get back to all of us.

He got up to leave and said, "Come on Lauren, we have to go."

"Think about it, okay? This may be exactly what you need." I gave him a hug. "I'll talk to you tomorrow."

James and Lauren left to walk next door to get Renee. She was playing with Keith's kids. They were teenagers now, and they adored Renee.

"What do you think?" Keith asked us all as he and Karen were getting ready to leave, too.

No one had much to say. "I'll talk with him tomorrow, and see if I can persuade him to at least give it try," I said.

"I don't think he'll go. Not yet. Maybe if he got arrested, and they offered him a choice. It might be better than jail, but if he doesn't have to be there, he won't go." Kylie said what everyone was thinking.

We thanked everyone for coming and said goodbye after that. There wasn't much else to say.

"Well, that was a waste of time," Paul said when we were finally alone. "I knew it would be."

"They just want to help. We had to try," I said as I heated up something for dinner.

"He won't stay anywhere unless he's locked up." Paul grabbed two beers from the fridge and handed one to me.

"So what do we do? Get him arrested?"

"Not a bad idea."

I tried talking to James the next day. I could tell he was clean. He always tried but never lasted for more than a few days at a time.

"It might not be all that bad, you know."

"It will be awful. They expect you to sit around and pray all day. Do you know they train you to be a pastor? And you have to sing in a choir. I'm not singing. You have to beg for money in front of stores. I'm not doing that either."

He knew more about it than I realized. "So let me get this straight. You have to pray, which you do, learn the Bible, which you are doing right now anyway, and beg for money which you do from me all the time. The only thing you're going to have to learn is how to sing. You might be pretty good at it, you know. Your father has a great voice. He sang in the church choir when he was young." I knew I was fighting a losing battle.

"Really, Dad in the choir? Did he wear one of those silly robes?" He laughed for a second. Then he was serious. "Lauren said she would support me, but she won't guarantee she'll wait for me. She said she wasn't sure we'd still be married when I finished."

"She said that? Seriously?"

"I don't blame her. I haven't been much of a husband lately."

This was becoming one of those rare moments when James opened up to me. I wanted to keep him talking.

"You know you can change all that. Start over. But you have to stop the drug use, and you haven't been able to do that for very long."

"I know I need help, but I can't leave for fifteen months. Richard was really bad, and he stopped all by himself." James had been talking to Richard a lot.

"I'm sure some people can do that, but most people need help. I don't want you to be one of those who has to hit rock bottom before you get help. You'll have lost more than just Lauren."

"I'm really going to try this time, and I am going to pay you back everything I owe you. I promise."

When my son was clean, the guilt ate away at him.

"How did you let this happen, James? After seeing what Kylie went through, I never thought I had to worry about you."

"Do you remember when I hurt my back when I was working at Roger's Heating Company?"

"I remember."

"The doctor put me on Oxycontin. It didn't heal right, and I had to have those cortisone shots. I was working here by then. The doctor kept prescribing more and more Oxycontin. Then, just like that, he stopped. It was awful. I was so sick. I couldn't handle it, so I made an appointment with a different doctor and got some more pills until he shut me off too. I tried to do the same thing again, but everything became computerized, and the doctors knew I had been prescribed it before and wouldn't give me any more."

"Didn't they try to put you on something else or cut down your dose slowly?"

"They tried prescribing less, but that only made me run out sooner."

"So you've been battling this addiction for a long time?"

It was beginning to make sense. Paul had mentioned James hadn't been completely normal in years. Not all the time, but some days he would be out in left field, as he put it.

"Yeah, I bought it off the street for a while but it's expensive. That's when I turned to drugs (we all hated to use the word heroin). It's cheaper."

He was ashamed of himself, and I finally realized this wasn't all his fault.

"James, you need serious help. You're so addicted. You may need medical help to wean off slowly. No wonder you can't stop cold turkey." I realized *Teen Challenge* was not the answer, just yet. He needed to detox under supervision. Prayers alone were not going to help.

"The only medicines I know are Suboxone and methadone, and I tried those," he said. "Richard, Uncle Keith, and Pastor don't think I should be on any medication. Richard didn't need any, he just prayed."

"Everyone is different. You have to find what works for you. Are the antidepressants helping?"

"I don't feel any different yet. I know it takes a while."

Just then Kylie came in from her apartment, and the conversation was over. James couldn't get out of there fast enough. I knew he didn't want another confrontation with his

156

sister.

"Is he going to go?" Kylie asked after he left.

"I don't think so. He's so addicted he can't just stop. Any ideas?"

"Suboxone was probably the best option, but he won't take it right. He may be addicted, but he also likes to get high."

Chapter Thirteen

The following week my focus shifted from James back to Kylie.

April was a little slower than the winter months, but we were still busy. Kylie tried to help when she felt up to it, but at least I was able to handle things on my own now. It had been almost two months since she had made the decision to get off methadone, and she wasn't doing well at all.

Kylie came in the office and sat at her desk. I smiled at her but continued with my phone call. I hung up and printed a ticket. Then I turned my attention back to the computer to enter invoices. After a minute or so, I noticed Kylie was just sitting at her desk, looking at me.

"I'm sorry, Kylie. Did you need something?" I asked.

She shook her head yes but couldn't seem to get the words out. Again, I had the feeling that something was very wrong. It was happening a lot these days.

"What is it, Sweetie? It'll be all right, I'm sure. Is it Tom? Are you two fighting?" She was crying now and stood up to go to her apartment, but I stopped her and held her until she had calmed enough to talk. "Whatever it is we'll get through it," I told her and waited until she was ready to tell me what was so horrible to get her this upset. My mind raced thinking of all the possibilities.

"I'm pregnant." Kylie finally got the words out.

Of all the possibilities, that thought never crossed my mind. She smiled at me for a second and I smiled back.

"You're going to have a baby?"

She shook her head yes, crying again.

"That's okay, we'll be here to help. You're going to be a mom. I'm going to have another grandchild."

I had questions about how this could happen. She was not naive about birth control. But it had happened, and now was not the time to ask.

She smiled again through the tears. Then she pulled herself together long enough to say, "You don't understand. I can't have this baby. I'm on methadone." She broke down again. When the door to the office opened, Kylie quickly made her way to her apartment just as a customer walked in.

Kylie managed to pull herself together while I was busy. When the customer left, she came back out to the office. We sat together on the little sofa.

"How does methadone affect a baby?" I asked.

"The baby will be born addicted to it, just like me. I can't put a baby through that."

"Can you get off the methadone before the baby is born?"

"That's worse for the baby. I would have to go back to a stabilizing dose and wait until after the baby is born to wean off. I can do that if it would help, but Tom doesn't want a baby born addicted to drugs. He's pretty adamant about that. I feel like such a loser." She was crying again.

This was not Tom's decision. This was up to Kylie. I was adamant about that.

"How do they treat these babies? They must have a way to help them."

"They give them some kind of opiates to stabilize them and then wean them off. The same as me. It's awful. It can take months."

"Okay. How do you know all this?"

"I was on the computer most of the night."

159

"How far along are you?" I wanted to know how much time we had. We had never talked much about abortion. We had talked about birth control, so we wouldn't have to talk about abortion. It was just understood if you got pregnant you had a baby. There were no other options in my mind. But I was never faced with a difficult decision like this.

"Not more than three or four weeks."

"How did you know so soon?" I asked, shocked it was so early in the pregnancy.

"I just felt different, so I took a test. It's only been about a month since the first time. I haven't had a boyfriend in over a year and a half, so I stopped taking the pill. I thought we were careful."

"I think we need some more education before you make any rash decisions. Let's look at it this way. You need to decide if it is better not to have this baby than it is to have it addicted to methadone. Are there long-term effects for the baby? Does the baby suffer during the weaning process? Are there developmental issues? I think we have a lot more research to do."

"Okay," she said, much calmer now that we had a plan.

We both went to our computers and began searching for any information on "methadone babies" as they were called. That's all we did for three days. We read good news and bad. We left Tom out of it. We actually told Paul. He came into the office and saw her crying and asked what was wrong. So for once, I just told him.

"Kylie's pregnant."

"So why's she crying? If the convict doesn't want it, get rid of him. We'll take care of her and the baby."

Kylie hugged him.

"Thank you, Daddy," she said in that sweet little

voice that melted her dad's heart.

"Unfortunately, it's a little more complicated than that. She's not off methadone yet, so we're trying to figure out what's the best thing to do," I told my husband knowing Kylie needed her father's support now more than ever.

"Well, I'm sure you'll figure it out," Paul replied.

"He took that well," Kylie said after her father left.

"He loves you, and he'll be there for you. But your timing could have been better, with James and everything else that's going on. Why now? You couldn't have waited a little while?" My feeble attempt at lightening the mood.

She smiled and said, "I know. You should write a book. You can't make this stuff up."

"Maybe I will someday," I teased. Then we got back to our research.

Kylie was leaning towards having the baby until she read one article that brought her to tears again. Her problem was not only that she was still on methadone, but she was in withdrawals from weaning off.

"Being in withdrawals during the early part of a pregnancy produces an unstable uterine environment. This results in birth defects," Kylie read from the internet.

The list of possible birth defects was long, and the incident rate was very high. She knew her baby would be addicted to drugs. Would it also be born with birth defects? Could she live with that?

We looked harder concentrating on the effects of withdrawals during early pregnancy. Every article we read said the same thing. There was a very good chance this baby would be born with some very severe birth defects.

And so, Kylie made the hardest decision of her young life. She made an appointment at the Family Planning Clinic. She would not bring this child into the world. We both cried for this unborn child conceived at the wrong time. There

161

would be other children later, I told her, but nothing can make a person feel better at a time like this.

The initial appointment was set for the next day. Kylie and Tom went together. They did an ultrasound to confirm the pregnancy, showing her the fetus about the size of a piece of rice. They set up a date for the abortion two weeks away, and Kylie came home to wait.

The next few days were quiet. There wasn't much to say. Kylie was getting sicker, probably from a combination of the withdrawals and morning sickness. Determined now to get off this awful drug even faster, she called Dr. Stevens. He said he remembered her as she explained her situation leaving out the pregnancy, and they set up an appointment.

My daughter walked into the office after her appointment looking horrible, pale, and thin.

"He told me to throw away the methadone I have, and he gave me a prescription for Oxycontin."

"Is he crazy? That's what started this whole thing. You don't want to do that," I told Kylie.

"He said it's the best way to get off the methadone."

"To give Oxycontin to an addict?" I didn't say it out loud. I had never called Kylie an addict. I wouldn't start now.

"But won't you be addicted to Oxycontin? Isn't that going backwards?" I pleaded with her to think this through. I didn't want to start over.

"I have to believe he knows what he's doing."

She filled the prescription and threw away her week's supply of methadone.

"I don't want to be tempted. I never want to be on that ever again."

***

The next day was awful, and the day after was even worse. I left after work on Thursday wishing this would all be over soon. She was so sick and in pain. Tom assured me he would stay with her all night as I said goodbye. I was sure it would be a long night for them.

I didn't see Kylie when I first got to the office the next morning. Not wanting to bother her if she was sleeping, I got to work and waited.

About twenty minutes later, I was surprised to see her car pull in and drive around to the back entrance of the apartment. A few minutes after that, she came into the office obviously in pain and very weak. She shook all over, and I had never seen her so pale.

"I need you to drive me to the New Beginnings Rehab Center right now," she said adding, "Please, they're expecting me."

There was no question I would do it, even if I had to close the office, but I called Paul's phone. Fortunately, he was still out back loading a van. I rarely asked him to cover for me especially at the last minute, so he knew something was wrong. I didn't take the time to explain. He came right up, and we headed out.

I had never seen my daughter in this condition. She was shivering and bent over in the car. She wouldn't tell me what was going on, so after a few questions that went unanswered, I drove in silence hoping to get her there before she got any worse.

We entered the familiar building and checked in with the receptionist. The nurse came right away and took us to the same small office we were at before. She took Kylie's pulse. It was one-forty. The nurse was just starting to take her blood pressure when Dr. Stevens came around the corner.

"What is she doing here? We've got to get her in bed right now. Come on, Kylie," he said, helping her stand up.

Dr. Stevens looked at me.

"She'll be fine. I'll have her check in with you tomorrow."

That was it.

I stood there and watched them walk down the hall and through the same double doors that had scared Kylie to death almost two years before. The nurse was talking to me, but my mind was back to that day. How different would things be today if she had gone through those doors back then?

The nurse was telling me I couldn't stay. She was an adult. I knew the drill. I remembered it well.

"We'll stay in touch. She should be ready to go home in a few days."

I thanked her and left.

I still didn't know what had happened last night, where had she come from, and where was Tom? She would tell me later. She usually did.

It was a really long day, and I never heard from Kylie or the rehab center. I guess I didn't expect to, but I was hoping for some news. I prayed for Kylie to get through this. She was where she needed to be, I hoped.

When the phone rang at home the next morning, I answered it quickly hoping it was Kylie or at least some news. It was Kylie, and she didn't sound much better.

"They want to put me on Suboxone. I don't want to be on any drugs anymore, ever."

I could tell she was near tears. Why wouldn't they let me stay? I just didn't understand.

"Sweetie, remember all the research we did on

withdrawals from methadone? It's the worst drug to get off from. The withdrawals last up to six weeks after you stop completely. I'm sure Dr. Stevens knows what he's doing."

"I don't want to. Look what it did to James." She was crying by now. All alone behind those dreaded double doors.

"You were the one who said it's a good drug if taken correctly, and James didn't take them the way he was supposed to." I couldn't tell if she was listening, but I went on, "I'm sure this will be temporary. If you need to take the Suboxone to let your body heal from the methadone, then that's what you need to do. A couple of months tops, then you wean off the Suboxone. I think that's the best way."

She finally said what was holding her back, "Tom will think I'm such a loser. He doesn't want me on any drugs."

"He won't think that. Besides, this is short term. Six weeks. I'm sure if he felt like you do, he'd do the same thing." I wanted her off drugs too but safely. "Kylie, your body needs to heal. I think it's the right move." I didn't care what Tom thought.

"Okay, I gotta go."

I could hear someone talking to her as she ended the phone call. I wanted so much to be with her. She would always be my little girl, my baby.

An hour later Kylie called back.

"I can't do this! It's not working! I need you to come and get me and take me to the methadone clinic. I know I can talk them into taking me back. I'm so sick. Please come and get me!" She was hysterical.

I tried to calm her down, but she wasn't listening. Then I remembered something I had read somewhere during all our research over the last few months for both of my children's issues. I could see the page and for some reason I knew it word for word.

165

"Kylie, listen to me!" I almost had to yell. "I read that when Suboxone is used to curtail the withdrawal symptoms of methadone cessation, sometimes a second dose is required." I don't know why I remembered it exactly, but I did. "You just need another dose. Tell them you need another dose. Do you want me to tell them?" How I wished I was there!

She calmed down a little. "No. I will," my all alone daughter said to me and hung up the phone.

It was just before eleven, and I didn't hear anything else until four in the afternoon. I was going crazy by the time the phone rang.

It was Kylie again but this time much calmer. "Mom, can you pick me up in the morning? I'll be ready to go home around ten."

"Sure, Sweetie, I'll be there. How are you feeling?"

"Much better. You were right. They gave me another dose and it worked. But I'm not staying on them."

"I know. You won't have to. I'm so glad you're feeling better. I'll see you tomorrow. Get some rest." I started to end the call, but Kylie stopped me.

"Mom." There was a long pause.

"I'm here, Sweetie."

"I lost the baby." She started to cry again.

She needed her mother now more than ever, but I wasn't allowed through those damn double doors.

"I'm so sorry. Are you okay? Do you want me to come down and stay with you?" I would make them let me in somehow. She shouldn't be alone right now.

"No, I'll be okay. I just wanted you to know. I'll see you in the morning."

She hung up and I cried.

I stood in my kitchen and cried for my unborn grandchild, for my daughter alone behind those stupid double doors, for my son who should be behind locked double doors, and for my husband and myself who were barely holding on. Then I pulled myself together and went to tell Paul.

I drove down in the morning to pick up Kylie. As I sat in the waiting room, I could see down the hall. She eventually came out through those awful double doors with Dr. Stevens.

"I'd like to talk to you for a minute," he said. We all sat down on a couch in the waiting room. "I'm sorry I wasn't able to explain things to you when you brought Kylie in, but I didn't know if you knew that she had been pregnant."

I just nodded my head.

"I have to protect her confidentiality. She's stable now. I'll be seeing her on a regular basis until she's off the Suboxone."

I wanted to scream at him for not allowing me to be with her at such a difficult time, but I bit my tongue and said, "Thank you for all your help."

"Kylie's a great person. I'm sure she'll make it through this. How's your son?"

I was shocked he knew James was my son. It had been months since James had gone to the clinic, and I never went with him.

"Kylie and I have been talking," he said with a smile.

"He's about the same. We're trying to get him help, but he doesn't want to go away. He's going to counseling. That's about it." What else was there to say? I was failing James.

"I run a place in Florida for people like James. I've given Kylie the information. I think we can really help him."

"Thank you. I'll look it over, but I don't think he'll

go to Florida. He doesn't want to leave his family."

"If he doesn't get help, he won't have a family to leave," Dr. Stevens said.

I believed he genuinely cared, but I was feeling uncomfortable and embarrassed that he knew both my children were struggling with addiction.

"I know," I said quietly. "Thank you for your concern and for all you did for Kylie."

Kylie said goodbye, actually gave him a hug, and we left.

I hugged her as we walked to the car. She was still fighting back tears. I wouldn't push her to talk.

She finally looked at me and said, "You're probably wondering what happened?"

"That's a little bit of an understatement, but I figured you'd tell me when you were ready."

"I'm sorry I didn't tell you on Friday. I couldn't talk because I was in such pain. It all started Thursday night. I thought the pain was from the withdrawals, so I asked Tom to take me to the clinic. When we got there it was late, so Dr. Stevens wasn't there. The nurse asked all the typical questions, and when she asked if I was pregnant, I said yes. She said she couldn't admit me, and I should go to the emergency room.

"Instead, I had Tom take me to the other clinic, the free one. I knew I only needed some of the drugs they give you to help with the withdrawal symptoms. We had to wait for a bed to open. They kept telling us it wouldn't be long, but we waited hours. I could feel something happening. I had such awful cramps.

"When they finally took me in, instead of asking if I was pregnant, they just gave me a pregnancy test. I guess that's their procedure. I was going to lie. By then I was bleeding and I told them everything. The methadone, the oxys, the abortion, and I told them I was losing the baby right then. I could feel myself bleeding, but they wouldn't help me. I begged them to take me, but they kept saying they couldn't."

"I'm so sorry. I wish you had called me." I held her hand as I drove and let her continue.

"It wouldn't have done any good. I needed their help. Tom was furious with them and me. He wanted to take me to the emergency room. I know he was just scared for me, but I kept yelling at him. By the time we left that clinic, it was after eight in the morning, so I called Dr. Stevens. I told him about the pregnancy, the miscarriage, and the pain I was in. I was crying, and Tom was yelling at me. Dr. Stevens said to come right in. That was right about the time we pulled into the office. I couldn't even look at Tom for another second. We were so mad at each other. You know the rest."

"Where's Tom now?" I asked.

"I don't know." She started to cry again. "I left him in the apartment. I ruined everything."

"Have you talked to him?"

"No, they won't let calls come in, and I didn't try to call him. I know he's furious. We said some awful things to each other. I think he's probably gone." She calmed down as we rode back to town in silence.

"If you really love each other, you'll get through this." I knew it had been said before, but I had to give her hope. She had been through so much. "So he doesn't know about the Suboxone?"

"No, he won't like it. I took a much smaller dose this morning. I'm not going to look like James. That reminds me, can we stop and fill my prescription?"

So we filled her prescription, and I dropped her off at her apartment. As I helped her up the stairs, Tom came outside and took Kylie's hand.

169

"I guess I'll head home." I hugged my daughter and whispered, "Are you going to be all right? Do you want me to stay?"

She smiled a little and said, "I'll be fine, thank you. I'll call you later."

"Make sure you do."

Tom had waited for her. That was a good sign.

Kylie did call an hour later to tell me everything was fine. They had talked. She had told him about the Suboxone, and Tom understood. She promised to get off it as soon as possible.

It had been a long couple of weeks, but now it was over. Kylie was now completely off methadone. It had been an extremely difficult accomplishment for her. I was hoping she would do well on the Suboxone while her brain healed. Dr. Stevens explained it may take a while for that to happen. He said something about the receptors being damaged. We would worry about weaning her off from the Suboxone later.

Kylie did not need to have an abortion. She would live with the guilt of not being ready and able to carry the child full term, but I was sure that was better than the guilt of actually having to go through an abortion. I knew the abortion would have been more traumatic for her. If she hadn't gotten pregnant though, would she have gone back to Dr. Stevens or would she have gone back to methadone? I would never know.

Chapter Fourteen

We were finally into May. Usually, a good time to be in the oil business. We almost always had a nice reserve of cash from the winter. We were just busy enough to pay the bills and not have to dip into the reserves. The atmosphere at the office was mostly lighthearted and sometimes, even fun.

But this year was different. James was still up and down. I asked him about the antidepressants. He said he didn't notice much difference, but at a doctor's appointment the other day, the doctor did some testing for adult ADD. Then prescribed Ritalin to see if it helped James concentrate.

I thought back to when James was younger. It was never talked about much back then, but now I was sure he had the signs. James would look past us when he talked, like he was thinking about something else. I remembered how cute I thought it was when he was four. Then in kindergarten, the teacher said he couldn't sit still, probably because he was so young, an August birthday. We were advised to keep him back. Sitting still and concentrating had always been a struggle for my son. Had I failed to get him the help he needed back then? Could this have all been avoided if I had done more?

Sam was frustrated with James as well and threatened to quit many times. We were now getting complaints about some of the work the boys had done.

Our reserves were much smaller, and Paul was still talking about buying a propane truck.

The only good thing I could see was Kylie. The Suboxone was working well for her. She was no longer running to her apartment in tears or counting and recounting the pens in each drawer. She was better than she had ever been on methadone. I had my old Kylie back, and she was improving every day.

Paul and I were both tired, physically and mentally. Paul was struggling to keep customers happy. We won bids on three new houses to install the entire plumbing and heating systems. There was plenty of work to keep the boys busy for the summer. However, Paul was discovering the reason we won the bids was because we under priced them. We wouldn't lose money, he told me, but after we paid for the materials and all the overhead, the company wouldn't make any money. It would, at best, pay the employees.

By the middle of the month, we knew we had to make some difficult decisions. We wouldn't survive another winter with the high oil prices if we didn't change the delivery business dramatically. Other companies were going to "cash only" or offering "prebuys" and "cap plans." The prebuys and cap plans involved buying oil on the futures market or protecting our prices by purchasing options. The futures market was a gamble and the options just added to the overall cost of our oil. Most larger companies could hire a person just to determine when and how much of each to buy. We had tried our hand at it a couple of times in the last few years, but we ended up losing money. However, we went ahead anyway and ordered pamphlets made up to sell a package deal of a cap price, oil burner cleaning, and insurance on the furnace. Paul decided to put a deposit on a propane truck, as well.

Within the next few weeks, things took a turn for the

worse. One customer threatened a lawsuit. His new furnace worked fine all winter, but now another company had told him a different system would work better. The cut-throat world of the oil service business had reared its ugly head.

A few days later, our service helper came into the office with all his uniforms and placed them on the counter in front of Paul. Then he put a syringe with a needle on top of the pile.

"Your son is on drugs, and I can't work this way," he said and walked out the door.

That weekend we got a call from the local police in the next town over. James had fallen asleep in our work vehicle in a store parking lot. The officer was arresting him on a DUI charge and wanted us to come and get our van.

I talked to Paul the next day. Obviously, he was furious with the fact that our name was all over the van, and James was doing drugs again. We were going to have to fire him, I knew that, but I said something I didn't think I would ever say.

"Paul, do you remember that lady who stopped into the office before we bought the new building, maybe two or three years ago? She was from that big oil company."

"The one who wanted to buy us out?" he asked.

"Yes, I don't remember her name, but I kept her card."

He was silent for a few minutes. I knew he was remembering the conversation. She had said they liked our business because we were not a cash business, we did not cut prices, we had a lot of automatic customers, and they were all in a nice compacted area and not spread out all over the state. We explained we were not looking to sell, but she said to keep her card and call her if we ever changed our minds.

"What are you saying?" he finally said.

"I don't know. I only wanted to put it out there." That

Jess Gallant

was the truth. I wasn't sure we should even think about it, but I thought it should at least be an option.

"Would you consider selling?" Paul asked. "Is that what you want to do?"

"I'm not sure, but maybe we should see what they think it's worth."

I didn't want to sell the company, but I was afraid there wouldn't be a company left to sell if we had another winter like last winter. James was on his way out the door, and Sam would be right behind him if his attitude didn't improve. I knew I would feel bad for Kylie, but we would take care of her somehow, and when I was faced with the truth, she hadn't worked all that hard for us most of the time. She had tried, but she had so many hurdles to climb over.

Our whole lives were wrapped up in this company. I wasn't sure if Paul would even think about it, and at one point I was afraid he would be upset with me for mentioning it. So I was surprised when he responded.

"It couldn't hurt to talk to her. Why don't you give her a call and set up a meeting? They may not offer us enough money to seriously consider it, but it'd be nice to know what financial level they're talking about." He added, "Not that I even want to sell."

"Okay, only a meeting then." What had I just done? There were five family members employed. Could we walk away? But it was just a meeting.

We confronted James about the DUI in our van. He begged us for one last chance. We thought being arrested may have smartened him up, so we gave in. By now, Lauren had kicked him out of the house, and he was staying with Sam.

"If there is any indication whatsoever that you took any kind of drugs besides an aspirin, you are fired! Do you understand? Anything at all!" That was Paul's ultimatum.

174

***

That one last chance didn't last. Sam called me in a panic a couple of days later.

"James is in really bad shape. I called 911. They're taking him to the hospital now."

"Which hospital?" I asked, trying to keep calm.

"Lakes Region General, I think."

"Do you know what happened to him?"

"I know it was drugs, but I don't know how much or what kind."

"Thank you, Sam. I'm glad you were there to help him."

I ended the call and told Paul. It was a Saturday morning. Like Kylie had mentioned once before, there are a lot of opportunities to buy drugs on a Friday night.

I rushed out of the house calling Kylie at the same time. Of course she would come with me, she said. She was worried too. A classmate of theirs had died of a drug overdose not too long ago.

I picked up Kylie at her apartment, and we headed to the hospital. We tried not to think the worst. If he survived, would this be enough to scare him? I doubted it.

He was hooked up to an IV and was getting morphine when we got there. He looked okay, even happy. I guess you could say "high" on free drugs.

We didn't stay long. He would be fine the nurse told us. I asked why they were giving him morphine. Did they know he was a drug addict? She said something about it opening up the blood vessels, that it was standard practice.

I walked out of the hospital room before Kylie. I sensed she wanted to smack her brother.

Back in the car, Kylie told me she asked James what he had done.

"Did he tell you?"

"Yes. He did heroin and coke, a speedball. It's really, really dangerous. I don't know why he would do that. He could have died. People die from that."

She was remarkably calm. I think she may have been coming to terms with the possibility of her brother's death.

I, on the other hand, was not calm. "What is wrong with him?" I screamed. "When will he stop this?" I knew she didn't have the answers. I just needed to vent.

"You know we have to fire him," I told Kylie. "Your dad gave him one last chance. He can't weasel his way out of this one."

"I know. You should have fired him a long time ago."

She was right. Maybe he would have stopped already. Maybe we wouldn't be thinking of selling the company.

We drove the rest of the way back home in silence.

On Monday, we fired James, Sam kicked him out, Lauren took him back, and we met with Marilyn about selling the oil company.

It would be weeks before a final decision was made. It was helped along by the fact that we were missing some very expensive tools. We hadn't changed the locks on the garage and basement doors, never dreaming James would help himself to our inventory. We'd never know exactly how much he took, but Paul figured at least a couple thousand dollars worth, maybe double that. We were crushed when Sam found our expensive, heavy-duty, right angle drill at the local pawn shop. How could he? James was staying away from all of us right now.

The offers went back and forth until we had one we

could live with. The price wasn't nearly what we wanted, but I think we were just emotionally drained, physically tired, and mentally exhausted. We asked for time to think it over. We'd get back to them in a few days.

Paul and I went home and talked. Paul was fifty and I was almost forty-five. Not exactly retirement age, and the money was certainly not enough to retire on anyway. We would have to start a new career. Easier said than done at our age.

"Well, what do you want to do?" Paul asked, reaching for a couple of beers from the fridge. It was a warm afternoon in June. We took the beers out to the deck.

"What do you want to do?" I put the question back to him.

"You're no help."

We laughed. This was not an easy decision.

"I guess we have to figure out what we're going to do for a living," I said.

"I've been thinking about that."

I knew it. Paul was always thinking.

"Well, go on. I'm listening."

"You know we've been buying a house for the guys to renovate every summer. If we were to do all the work ourselves and do two or three houses a year, we can probably make almost the same money we made in the oil company after we finished paying all the expenses, the payroll, and the overhead."

"And we wouldn't have all the headaches." I liked the idea.

"You'd have to do a lot of the cleaning and painting. I can teach you how to do some repairs. I can do all the plumbing, heating, landscaping, roofing, and general maintenance."

He was right. Paul had been working on homes for

177

most of his life. He bought his first one when he was only twenty-one, and he loved real estate. This could work.

"It would be nice not being tied to an office all the time. And the cell phone. But I know the oil company is your dream. I don't want to sell it now and regret it later. You have to be sure. We can hire new people, get involved with propane, and keep going. Maybe next year will be better."

I wanted Paul to be sure. I had brought up the possibility of selling because of all the stress we were under, both of us, but Paul was the one who had done the bulk of the work to get us where we were today. I would be okay if we kept the company, but would Paul be okay if we sold it?

"I like the idea of doing everything ourselves." Paul sighed and continued, "Not relying on other people to get the job done and then being responsible for their mistakes. I've spent too much time in the last few years fixing other people's screw-ups."

"So you want to sell? You're really sure?"

"Yes, I guess so. Making this company a successful, full service, family company, able to support us all well into our retirement was my dream. I felt like it was within reach. That's why I didn't want to fire James a long time ago. He was part of that dream. I felt like if I just gave him more time, he would snap out of it. Kylie and Sam too. I thought they would become more responsible. Maybe they're just too young. They don't have the same work ethic as I do. We've probably spoiled them. I guess this isn't their dream, or they would have tried harder."

I was glad he was opening up. He had to be sure.

"I feel bad for you, too," Paul continued. "Up all night with those phone calls. Even this time of year you're still getting them. We can't trust anyone else. Look at what the drivers did this winter. Wendell let thirty gallons of oil pour into a customer's basement. I spent weeks cleaning it up and trying to get the odor out. It was a good thing she was nice and had been with us a long time, or we would have been sued. Then Mike spilled all that oil at the terminal while he was loading the truck. That cost us over two thousand dollars to clean up, plus we had to pay for the fifteen hundred gallons of oil we never got.

"Speaking of mistakes, do you remember a few weeks ago when we found out Sam moved a customer's freezer and put it back forgetting to plug it in? A few weeks later, she opens it to find everything's spoiled, and she wants a new freezer as well as the cost of all the meat and everything else she had in it. Another thousand dollars."

I wondered if Paul was trying to convince himself.

"And don't get me started on the fallout from James' actions these past six months. I've tried to make sure he was never on a job impaired, and I checked and double checked everything he did, but I'm not a burner man. I'm afraid something he did will come back to haunt us. Then he steals from us while we continue to pay him, hoping he'll straighten out." He stopped talking and looked out over the lake.

"Yes. I guess it's time for another career, another dream." He was sure.

"I'll call Marilyn in the morning," I said. We sat quietly for a while lost in our thoughts watching the sunset over the lake with a mixture of emotions.

Things moved quickly after that. Marilyn required massive amounts of paperwork from us. She wanted receipts for all the oil we purchased over the last three years, bills of sale for all the vehicles, and all kinds of records relating to our customers. I was glad we had been completely honest about our sales volume and customer base. We had run our business with honesty and integrity from the beginning, and we would end it the same way.

We canceled the order for the propane truck and lost a rather large deposit.

The hardest part for me was telling Kylie. I knew she would be devastated. We had worked side by side for years. She thought she would be at the oil company forever. Fortunately for her, we were not selling the building, so she could stay in her apartment. The new company wanted to hire her at the same salary and benefit package she had with us, as well. I hoped that would soften the blow. It didn't.

"Are you serious? You're going to sell the company? How could you?" She stood there looking at me as if someone had just died.

"I'm sorry, Sweetie, but you've seen what we went through this past winter. I don't think we'll make it through another one. You know how much people are struggling to pay for their oil. It's going to put us under." I had decided it would be easier for her if I blamed it all on the price of oil which was something no one could control.

"It's all James' fault, isn't it?" She wasn't buying it.

"Okay. He helped make the decision easier, but your father and I are afraid even if we hire someone to take his place, we'd still have to deal with the price of oil. Do you know when we started in business, we could fill a three thousand gallon oil truck for less than $1500? Now it's over $9000. That's each truck load! We don't have pockets deep enough to cover that when people don't pay. The oil business has changed and not for the better. I wouldn't want to stick you kids with that kind of business." I hoped she understood, but I didn't think she was even listening.

I could see tears form in her eyes. It was breaking my heart.

"It will be all right." I reached over to hug her, but

she pulled away.

"How can you do this to me?" Kylie yelled.

Her shock was turning to anger. I half expected it to, but I was hoping it wouldn't.

"What's going to happen to me?" she cried.

"They want to hire you. Same pay including the raise I just gave you."

"You gave me a raise?"

"Yes, last week. It will be in this week's paycheck."

That idea suddenly came to me. I was trying to cheer her up. I hoped I could get a raise through before the details were firmed up.

"So I'll work right here?" She had stopped crying.

"No. They don't want the building. You'll have to go to their office, but that means you can keep your apartment."

"Are they nice?"

"You met Marilyn the other day, remember?"

"Yes. I guess you failed to mention what the meeting was about." She was being sarcastic now, but that was better than tears.

"We hadn't made any decisions yet. She seems pleasant. You'll work with her and help with all our customers. They want a familiar face."

"What about Sam? Are they hiring him too?"

"Dad talked to him this morning. He said he'd rather go on his own. He has his master plumber's license now, so he can do that. They wanted James, but we told them he had other plans."

"Good. I wouldn't want to work for them if they hired him too."

She was much calmer now as we continued to talk about where they were located, how many people worked in their office, and of course, their dress code. I promised to take her shopping before she started work for them. I wanted her to be happy. Kylie was my biggest concern. It had been a rough few years, and I hoped this would be a new beginning for my daughter. Get her out of her comfort zone and into the world. I hoped she would make new friends and have a more normal life.

So it was settled. They wanted to close the deal in a month. We had a lot to do. We had to draw up notices to all our customers and train Marilyn on our computer system. The plan was to use our system until eventually converting our customers to their own system. Marilyn wanted Kylie to help as much as possible since she would be the one staying on.

Paul was busy getting all the inventory ready and accounted for. Every day, he discovered more and more supplies missing.

Then he tackled the vehicles. Paul was always one to make sure everything he sold he could be proud of. This company was no different. All the vehicles would be cleaned, maintained, and in good working order. He would clean James' van himself since he was afraid of what someone else might find.

It was a good thing. The van had been trashed because James was obviously driving too fast and letting the equipment smash around in the back. So the van and everything inside it was in rough shape. But that was not the worst. When Paul checked the glove compartment, he found needles and syringes under the registration papers. Dozens of them. There were more over the visor and even more under the floor mats. He searched every hiding spot he could think of in the van. We hated to think what would have happened if Paul had not found them all himself.

We purchased a house at a foreclosure auction in

June. Initially, we looked at it for the drivers to work on over the summer. Now it would be our first "project house." The work would begin after the sale.

I hadn't seen James in a while. I'm sure he was aware of what we were finding out about our inventory and his van. However, he eventually stopped in the office. Somehow he knew his father had left for the day.

"Are you really selling the business?" he asked.

"Yes, we are."

"Is it because of me?"

How do I answer that? I wanted to tell him it was all his fault, but I was afraid of what that might do to him. If he managed to turn his life around, I didn't want him living with that kind of guilt. But I also wanted him to know his actions had played a significant part in the decision. I tried to choose my words carefully.

"Partly. You certainly didn't make it easy on us this winter, and the money we don't have, thanks to you, is making it very difficult to pay our bills. But you weren't the only reason." I went on to discuss the price of oil and all the other issues that led to the decision.

"Good, so it wasn't my fault."

He left the office hearing only what he wanted to hear. I had just eased his conscience.

I didn't have a chance to confront him about the missing inventory. We would never be paid back for anything James had taken. All the promises to pay me back when he sold the snowmobile were never going to be kept. The snowmobile was repossessed a month ago. I didn't know he had financed it since he neglected to mention that. I didn't dare add up the total amount James had cost us over the last eight or nine months. I guessed it was somewhere

183

between twenty and thirty thousand dollars, probably more.

I didn't have a chance to ask how he was or what his plans were. I knew his mortgage hadn't been paid since February. The house would be foreclosed on soon. Was he close to hitting bottom? Then would he get help?

A week later Kylie informed me she was stopping the Suboxone, wanting to be completely drug-free before starting her new job. She was afraid of having withdrawal symptoms while working for the new company.

Kylie was taking two pills a day, which totaled four milligrams. She was prescribed twelve milligrams a day but had never taken more than the four milligrams she was still on.

"I'm just going to stop. It's not that high a dose. I think I'll be fine."

She wasn't.

After a week of feeling the same type of withdrawals she had before, my daughter came to me. I heard those now all too familiar words.

"Mom, I need your help."

I wanted to scream, "Kylie, I need your help!" We were trying to get everything done to turn the business over to the new owners. The closing was in less than two weeks, and Kylie once again was trying to detox. But I simply asked her how I could help.

"It's awful and the worst part is I can't sleep. Can I stay with you tonight? Can you help me through this? Please?" begged my all grown up daughter.

"What about Tom?" I knew he was staying with her most of the time now.

"He doesn't understand. He thinks I'm just being a baby. I think if I can sleep I'll make it."

"Okay, we'll have a sleepover," I said, thinking about how I was going to tell Paul his daughter had to detox again. He just couldn't seem to keep up. It had been more than two years since the first time she asked for help to detox. We had gotten through it then with hot baths and leg rubs. I was sure we could do it again. I was wrong.

She stayed with me for three nights. She jerked, and twitched, and never slept. She was better during the day when she kept busy, but the nights were difficult for both of us. The last night she stayed with me she cried most of the time. When she confided in me she had thoughts of driving her car into a tree or off a cliff, I decided she needed more help than I could give her.

"You need to talk to Dr. Stevens."

"He'll want me to stay on the Suboxone, or he'll tell me to wean off slowly. He doesn't know I'm already so low. I don't understand why this is so hard. It's such a small amount."

We talked as we headed to work the next morning. Neither of us had slept much in days.

"I'm concerned that you're depressed. Maybe you could call your primary care doctor. Tell her what's going on."

I couldn't remember her name. Kylie could no longer see Debbie since she was officially an adult in their eyes now.

"I guess I could call her. Maybe I won't have to go in."

"Call early. They sometimes take a long time getting back to you."

The return call came in shortly after noon. Kylie was on the phone for quite a while. I tried not to listen, doctor/patient confidentiality and all.

"She thinks I should go back on the Suboxone until the feelings pass, then wean off really, really slow," Kylie said after she hung up. "She thinks going from four milligrams to nothing like that was too drastic for me especially after a year and a half on methadone. I'll never be drug-free, and I start the new job next week." Tears were beginning to form in those beautiful brown eyes. Again.

"You're just going to have to take it slow. Dr. Stevens said your brain needs to heal, remember?" All she wanted right now was to be normal, and I couldn't help her.

So Kylie went back on Suboxone. This time, she took only one pill, two milligrams a day. She figured the last week and a half must have helped a little.

It must have helped because Kylie did great on the one pill. She was better than I'd seen her in the last two years... back to her old self, although still nervous about her first real job. It would be the first time she worked for someone other than family. But my daughter was happy and self-confident again. I'm sure the new wardrobe helped a little.

We closed the sale of our business on July 31st, 2005. Kylie ran our office for the new company for a week by herself, just to keep it open for anxious customers. I was not supposed to be there. She had to explain they would still get the same service and pricing they had with us, but our office would be closed. We had been a fixture there for seventeen years. We were the only oil company in our small town.

Some people were shocked, some saddened, many had been friends. I think others saw it coming... the people who had seen James deteriorate, the companies he bounced checks at, the people at the bank.

After the new company had taken everything they wanted out of our office, basement, and garage, Paul and I started cleaning and figuring out what to do with the rest of the office furniture. We would be renting the space soon.

The last thing to go was the workstation that Paul and James had built since it was of no use to anyone else. It had been custom made to fit our space and our needs. Paul was able to dismantle most of it in the office, but the top that James had laminated had to be taken outside and cut up with a saw. Then we loaded all the pieces into Paul's pick-up and took them home. That night we burned the pieces of that workstation in our outside fireplace. It was the last remaining remnants of our company. The company Paul and I had started with one oil truck and a dream seventeen years before.

We sat and watched the fire in silence. My thoughts turned to our son and daughter. Drug addiction and recovery. James was falling further into addiction, while at the same time, Kylie was well on her way to a full recovery. The last two years had been a roller coaster ride of ups and downs. I knew now I would never be sure of what was just around the next curve. I wondered what Paul was thinking.

Chapter Fifteen

Kylie made the transition to her new job well. She had grown up in our oil company, so she knew the ropes. It wasn't long before they moved her from answering the phones in the front office to scheduling all the service calls in the back office. She thrived in the busy atmosphere and worked well with all the technicians. It was a good fit for her. I was so relieved.

Paul and I started work on our first project house. I was stripping wallpaper while Paul was replacing windows. I had a lot to learn, but I loved the idea of making things better. We were taking something that had been abused and forgotten and were bringing it back to life. I was excited about it.

We started early and went home after lunch to let the dogs out. If it was a nice day, sometimes we didn't go back. Those few afternoons a week to enjoy the lake we had been hoping for, finally came to be. For once we weren't in a hurry and no one ran out of oil. No one complained. Life was good, but not great.

I worried constantly about James. I worried about Renee and Lauren too. I didn't know what they were going to do for money or a home for that matter. I hoped something would make James wake up and see what he was doing to himself and his family.

Something finally did.

***

James wouldn't give me all the details, but as I understood it he got picked up by the DEA, Drug Enforcement Agency, another unfamiliar term. They didn't want him. He was small time, but they were onto him and would be watching. The next time they picked him up he would go to jail, they told James. He had better clean himself up or else. He hinted there was more, something he couldn't tell me, but he was scared and going to get clean, so he said.

He had stopped at the house we were working on. Paul disappeared into the garage, still very angry with James for everything he had done to our business. I was angry too, but I still talked to our son. Paul didn't.

"I know I can get clean. Then I'll get a job. I have to make it this time," James said.

"What about the antidepressants and the Ritalin? Are they helping?" I asked.

"No, I stopped taking them."

I wasn't surprised, Kylie had mentioned he was probably abusing the ADD medication, and if he was still depressed, why bother with the antidepressants.

"Don't you need help to detox?"

We hadn't canceled his health insurance yet. I'm not sure if I was holding on to the hope he would use it to get clean or the fear he would need it if he ended up back in the hospital.

"No. I can do it. Lauren will help. I already asked her."

"It's not easy. You've seen what Kylie's gone through."

"Don't worry," he said as he walked out the door.

I was worried.

Paul came out of the garage after hearing the door close.

"What does he want? I hope he wasn't asking for

money."

The anger was boiling over. I wasn't sure if Paul would ever forgive him.

"He wanted to tell me he is going to clean up his act and get a job," I said, keeping it simple. We had been arguing about James a lot lately. Sometimes, it was easier if his name just didn't come up.

James did get clean this time. It took two weeks and a lot of hot baths and back rubs. I caught him in one of those baths. I stopped by his house to bring some of his things that were left at the old office. We had renters coming in and everything had to be out.

I asked Lauren how he was doing.

"See for yourself. He's in the tub," she said.

I made my way through the kitchen and down the hall. I couldn't believe the way they were living. Friends and family had tried to help Lauren keep house, but she just got angry with them. Lauren and James were grown-ups. If they wanted to live like this, that was fine, but it was not okay to have a child live in this filth.

I had talked to Lauren's father once about it. We were having a conversation about James' drug issues, and Lauren's housekeeping came up. Richard admitted his daughter needed as much help as James. He had cleaned the house a couple of times himself, but it never lasted. She just doesn't see it, he said.

So I tried not to look, and when Renee ran around the corner to greet me, I grabbed her and picked her up wishing I could take her home with me. We walked to just outside the bathroom door, and I called out James' name.

"I'm in here. It's okay, the curtain's closed."

I peeked around the corner to see his trembling hand

holding the curtain open a little. He looked pale, and his face was even thinner than the last time I'd seen him.

"I brought your things from the office. How are you doing?" I realized once again I was looking at one of my children in the throws of withdrawal.

"I've been better," he said with a chuckle.

"You don't look so good. Is there anything I can do?"

"No. I'll make it. I have to. I've e-mailed a few job applications."

"Seriously? Isn't that a little soon?"

There was no way in my mind he would be ready for a job interview for weeks.

"Incentive," he answered with a small, shaky smile.

I wished him good luck, told him I loved him, and gave Renee a big squeeze. I said goodbye to Lauren as I walked out the door. I said a prayer in the car that he would indeed make it this time.

He did. And he got a job at the first interview he went to. It was a large plumbing and heating company in the city.

It lasted six weeks. He had gotten clean but couldn't resist the cravings. I would never understand what that meant, only that it was true, and those cravings were uncontrollable.

The first time I saw him after he lost his job, I was shocked again. I had seen him two or three times during the past six weeks, and he was looking better. He had gained a little weight, and his eyes were open and clear. But his downfall was fast. When he messed up while working for us, we kept giving him another chance. Chance after chance after chance to get his act together. It doesn't usually work that way in the real world. It happened suddenly. One week he was doing great. The next week he was a mess, with no job and strung out on drugs.

I saw him walking up the road. I wasn't sure where he was headed, but I stopped and picked him up.

"You look awful," I said to James as he got in the car. "Where are you going?"

"I don't know. I just had a fight with Lauren."

I could tell he was angry, but I was thinking he was more hurt and ashamed.

"Do you want to talk about it?"

"No. Can you just take me back home?" He was miles from his house. He must have been walking a long time.

"Sure." I turned my car around. "What are you going to do now?"

"I don't know!" he yelled.

I pressed on, "You need help, James. Serious help. Long-term help."

"Don't start! I don't want to hear it! That's all I keep hearing!"

"What do you want us to say? 'Hi, James, you look great!' You look awful, and you know it. You lost your job because you were doing drugs. You're bouncing checks all over town again. You must be looking over your shoulder waiting for the police to catch up with you. I'm sure you're waiting to get kicked out of your house. No wonder you're fighting with Lauren. What do you think this is doing to her?"

I was trying to get through to him, but I knew he had probably blocked me out. I continued anyway.

"You have no money, no job, no home soon, the police are looking for you, and Lauren will probably leave with Renee! How much further do you have to fall before you get help?" I was almost screaming at him by now.

He screamed back, "Don't you think I know that! It's

all I think about!"

"Then do something about it!" I didn't raise my voice often with my children, but I had tried everything else.

"Don't yell at me. That's all I get at home," James said quietly. "I don't know what to do. I can't go away for a long time. I'll lose everything, and I don't think I could handle it."

"What about going back to Dr. Stevens? Maybe back on Suboxone?"

I was thinking about how well Kylie was doing. Maybe he was ready to try it again, but I knew he had to want to get better for it to work.

"He won't take me back. Besides, it didn't work for me."

"It didn't work because you weren't ready. Look how well it's working for Kylie. I also think they gave you too much. Kylie's doing really well on an extremely low dose. Why don't you try it again? It can't hurt if you use it right."

Then I realized he wouldn't be able to use it properly. He was an addict. If he had a full prescription in his hands, he would surely abuse it.

"I said he won't take me back!"

He was getting angry again, but I was not giving up. A plan was taking shape in my mind. I knew Kylie was filling her prescriptions for far more pills than she was taking. I once asked her what she was doing with the others, afraid she would try to sell them and get herself in trouble. She assured me she was keeping them in case she was ever in a situation where she couldn't afford to pay for them. What if she lost her job or insurance? She was simply planning ahead for a rainy day.

"Look, I know your sister has a few extra pills from when she tried to get off them last summer." At this point, I didn't want to let on about how many extra she was getting.

"What if I were able to get some from her? I'll hold them and give you only two a day, four milligrams. Last time Dr. Stevens prescribed you twelve milligrams, and you couldn't keep your eyes open. Take one in the morning and one at night. I'll watch you take them. You won't be able to abuse them. Try it for a few weeks and see if it works for you. It couldn't hurt."

I hoped I knew what I was doing. The thoughts were coming into my head now. What if something went wrong? Would they ask where he got the pills? Could I get Kylie in trouble? I would take the blame. I would say I stole them. I had to try something. If I kept the pills, he couldn't abuse them, I reasoned. He had been on them before so I figured it was safe to try again, and his dose would be so much lower. But I wasn't a doctor. I shouldn't even be thinking of this.

I finally told my brain to shut up, and I looked at my son sitting next to me. A mess, high, probably just coming off a dose of heroin, I assumed. He was going to die soon if something didn't change. I couldn't live with myself if I didn't try.

"Well, what do you think? Do you want to give it a try? I'll call Kylie and ask if it's okay with her."

"Okay." He sounded just a little better when he answered. "Maybe it will work this time."

It did.

I made all the arrangements with Kylie. She was great. She loved her brother even though she blamed him for losing the oil company and her job. She wanted to help.

"I'll keep you completely out of it," I assured her. "We'll try it for a few weeks, and if it works we'll figure out where to go from there."

I picked up some of the Suboxone pills from Kylie

and gave one to James that night. I watched him put it under his tongue the way Kylie told me he was supposed to take it. I made him wait until it was dissolved. He came over in the morning for another one. I watched again until it was gone. He already seemed a little better. After three days, he was almost normal. Within a week he was gaining some weight and looking for another job. The following week he had one. This time, it was with a small company in a small town a little to the north of us.

The Suboxone was working well for James. Only four milligrams a day, and he was almost normal. I wondered why they had given him twelve milligrams last winter. Maybe things would have been different. Probably not, he wasn't ready. Kylie had said he still wanted to get high then. I hoped his brain was healing.

As much as I wanted James to go back to Dr. Stevens to get his own prescription and get into counseling, I didn't think it would work. We finally had to cancel his health insurance, and Suboxone was very expensive. The company he worked for didn't offer insurance. Lauren was supposed to be signing them up for the local free care for children and families.

But I was more concerned with the amount of Suboxone Dr. Stevens would prescribe. I couldn't trust James not to abuse it. So we continued the way we were. I got the pills and gave them to my son, one at a time. He continued to work and was getting better. We were all hopeful the nightmare was over.

Then I told Paul what I was doing.

"Don't get involved. He's on his own." His anger at James hadn't subsided. In fact, it had gotten worse.

Paul was starting to become a hermit. He didn't want

to see anyone except a few close family members. If we needed something for the project house, I went to the local home improvement store alone. In fact, I ran all the errands. He would work at the project house and go home and work at our house. That was it.

"You don't understand. I don't want to run into anyone. Half the people in town owe us money, and the other half know about James and are angry with us or just feel sorry for us. I can't hold my head high and walk down the street anymore. I worked so hard to have a good reputation for seventeen years, and James ruined it in six months. I don't even want to be in this town now."

I understood. Everyone knew Paul. He was the face of our company. I was simply a voice on the phone to most of the customers. I could live my life anonymously. So I didn't push.

I did push for a vacation, though. We had been to the Caribbean eighteen years earlier, before we started the oil company, so I begged Paul to go back. We hadn't had a vacation in over fifteen years.

"Just for a week," I pleaded. "I'll make all the arrangements. You won't have to do anything."

"What about the dogs?" he asked.

They were like our children. I loved them as much as the kids, but I think Paul loved them more, especially now.

"Tina will watch them. I already asked." We have taken her four dogs at least twice a year since long before we had our dogs. I knew she would be happy to have a chance to repay the favor. But more importantly, she loved her dogs and ours as well. I knew they would be safe with her.

Reluctantly, Paul agreed. I made the arrangements to fly out the day after Thanksgiving. We would have to drive to Boston on Thanksgiving Day. It was a good excuse not to have a big meal at our home. Paul wasn't ready for that, so I had the kids make other arrangements.

It was getting harder to meet with James twice a day, so he was now stopping at Kylie's apartment sometimes instead of our house. Determined to stay on top of the situation, we made sure he wasn't stopping at both our places. Now I knew James would be fine while we were gone.

It was a great feeling to leave for a vacation without worrying about either of the kids. They were both doing well. I had hopes that with time Paul would forgive James, and we could all be one big happy family again. But Paul's feelings of anger, betrayal, and shame ran deep. I didn't realize how deep. And how our one week trip to the Caribbean would change our lives.

The first few days were nice. After a mix-up with our reservation, we settled into our room overlooking the beautiful blue-green ocean. We played tennis, sat in the sun, and went to nice restaurants for fancy dinners and cocktails. However, after four days, Paul began to miss our dogs. He'd had enough vacation and wanted to go home. I tried to explain I'd had those same feelings every time I left our children when they were young, but it didn't help.

"They'll be there safe and sound when we get back, and after being home for an hour with them, you'll regret you didn't enjoy yourself more now." It wasn't any use. We would finish our trip, but he wouldn't be any fun. I gave up.

Something changed a couple of days later. Over breakfast, Paul read an article in the English version of the local paper about people from the U.S. living on the island. He showed me the article.

"I didn't know we could buy real estate here," Paul said. His attitude had suddenly changed. We were flying out

197

the next day.

"I didn't think so either," I said cautiously, not exactly sure I liked how the conversation was going.

"What if we bought a home here to renovate during the winter?" He was getting excited. I wondered about the dogs.

"You would want to do that? What about the dogs?" I liked the change in his attitude. I also liked the way he had been here on the island. Much more open and inquisitive, I guess you'd call it. He talked to people. He was interested in their culture. We went to restaurants and casinos and walked on the beach. We sat at the hotel bar a few times and talked to the "locals." The first few days on the island had been nice. I saw a side of Paul I hadn't seen in a long time. We had stopped going out soon after we started the oil company because Paul never wanted to run into customers outside of work. So as he talked about buying property here, my thoughts were all over the place.

"I thought about that," Paul said. "I think we may be able to bring them. We'll have to check. Shadow is almost seventeen and Pebbles is fifteen, so they won't be around much longer. That's why it's so hard to leave them. Even if we wait until they're gone, I'd still like to check out our options. Get an education. It would be great. Don't you think?" Then he said what he really meant, "I never want to be cold again."

Now I understood.

"How do we check it out? You know we leave tomorrow." I was still not convinced, but what harm could come from checking it out.

"I saw a real estate company down by the supermarket. We can walk to it."

We hadn't rented a car. We were staying at the same time-share resort we had stayed at eighteen years before, so we knew we could walk to get what we needed.

"Hurry up and get dressed. We need to get going. It's a long walk."

And so we walked to the Remax Realty office. It was indeed a very long walk, but when we saw the name we were encouraged.

"It must be legitimate if it's an American company," Paul said.

There we met Tony, a short, slightly overweight, gray-haired man approaching sixty.

He drove us around to some of the properties for sale and explained how buying property worked on the island. He spoke English well, so we asked a lot of questions. He dropped us off at the time-share late that afternoon.

Tony had given us quite an education along with folders full of properties and land for sale. We explained we were leaving the island the next day, and to my surprise, Paul said we'd be back soon. We talked over drinks for hours sitting out on the lanai overlooking the ocean. It was a beautiful evening with a warm breeze and a magnificent sunset. I hadn't seen Paul this happy and excited in a long time. Was another dream taking shape?

On the flight home, Paul asked me to search for another vacation package. Within a few days, I found a last minute trip for the first week of January. Two weeks in the Caribbean in two months after not having any time off in years would be great. I thought we deserved it, but I wasn't sure yet how I felt about buying property in a foreign country.

The dogs were fine as I knew they would be, and James was still doing well. Kylie was the one who had a difficult time with our one week vacation. I was her best friend, she said. How could I go away again so soon? She whined and carried on like a young child with separation anxiety. I knew she needed to let go of me and expand her circle of friends. I told her just that, but she still did that little girl pout that usually helped her get her way. Not this time.

Before we left for the next trip, James informed us that Lauren was pregnant. I was furious with her, actually with both of them. James had been doing well, but it had only been a couple of months. I knew since his recovery was still fragile, he didn't need any more stress right now. They were still living in their house, but it had been foreclosed on, and it was only a matter of time before they would have to move. Their marriage was rocky as well. Not the best time to have another child.

I wanted to be happy about a new little baby on the way, but it was hard to get excited. I tried to reason that it was their lives, but when it concerns helpless children it's not that easy.

Our next trip to the Caribbean was nice, except for a little panic at Logan airport.

We decided to bring the company laptop that had once been James' so we could search the real estate market while we were there. The laptop was in rough shape after James used it for almost two years. Tina was able to get it working for us, and I put it in the laptop bag to carry on the plane before we headed to the airport.

For some reason while standing in line at security, my mind wandered to James and some of the things he was able to hide from us. I remembered the needle in his coat lining. Then I panicked! Could he have hidden a needle in the laptop case I was holding? I had emptied it of papers and folders, but he was sneaky. My heart began to pound.

"Paul, I have to go to the bathroom."

"Now?"

"Yes."

"Can't it wait? We're almost through the line."

"I'll hurry."

I left without giving him another chance to speak. I rushed to the restroom and into a stall, where I searched through all the little pockets and the larger ones for files. At the bottom of the large front pocket near the seam, I could just barely feel something with my fingertip. It took longer than I expected, but I was finally able to pry out a needle. I continued to search for more but couldn't find any others, so I headed back to the security line and Paul.

I could only hope and pray there were no more needles in the bag that would show up on the x-rays. I did not relax until we were finally on the plane.

The next day we toured the island with Tony and looked at a few homes. We were able to unwind and enjoy the beach and the sun. Paul was not as anxious about the dogs this time.

As the week flew by, Tony put the pressure on us to purchase one of the properties we had viewed. Explaining that we were only beginning to look for a warm weather property didn't sit well with him.

Realizing once we were off the island, his chance at a sale was slim, he continued to push until we flat out said, "not this trip." He was obviously disappointed, but we told him we'd be back.

We decided on the flight home we were premature in purchasing a property so far away. The dogs were too old to make the trip, so we thought it was best to wait a few years. But the idea was planted in our minds, and we were excited. We began researching other destinations, in the U.S. and the Caribbean. As long as it was warm, we were open to any

Jess Gallant

location.

Chapter Sixteen

W̲e got home and back to work on our project house. I was learning a lot and making my share of mistakes. I did all the running around while Paul did all the hard work. Kylie stopped by a few times to give us her opinion on the progress. We tried to stay neutral with paint colors, but she insisted it should all be pastels. She was a girly girl even at twenty-two. I hoped she'd never change.

The house was coming along, and we decided to advertise it for sale at the end of January. After a couple of low-ball offers, we had an offer that was full price, but the buyer wanted us to owner finance.

"What do you think? Should we consider it?" Paul asked me.

Tina had done many owner financed home sales, and she was doing okay, but we had always sold our project homes outright.

Some sales worked well for Tina, but many others didn't. Paul always thought his sister was crazy to sell the way she did. A lot of buyers walked away from the property when things got difficult, but she simply sold the property again to someone else, after another rehab of course.

"Why would you want to do that?"

"I'm asking you," he said. "Obviously, we'd have to do a credit check and get a large down payment."

"It wouldn't hurt to check them out."

It was a good thing we checked them out because

their credit was terrible, but I had an idea.

We had helped James and Sam get their first homes. Was it Kylie's turn? I knew she loved the house. Kylie and Tom had gotten engaged at Christmas. With her job and Tom's income, I was sure they could afford it. They only needed the down payment.

"If you were thinking of owner financing for a stranger, why not owner finance the property for your daughter?" I asked Paul a few days later.

"Because she doesn't have a down payment. We have to get some money to pay for the improvements."

"What I'm thinking is that we finance the down payment, and she gets a conventional mortgage." Now I had his attention.

"I'm listening. You've obviously been thinking. How would that work?"

"I've been 'researching,' " I corrected Paul with a smile. "Because she's our daughter we can give her a gift of equity. It should be twenty percent so there won't be any mortgage insurance. Then she goes to the mortgage company and gets a regular mortgage on this property with a twenty percent down payment." I knew that meant we would not be paid for any of the work we had done to the property, so I quickly added, "She'll have to pay us back of course."

"Would she qualify?"

"I can check with Sharon. She handled the mortgage on our home. I think there's a way to use Tom's income even though he won't own the home. Sort of like a renter. I would want to talk with Sharon before we mention it to Kylie."

That was January of 2006, and banks were pretty much giving money away.

"How would she ever pay us back?"

"I thought of that." I had tried to think of everything over the last few days, preparing myself for all his questions. I was hoping he would go along with it. We had taken Kylie's future away when we sold the oil company. Maybe this was a way to help her move forward and ease our guilt at the same time.

"If she qualifies," I said to Paul, "and we go through with it, we put a lien on the property for the amount of the down payment, so she can't get a home equity loan like James did.

"We give her seven years with no payments to us. Chances are she'll sell the house before then and pay us back at the sale. Most people sell their first homes within a few years anyway. If she still owns it after seven years, she can make monthly payments to us. She should be making more money by then."

"We'll be giving up all of our profit. That's a lot of money."

"I know, but we'll get back our initial investment, and we can move on to another property."

Although we didn't mention it, we both knew there was a very good chance we would not see anything more than that initial investment, the amount of Kylie's mortgage. But I would rather take that chance with our own child than with a stranger.

"Go ahead and check into it. Don't say anything to Kylie just yet. Let's think about it some more."

He added, "It's going to be hard to make a living if we keep giving away all our profits, you know."

But he was smiling. He would go for it. I knew Paul, and he loved his daughter.

After a few phone calls, I was confident Kylie could

get a mortgage. It was time to ask her if she was interested.

She screamed, jumped up and down, and then cried. She was interested.

We had thirty days to finish up the improvements. I wouldn't let her change the paint colors yet. I tried explaining about investment property and neutrals. But it would soon be her home, and she could do whatever she wanted. I suggested bringing in her favorite colors with accessories since Tom was going to be living there too. To my surprise, she listened.

The closing was scheduled for two weeks away. Kylie was busy packing. The plan was to help her move and then get the apartment she was living in ready to rent. We agreed to let her put a few things in one room of the house, but she couldn't move in until after the closing. So when she stopped by with a few boxes, I wasn't surprised, but as soon as she got out of the car, I knew something was wrong.

"What is it, Sweetie?" I asked as I walked toward her. I could tell she'd been crying, but now she was smiling.

"I'm pregnant." Now she was smiling and crying. "I don't know how it happened, but I want this baby so much."

"That's great!"

I hugged my now expecting daughter wondering whatever happened to birth control.... "Why all the tears?"

"Can I still buy the house? I want the baby more than the house, but I really want the house too."

I didn't have an answer right away. I was quickly trying to add numbers in my head.

"Let's do the math. Come inside and we'll talk." And we did talk and talk and talk. We made a list of expenses, utilities, car payments, and baby needs. In the end, it all came down to choices. She would have this baby. That was a given. But could she afford the mortgage with a baby too? Would Tom stick around to help? She would have to work after the baby came, but most people did now anyway. It would be a struggle, but it could be done.

"It's up to you, Kylie," I finally told her. If she had waited two more weeks, she wouldn't have had a choice. She would have already owned the house anyway.

"I want to buy the house. I know Tom will be with me. We'll be getting married someday." They hadn't set a date. They wanted to take their time.

"You know you're doing this backwards. Most people get married first, then have a baby, and then buy a house." I hoped it wouldn't be too much for her.

Then she said something I had forgotten about.

"Mom, I'm still on Suboxone."

During my many hours on the computer looking for answers to all the problems my children were having, I was sure I had read that Suboxone was safe for pregnant women and newborns. But I hadn't actually looked for it specifically.

"Call Dr. Stevens right now." I wanted her to know right away.

She called and he confirmed that Suboxone was safe. He would switch her to Subutex because it only has the one ingredient, buprenorphine. The other ingredient was to prevent abuse and was not necessary for Kylie, especially at this time.

"He said it was safe thinking I'm taking twelve milligrams, so I feel even better taking only one milligram. You know the only thing that upsets me now is Lauren's pregnant too."

"That's right! I'm going to have two new grandchildren this year."

"I already decided my child is going to call you

'Mimi.' What do you think?"

"I love it! And I love you, too." I hugged her again thinking it was going to be a busy year.

It was.

Chapter Seventeen

Kylie and Tom moved into their new home in April, and James and Lauren moved out of their foreclosed home the same month.

James was still doing well but had changed jobs and was working in a town about an hour south of us. He and Lauren decided to get an apartment closer to where he worked.

In June, Paul and I made another trip to the Caribbean. The idea that we could own a piece of paradise just wouldn't fade away. We ended up purchasing a small home that needed a lot of work on the Island of Aruba. It would be an adventure, we told ourselves. It would be years before we could spend much time there. We knew that. The dogs came first, but a week here and there wouldn't hurt.

Lauren's child was due at the end of August, and Kylie's was due the first of November. The pregnancies were going well. Kylie had an obstetrician who specialized in high-risk babies and was familiar with Subutex. He constantly assured Kylie her baby would be fine.

The problem came when he asked her halfway through her pregnancy how much Subutex she was taking. She told him the truth, one milligram.

"Dr. Stevens has you down for twelve milligrams," Dr. Gutenberg said to Kylie.

I was with her at that appointment. She wanted me to meet him since I was going to be with her during the delivery. She had asked me a few months before. Tom would be there too, of course, but she wanted her mom as well.

Kylie looked at me for help. We had been caught.

Before she had a chance to answer, Dr. Gutenberg said to her firmly, "It doesn't matter how much, but I need to know the exact amount so we'll be prepared in case of any complications."

He was a large, tall man about fifty years old. Very nice but right now a little scary.

Kylie was quick on her feet. "I started taking twelve, but I cut down slowly. I've been taking only one milligram since before I got pregnant."

I could see her hands begin to tremble like a little girl caught in a lie, afraid of what he would do.

"I didn't tell Dr. Stevens because I wasn't sure I could maintain that low a dose," Kylie continued.

"But you have been that low for more than six or seven months?"

"Yes."

"That's better for the baby."

That was all Dr. Gutenberg said about it.

Dr. Stevens, on the other hand, was not so happy.

Obviously, Dr. Gutenberg shared the dosage information with him. He gave Kylie a stern lecture and dropped her prescription amount down to one milligram a day. Fortunately, she still had some stashed away for James, but she no longer had an unlimited supply. We would have to deal with that eventually.

The ultrasounds confirmed that both Lauren and Kylie were having little girls. Gabby came into the world the first of September with the cutest chubby cheeks I had ever seen on a newborn and light brown hair that stood straight up about an inch long. James was a proud daddy again, and they made a cute family. I prayed James would continue to do well and Lauren would learn to clean.

James had been doing some work in Florida on and off over the summer for the company he worked at. A few weeks after Gabby was born, he told me they offered him a job down there.

"Are you sure you want to do that?" I asked. "How does Lauren feel about being so far away from her family with two kids?"

"We've talked about it. I'll go down now and come back at Thanksgiving. Then we'll move down together. She'll come back next summer. Maybe I'll be able to come for a week or so, but she wants to stay longer. Lauren's okay with it as long as she can come back with the kids. Then you can see them too."

It was clear they had already decided, so I kept my doubts to myself. "What about Suboxone?"

"I'm going to wean off. Kylie's going to run out soon anyway, and I think I'm ready."

He looked good. He had gained weight and appeared to be doing well, but I worried it was too soon.

"I'm going to miss you." I hugged him. "And my grandchildren. How can you take them away?" I was teasing him, but it was the truth.

"I'll call, and Lauren will be back in the summer with the kids," he said, putting his arm around my shoulder. He had matured a lot in the last few months.

So James headed off to Florida to work and get things ready for his family to join him. Lauren and the kids spent most of the next couple of months bouncing between their apartment when James came home every few weeks, and her dad's home, when James was gone.

Ten weeks after Gabby was born, little Bree entered the world. Her entrance did not go as smoothly as Gabby's.

It was four-thirty on a Sunday morning when I got the call that Kylie's water had broken, and they were heading into the hospital. She was a week past her due date, so I wasn't surprised. I told her I'd be right behind them. The hospital was a half hour away for them. Forty-five minutes for me. So I rushed to shower and dress hoping there would be no baby before I arrived.

When I got to the hospital, all was going well. Tom was joking about getting this over with before the football game came on, after all it was a Sunday in November. Kylie was feeling the contractions getting stronger. They had decided on an epidural so it was time. I don't do well with needles, but I offered to stay with Kylie. Unfortunately, I turned white as a ghost, almost passed out, and had to leave the room. Tom stayed with her after that until they had inserted the needle in her back, and we all returned to watching the monitor and timing the contractions. The monitor was also showing the baby's heart rate.

We watched as Bree's heart rate began to slow down. It dropped down to the sixties when the door to the hospital room opened, and three people came in. One was the woman doctor who would deliver the baby. Dr. Gutenberg was not on call that Sunday morning.

They moved Kylie to a different position and checked her cervix. She was seven centimeters dilated the doctor told us. The baby's heart rate went back up, and they all left the room. This happened three more times in less than an hour. The last time the heart rate dropped down into the forties.

The doctor checked Kylie's cervix and said she was

ready to push. After twenty minutes of pushing, and with the baby's heart rate continuing to drop, the doctor decided to prepare for a cesarean delivery. The obstetrician would try one last time to suction the baby out of the vagina, but she was moving Kylie to the operating room. Tom and I were given surgical gowns, caps, and shoe covers, and told to hurry if we wanted to be there. If it became necessary for a cesarean, we would have to leave, but they were still hoping for a natural birth.

We made it to the operating room to see them try to suction the baby and hear Kylie scream. The doctor scolded her, saying there would be none of that. I was shocked by the doctor's words, but extremely glad Kylie had opted for the epidural. We tried to reassure her everything would be okay but were quickly led away. They would have to operate. Kylie looked at us one last time as they put a mask over her face while at the same time, asking her permission to do a cesarean. I will never forget the fear in my daughter's beautiful brown eyes.

Tom and I waited quietly in the hospital room for news. It seemed like hours when finally a nurse came to tell us a baby girl had been born, and the baby was doing well. She brought little Bree in a while later. There was no news on Kylie.

Bree was adorable with just a little bit of very dark hair and almost black eyes, like her mother's. Tom's mom had made it to the hospital by then, so we took turns holding the baby, but my thoughts were on Kylie. We were assured she was fine, but I was getting worried that it was taking so long.

My worst fears materialized when they wheeled Kylie into the room on a gurney. She was hooked up to IV's and monitors, and she was in extreme pain. Kylie was just waking up, but she was shaking all over. I went to her side reassuring her she would be fine while Tom was asking about pain medication.

"She has a morphine pump," the nurse said. Then she explained how to use it.

"Kylie, can you rate your pain on a scale of one to ten with ten being the worst possible pain you can imagine?" the nurse asked Kylie.

"Ten! Ten! Ten!" She was crying and holding her side.

The nursed pumped more morphine into the IV by pushing the button. She handed the control to Kylie to use as needed explaining it wouldn't give her more than what was allowed in a given amount of time.

I stood there holding her hand and praying the morphine would kick in quickly.

"Mom, it hurts so bad," Kylie whispered to me through her tears. "I feel like I'm being stabbed with a knife while someone's twisting it."

I fought back my own tears as I reassured her the pain would go away soon. Tom brought little Bree over as we all said how beautiful she was. But Kylie couldn't see her through the pain. She had exhausted her morphine allowance for the time being. Tom went for the nurse.

Again the nurse asked Kylie to rate her pain.

"Ten!"

"Still?"

"Yes! If I could go higher, I would," she told the nurse showing her exactly where the pain was.

Hours would go by before Kylie was taken to a hospital room and out of the labor and delivery area. They didn't know what was wrong, and her pain was still a ten.

As they had her move into the hospital bed from the gurney, Kylie screamed out in pain. The new nurse in this ward chastised her.

"You had a baby. It's going to hurt, but it's not that bad."

I didn't understand why these people were being so mean to her. Couldn't they see something was drastically wrong? Kylie wouldn't be making this up. She hadn't even been able to hold her new baby.

Just then, a new doctor showed up. He was the first person to really talk to Kylie. He had read her chart and was going to up the amount of morphine. Only a little, he said. It should take the edge off. He explained the use of opiates like Oxycontin, heroin, and methadone cause you to build up a high tolerance to morphine. That was why she was not getting any relief, but they still had to find the cause of the pain. He was scheduling a cat scan.

"Now?" Kylie asked him. She had just been moved into the hospital bed and was in no mood to be moved again anytime soon.

"I'd like to do it right away."

"I can't." Kylie started to cry again. It had been an extremely long day.

"Can you do it in the morning?" I asked. "Will it make much of a difference?"

"I guess we can schedule it for first thing in the morning. I'll be by to talk to you after the scan. Okay?" He smiled at Kylie and took her hand. "You have a beautiful little girl over there." He pointed to Bree sleeping peacefully in her father's arms.

"Thank you. I haven't held her yet. It hurt so much," Kylie said.

Tom brought Bree closer.

"Well, I think it's time. Is the pain a little better now?"

"Maybe an eight," she answered and tried to smile.

"Good. I'll let you hold your baby, and I'll see you

tomorrow."

He left us alone while Tom put a sleeping Bree on Kylie's chest, far away from the spot of her pain.

This was the moment I had been waiting for all day. To see my smiling daughter holding her sleeping little princess. A moment I'll treasure forever.

I went home a little later, after making sure Kylie was comfortable. She was still in pain, but it was bearable. The bed next to her was empty, so Tom could stay the night as long as they didn't need it for another patient. I would be back early in the morning, I told her as I left.

I had called Paul many times during the day but told him not to come in. "It won't do any good. I'll see you at home later," I said. Then when I saw him I fell into his arms and cried. He held me for a long time until I stopped sobbing and pulled myself together. Then I showed him pictures from my camera of his new little granddaughter.

Always ready with a joke, Paul said, "She looks like a convict."

He was right, she looked exactly like her dad.

I was back in the hospital the next morning.

"How are you this morning, Sweetie? And how is little Bree?" The baby was sleeping on Kylie's chest.

"I've been better. It still really hurts. They're coming to get me in a few minutes, and it hurts so much to move. One nurse keeps yelling at me. She thinks I'm making it all up."

Kylie was better than yesterday but not by much.

"I'm sure she doesn't think that," I said. "Can I hold her for a minute before they come to take her?" I asked as I was already picking up Bree. "Tom and I will help you move to the gurney."

Tom interrupted, "I asked if she can be wheeled down on the bed since she'll have to move again in the cat scan room and then back to the gurney and back in bed again. That will save her two moves."

"Good idea, Tom. That will save Kylie a lot of pain."

They showed up a short time later and took Bree to the nursery. Then a very nice nurse wheeled Kylie's bed down to have the cat scan.

As we waited in the hall with Kylie, Tom noticed her chart on the end of the bed. He opened it. I gave him a look that said, "don't do that." He gave me a look that said, "you better come look at this." So I read the chart as Tom played lookout and kept Kylie distracted.

I couldn't believe what I was reading. They had labeled my little girl a "heroin addict." Page after page right under her name were the words heroin addict. It all made sense now. Why some of the nurses treated her badly. Of course, they would think she was an awful person to have a baby under the circumstances. I probably would have thought the same thing a few years ago. When Tom coughed loudly, I closed the chart quickly. Someone was coming.

Tom and I talked about the chart while they did the cat scan. We wouldn't say anything to Kylie right now, maybe never. But we would talk to one of the nicer nurses and explain the facts of Kylie's addiction and most importantly, her recovery.

The cat scan revealed a cut in Kylie's right ureter, the tube that carried urine from the kidney to the bladder. The doctor explained that the pain she was feeling was probably similar to, but way worse than a kidney stone. They would have to go in and put a stent into the ureter until it healed and then go in and remove it, probably six weeks later.

We finally had an answer, but it meant another procedure and an epidural again. The soonest they could do it was later that evening. Needless to say, Kylie was frightened. So was I.

What should have been the happiest few days of her young life had become a nightmare. She was swollen and sore from the attempted vaginal birth and failed suction attempt. Her lower abdomen had been cut open and stitched up from the cesarean. And she was suffering from excruciating pain in her right side caused by a cut to her ureter during the operation. Now she had to go through another procedure to repair the damage and then heal from all three areas. On top of all that, some people in the hospital were treating her like garbage. It just wasn't fair.

I knew I had to stay calm and positive for Kylie. It wouldn't do anybody any good to get angry now. So Tom and I, as well as his mother, tried to keep Kylie distracted during the long wait for an operating room. We changed and dressed the baby, took lots of pictures, and encouraged Kylie to try nursing. A difficult task under the circumstances.

Tom talked to one of the nicer nurses about Kylie. His mother didn't know about Kylie's past either, and Kylie wanted to keep it that way. We respected her feelings and asked the nurse to do the same. Now that they knew Kylie was really in pain, they seemed to be nicer, all but the one. Kylie began referring to her as "the witch."

The day passed as well as could be expected. I thought Kylie was going to wear out the morphine pump, but she made it through all right until they came to get her. She had a minor meltdown then, but the staff was great and assured her and us everything would be fine. We were not allowed to be with her even for the epidural this time. She was more frightened of that than the procedure itself. But she did well, and the stent was placed in her ureter successfully.

***

They brought Kylie back from the operating room at 11:00 that night. They took Bree to the NICU at 3:00 the next morning.

I had stayed at the hospital until Kylie's procedure was over. Once I knew it was successful, I went home. Tom was going to spend another night in her room. When I arrived back at the hospital the next day, Kylie was crying again. I tried to calm her down as Tom filled me in.

"Bree was fussy during the night. They took her to NICU because of the Subutex. They think it's withdrawals," he said.

"The witch said I should have expected it if I was going to live that lifestyle! She told me not to be such a baby and to think of Bree!" Kylie was hysterical now.

"It'll be all right. They have to do what's best for Bree," I told her as I held her hand. I knew a hug was out of the question with all the IV lines, pumps, and monitors she was hooked up to.

"You don't understand! They'll give her opiates! They'll addict her, and she doesn't need that! I do want to do what's best for Bree!"

"Okay. Why don't we talk to them and tell them how low a dose you're on? We'll make sure they have all the facts before they do anything. I'll see if I can find someone. I'm sure we can talk to whoever is in charge of Bree's care." I left the room to look for anyone who could get a message to the NICU.

Kylie was a little calmer when I got back.

"They're going to send someone down from the NICU," I told her. Then added, "You must be feeling better to be yelling like that."

She attempted a smile. "I'm so afraid for her." The tears started to flow again.

"That's what it feels like to be a mom." I hugged her then, wires and all.

When the doctor in charge of Bree's care came to talk to us, he assured us Bree had only been given a mild sedative so far. Her condition could be a result of the difficult birth, and he was glad to know the dose of Subutex that Kylie took was so low. They would watch her for now, but because Subutex is a relatively new drug they wanted to keep her in NICU for a few days.

Bree never needed anything else. A few days later Kylie and Bree were both ready to go home. It had been a rough few days. Kylie's bad choices at nineteen had come back to haunt her again at twenty-three.

Chapter Eighteen

A few weeks later, on Thanksgiving Day, Tom picked James up at the airport, and they came to our house for dinner. Kylie and Bree were already there, while Lauren and the girls were at her dad's. Paul had softened a little over the past year, but I wasn't sure he would ever really forgive James. It was, however, a nice quiet dinner, and James got to see his new niece for the first time. He was moving his family to Florida over the weekend.

We stayed busy that winter with a new project house. Actually, it was a very old house. It had been abandoned years ago, but it had "character" as we called it. I cleaned and painted while Paul repaired the chimney, installed a woodstove, and replaced the kitchen cabinets. We were now bringing the dogs with us since the older one needed constant care. He was almost eighteen.

James called often from Florida. He sounded good and said he loved it there. They were now renting a house with a pool in Cape Coral, and Renee was learning to swim. Knowing I worried, James assured me the pool had a baby gate around it. During one of these calls, he told me how great he felt.

"I feel like I was living in a fog and now it's lifted. Everything is so clear, and I actually have money in my pocket."

I was happy for him. I believed he had finally made it.

***

We lost Shadow in May of 2007. I cried for weeks. Paul cried for months. It was heartbreaking for both of us. At eighteen, Shadow had lived with us longer than either of our children. We still had Pebbles, but she was almost seventeen. We knew it wouldn't be long before we lost her too.

We talked more and more about the house in Aruba. Paul was determined we would not be spending many more winters in New England.

I was excited about Aruba too, but I wanted to keep a home in New Hampshire as well. I hoped to eventually buy a smaller camp on the lake we loved so much. Paul's family had been coming here since he was six years old. My family started camping at the local campground when I was in my early teens. This was where Paul and I met so many years ago. I couldn't imagine summers anywhere else. And summer was just around the corner.

Kylie hadn't gone back to work after Bree was born. She was now working from home. They were struggling financially but still getting by. With her flexible schedule, I expected her to be around a lot in the warmer weather. Lauren and my other two granddaughters would be home in a few weeks. I was eager to see the girls, but I was not happy about James being left behind, especially after I found out Lauren and the children would be staying alone with a young single man. It just didn't feel right, and people were beginning to talk.

Lauren told Lindsey, Keith's daughter, who told her father. Then Keith confronted Paul. Karen told me, and I told Kylie who was not shy about expressing her feelings. I won't repeat her exact words. Most people were a little more tactful, but it was an uncomfortable situation, to say the least.

I decided to find out how James felt, so I asked him flat out. Sometimes there's no other way.

"Hi, James. How are you?" I asked the next time he called.

"I'm good. Lauren and the girls will be there next week."

"That's great. I can't wait to see them. Gabby must be so big." Then I asked, "Are they really going to be staying with Tim?"

"Yes. It's okay. They're just friends."

"Are you sure you're okay with that?"

"Yes, Mom, I'm sure. He's my friend too."

"How long are they staying?"

"I don't know. Lauren hasn't decided yet. She's not making plans to come back for a while."

So James didn't know how long his wife and girls were staying either. I didn't like the way things were shaping up at all.

Lauren and the kids arrived back in New Hampshire on the eighth of June 2007 to begin their summer vacation. I can't say I wasn't excited to see the girls. Renee had gotten taller. At almost five, she was now a little girl who loved everything princess. I had referred to her as "the baby" for four years, but she would be starting school in the fall. She looked so much like her father, if it wasn't for the pink dress and long hair, I would have thought they were the same child. Gabby was cute as ever with those pinchable chubby cheeks. She looked even more like her mother now. As I feared, she didn't remember me, and at nine months old she clung to her mother.

Lauren was definitely a different kind of mother, though. She just handed Gabby to me and went over next door. It didn't matter that Gabby was screaming as she walked away. Lauren had been that way with Renee too. She left her with anyone who would take her. I bit my tongue and kept my mouth shut.

Fortunately for me, Gabby didn't cry for long. I figured Lauren had done this before.

It was fun to have the two babies and Renee at the lake. Renee was almost swimming alone now, and we bought floating baby seats for the little ones. But I was worried about James.

I had that feeling again, something you can't put your finger on. He called every couple of days to check on things. But he was beginning to sound different. A little distant, a little depressed, and maybe a little angry. Just a little at first.

And then he started asking for money. That was a red flag. He hadn't asked for money in over a year, and he was making good money in Florida. He blamed it on Lauren and the kids, but I was sure there was more.

When he called at night a couple of times, I could tell by the slurring words he was doing something.

"James, you sound high."

"No, I'm not high. I only had a couple of beers after work. There's nothing wrong with that!"

He was defensive. Paul had told him many times to have a couple of beers instead of doing drugs. Beer was legal and cheap compared to the alternative. "As long as you don't drive, just have a few beers," Paul would often say to James.

"Don't bite my head off. I just worry," I said, wishing he wasn't down there all alone.

James called again a few nights later. He was on Alligator Alley, on his way to Miami. I certainly didn't like the sound of that.

"I'm going over for a job. That's all."

"At this time of night?"

"It's a three hour drive. We'll stay in a hotel tonight, so we can start early in the morning."

"Is someone with you?" I asked. It didn't make sense.

"Yes, John. He's a guy I work with. The thing is they didn't give us any money to eat tonight or tomorrow. I'm broke and so is John. Can you give me a credit card number so we can get some food? I promise I'll pay you back."

Major red flag. How stupid did he think I was?

"No, James, I'm sorry I can't do that. You'll have to make do." He begged a little more but not too much. I think he knew before he called it was a long shot. But he was up to something, and it wasn't good.

I tried to talk to him a few days later since it was always easier to talk during the day. He just kept reassuring me everything was fine. Money was tight, but he was doing well. Without being able to see him, I couldn't tell if he had lost weight. Was he shaking? Were his eyes half closed? I only had the voice on the other end of the phone. Sometimes, he sounded fine. Other times, not so much.

And then it happened. It was a Saturday night at the beginning of August. Lauren and the girls had been here for eight weeks with no indication of when they would return to Florida and James. We had company that day. Paul's sister and Alex were still at the house. Kylie, Tom, and Bree had been there earlier but had long since gone home. Paul had gone to bed. He was never a late night person. Anything after eight was too late for him. We were drinking wine and discussing drug addiction. Alex knew I was worrying about James again.

"My brother was way worse than James ever thought of being, and he turned his life around. Do you know he actually took a knife to Paul once?"

Alex and Tina are a couple and have been together longer than Paul and I have been married, so she has been a part of my husband's family for a long time. I met Alex when I met the rest of his family. We became good friends.

I knew she had a brother who had done drugs, but we rarely talked about it.

"No. I didn't know that. Paul never told me."

"Steve was bad. Really, really bad. He didn't hurt Paul, but that was the last time Paul had anything to do with him. I had to shut him out of my life a few years later. He would call at all hours of the night asking for money. I kept sending him some even though I couldn't afford it. He would tell me he was sleeping on the street, and I would feel bad."

"Sounds eerily familiar." I could picture James doing the same thing.

"I didn't talk to Steve for nine years," Alex said, emphasizing the nine.

"Then what happened?" I asked. I hoped I could somehow help James long before nine years had elapsed.

"Steve had a dream that he died and was going to Hell. It scared him so much he started going to church. Now he's a born-again Christian and has been clean for five years."

She didn't need to mention that he is also HIV positive from all the drug use and probably won't live a long life. That much I already knew. It was heartbreaking for Alex to finally have her brother back in her life knowing his life would most likely be cut short. I knew she prayed every day he would stay healthy a little longer.

"Maybe James will find his own way to beat this. His own nightmare that will make him stop," I said. It was all so very sad.

We were still sitting in the kitchen talking when the phone rang. Never a good thing this late on a Saturday night.

I looked at Tina and Alex, took a deep breath, and answered the phone. It was James.

"Mom, I need your help," he sobbed.

"James, where are you?" My first thought was that he was in jail.

"I'm sitting in the middle of the road in downtown Cape Coral." His words were definitely slurred.

"Listen to me James. The first thing you need to do is get out of the road!" I yelled. "Are you out of the road?"

"No."

"Get out of the road! Then we'll talk! Okay?" I tried to calm down.

"Okay. I'm out of the road. I want to come home. I need money to come home. I need help," he pleaded through sobs.

I knew the answer but had to ask, "What's going on, James?"

"I lost my job. Please help me come home. I'll go straight into a program. I'll go to *Teen Challenge*. I promise. I can't stay here."

Then he tried again. "Can you give me your card number so I can take a cab home?"

"James, I'm not giving you a credit card number. But you get yourself home and call me tomorrow. We'll figure out what to do then." The phone was silent. Then I heard sobs. "James, did you hear me?"

"Yes," he managed to say.

"Can you get home?"

He mumbled something and the phone went dead.

I had been walking around the room while I talked to him. I sat down on the floor right in the middle of our kitchen and cried. James was high, alone, and depressed in Florida. His entire family was here. I was afraid he wouldn't even make it through the night, and there was nothing I could do.

Alex helped me to my feet as I apologized for the

227

breakdown. They had heard everything so there was no need to explain.

"I don't know if I can go through this again," I said after I pulled myself together.

"Sometimes the best thing to do is nothing," Alex said and Tina agreed.

"I had to shut my brother out of my life for nine years. He finally got better."

"What if it was your child? What if we were talking about Melody?" Melody is Tina and Alex's nine-year-old daughter.

"I don't know," she answered quietly. But when they left the house a few minutes later, Alex looked back at me from the doorway and said, "Nine years, Jess, nine years."

I told Paul about James' call early the next morning.

"It's all because of Lauren," Paul said. "What was she thinking leaving him alone down there for two months, and she's here doing who knows what with that guy she's staying with. That's enough to make anyone do drugs. I have no respect for her. I think she's the cause of all his problems. Now he's doing drugs again, and there are two kids to worry about this time."

I knew he could go on for hours. He had never really warmed up to Lauren to begin with, and she hadn't done much to change that in his mind.

"I know, Hon, but what do we do now?"

"I don't know. Do you think he'll really get help?"

"He said he wants to." I knew that didn't mean very much.

"Well, get him home then. What else can we do?"

I would soon find out that wasn't going to be easy.

***

When James called later that morning, I was relieved to hear his voice. At least he was still alive. But I wasn't prepared for his question.

"Three thousand dollars! Are you kidding?" I responded to my son's request.

That was what it would cost to move him home, and he had no money. There was no way we were going to pay that.

"What do you want me to do? I can't just leave everything here," he said.

"James, we don't have that kind of money to give you every time you make a mistake."

"I'll pay you back."

I had heard that so many times before and not once had he followed through.

"No you won't. You don't even have a job." I didn't know what else to say. He got himself into trouble and expected me to bail him out. "You're going to have to figure out something else."

"Please, I just want to come home," he pleaded.

He was getting emotional again. I did want him to come home. I wanted to help him but not for that kind of money.

"Look, see if you can rent a small trailer and only bring some of your stuff. Take the rest to the Salvation Army or something."

I had a feeling most of their stuff was not worth bringing home anyway. The Salvation Army probably wouldn't want it either.

"If I find something cheaper, will you help me?" he begged.

"See what you can find out and call me back." I caved.

＊＊

So James rented a small trailer that he was able to tow behind the van they had bought back in the early spring when Lauren insisted they needed air conditioning in their vehicle. I paid for the trailer on a credit card. I didn't tell Paul. He had insisted we "not help" James this time. But how could I "not help" him when he was so far away?

I would "not help" him when he got back, I told myself. But that was going to be difficult when two little kids were involved.

When James finally made it home about a week after that Saturday late-night phone call, he was a wreck, but he wasn't high. He had no money to get high, or for anything else for that matter. No money for food, gas, or rent. He left what he was able to bring home in Lauren's father's garage. Lauren and the girls had been staying with him for the last few days. Young single guy had kicked her out. I didn't ask why.

James had promised to get help, so we insisted he follow through. I knew he didn't want to go, but Lauren took him to the *Teen Challenge* outside of Augusta. Kylie and I offered to drive him, but Lauren insisted she would do it. This time, we didn't have the energy to argue.

We all said goodbye and gave words of encouragement again. Keith had James over to his house for prayers before he and Lauren headed out. We were not supposed to hear from him for thirty days. I'm not sure why all the rehab places do that, but they must have a reason. I had heard this place was a big old farmhouse out in the country. I hoped he would fit in. I hoped he would stay.

He didn't.

230

***

He called after two days and begged someone to come and get him. We all said no, even Lauren this time. He left anyway with his suitcase. A nice police officer saw him walking and stopped to make sure he was okay.

When the police officer got back in his car, he ran James' name through his computer. He promptly got back out of the car and arrested James on a charge of passing a worthless instrument. It had happened back when we owned the oil company. When we heard he was in jail, Keith reminded us "God works in mysterious ways." I think some people, including Paul, got a good laugh at that comment and James' unfortunate predicament.

So James spent the next three days in jail. Evidently the check had been paid by my mother a long time ago, but James had to either pay the $500 fine or spend three days in jail. No one offered the $500.

Lauren did finally pick James up. He could not go back to *Teen Challenge*. They didn't want him. He wasn't ready.

For the next few weeks, James, Lauren, Renee, and Gabby lived in their van. Everyone tried to "not help" hoping to force James back into rehab. Fortunately, it was August, but there had been a few chilly nights. I gave in on one of those nights and let James and the girls stay with us. Lauren was at her sister's.

I woke up to noise in the kitchen at two o'clock in the morning. Assuming it was James, I went out to see what he needed. He was washing Gabby's baby shoes in the sink. He had already washed Renee's shoes and had cleaned the entire kitchen, even the floor. He would have vacuumed but didn't want to wake me up, he said. I thanked my son for helping but told him to go back to bed. I thought he was hoping to stay with us longer by being helpful. It wasn't going to work. I was determined to "not help."

It wasn't until the next day when Kylie came over with Bree that I found out what had happened. I told Kylie about James' cleaning frenzy in the middle of the night. I thought it was sweet, I said.

"Mom, James was doing cocaine."

"How do you know?" I was shocked. He looked fine. Wouldn't I have noticed?

"Cocaine makes you want to do things. You're alert, wide awake. You can't sit still like you've had twelve cups of coffee."

I was being educated on cocaine this time. Apparently, James had come home from Florida with a new "drug of choice."

"You know," Kylie continued, "it does make sense. He wasn't having withdrawals this time. You don't get them with coke. You feel awful for a day or so, and you usually feel awful about how much money you spent, but you don't have physical withdrawals like you do with opiates. The problem is you don't want to stop. You keep chasing an imaginary high you never get."

"How expensive is it?"

"Very. Someone could spend a week's pay in one night."

"James didn't have any money."

"Where's your pocketbook? Did you have any cash last night?"

She was making me nervous.

"I keep it in the bedroom now. I do have cash. Roger paid his rent in cash, and I haven't been to the bank yet."

Roger was renting the apartment Kylie used to rent behind the office. I was heading to the bedroom while I talked, afraid to open my wallet.

"Well?"

Kylie was right behind me. I should have had eight hundred dollars. I had five hundred. I was crushed. I was trying to give his kids a warm place to sleep, and James was stealing from me. Stealing from me to buy drugs for himself. Not food for his kids. Drugs, cocaine, for himself!

"Three hundred dollars is missing!"

"That jerk! You wait til I get a hold of him. Where is he?" Kylie always tried to protect me from James. She knew I didn't like confrontation. But I was his mother, and he had stolen from me. I would handle it, I told her.

"What I don't understand is how he got the money and the drugs?" I asked my daughter. "He was here all night with us."

"Drug addicts are sneaky. It only takes a minute to sneak into your bedroom. And how do you know he was here all night? After you went to bed, he could have left and come back."

Kylie was much more worldly than I was. I wanted to trust everyone. She trusted no one.

"So what do I do?"

"Don't let him in your house."

"How do I do that? He's my son."

"It doesn't matter who he is. Do you remember when I was going out with the guy who gave me the black eye?"

Did I ever. Loser boyfriend. "How can I forget?"

"We went to his friend's mother's house. She met us on the porch, and we talked for a while. She told me that even though she loved her son, he was not allowed inside her house. Ever."

"So stealing from your parents is common among drug addicts," I said to no one in particular. It had been over two years since the last time James had stolen from us. I was so sure it would never happen again.

233

"It's a shame, but you have to protect yourself from your son," Kylie replied.

I confronted James and told him he was no longer allowed in the house. He tried to make excuses, but I told him not to bother since I didn't believe anything he said. For some reason, I didn't tell Paul. Even though James was Paul's son too, I felt responsible. I should have kept a better eye on him and my pocketbook.

They slept in the car for a little longer, but Renee needed to start school, and James was looking for a job. As grandparents, the guilt was too much to handle. We finally gave in and offered to give them the first month's rent and security deposit for a "winter rental" on a lake. Winter rentals come already furnished and were usually available from September until June. It was obvious James was not going anywhere, and the kids needed a warm place to call home. They enrolled Renee in school, and James got a job.

We tried to have James do some work for us at our new project house, but he never showed up when he said he would. Paul got frustrated and again didn't want anything more to do with him.

James lost his job after three months. He said he had been late a few times, but I was sure there was more to it than that. We weren't really speaking much. His van was repossessed shortly after he lost his job. Now if he lost the camp he was staying in, he really had no place to go.

But James was fortunate. My mother was living in the same town and was stopping in regularly to see the kids, her great grandchildren. When James lost his job and his van, she bought food and drove them around. She made sure they had heat and tried to help Lauren keep the house clean. She even did their laundry. When we had given up on him, my mother had taken over.

I didn't realize how much she was doing for him at first, but she told me she wanted to help. It was her turn, and she thought she could save him somehow. She was happy to do it, she said, so I stayed out of it.

Halfway through the winter, James got another job. His grandmother paid to renew all his plumbing and heating licenses. It cost almost a thousand dollars. He said he would pay her back, but I didn't think he ever would.

Chapter Nineteen

He did well at that new job for a while. They loved him and bought a new truck for him to use. Things were looking up, and we gradually let down our defenses again.

In July of 2008, Kylie informed me she was ready to get married to Tom. They had been engaged for two and a half years. Together for almost four.

"I don't want to plan a wedding for a year. I want to do it right away. But I want it nice."

She was telling me this as I was thinking how Paul was going to feel about Kylie finally marrying the "convict."

I took a deep breath and said, "Slow down. You can't decide when to have it until you find a place to have it and then see what's available. To find a place you need to have a budget and an approximate head count. So let's start at the beginning."

"Okay. What do you want to know first?"

"How many people?"

I knew Kylie always wanted a small wedding so I wasn't too worried about the cost.

"I don't know. I don't have many friends."

"Well, let's start a list to get an idea."

And so we began to plan her wedding.

Kylie wanted to get married in the small Congregational Church on Main Street where Paul and I got married. We found a banquet hall on a golf course about twenty minutes away. They had an opening on October 4th. It was settled. Sit-down dinner with seventy-five guests.

Bree was the flower girl, and Tom's older daughter, Hannah, was a junior bridesmaid. Tom had reconnected with the child he had at twenty, and Hannah was now spending one weekend a month at Tom and Kylie's home. At almost eight, she was a wisp of a thing with long, light brown hair and sparkling eyes. Hannah adored Bree and was adjusting well to her new circumstances.

Kylie decided to have James and Lauren in the wedding to avoid hurt feelings. She loved James when he was clean, and she was trying to accept Lauren for who she was. Their children were cousins and so close in age that it was better to try and get along.

Kylie and I had fun picking out dresses. We found Bree a dress exactly like Kylie's. Bree would be almost two when they got married and was now looking just like her mother. She had Kylie's long, very dark hair and almost black eyes. Everywhere they went together strangers would comment on how much they looked alike. Kylie starter referring to her daughter as "my mini-me."

We laughed a lot that summer. Life was good. Would it last?

We began to see the occasional red flag again in August. James and Lauren had moved out of the winter rental and into another small camp not far from our house. My mother had cleaned the last place after James assured me he left it clean. Mom said it hadn't been touched in months. She was old school, and you left a home cleaner than when you moved in. That place had never been so clean. They were able to get their security deposit back to put down on the new place. It was supposed to come back to us but should probably have been given to my mother. However,

James and Lauren ended up with it. Nobody argued, we all wanted the kids to have a home.

It wasn't long after that, when Lauren would call looking for James. He was late. Had I seen him? The next day everything would be fine. But before long Kylie saw him looking sleepy at times, not all the time, only once in a while. She began to regret asking him to be in her wedding.

"I don't care what he does before or after, but please make sure he's clean at my wedding," she asked me as if I could control it.

"I'll talk to him. Don't worry." I lied. I was worried.

"He told me he was on pain pills, a non-narcotic type for his back," Kylie said. "I think he's either taking too many or taking them the wrong way because he looks high when he takes them."

I tried talking to James, but again, like always, he assured me everything was fine. It wasn't.

James was high at Kylie's wedding. A groomsman had to keep nudging him to keep him from falling asleep during the ceremony, and his eyes were half closed in all the pictures. Fortunately, the rest of the wedding was lovely. Little Bree stole the show, and I'll never forget Paul walking Kylie down the aisle. She glowed as every bride does, and Paul had to choke back tears. He had warmed up to Tom, a little. Tom was pretty responsible, but more importantly, he loved Kylie and adored Bree. He was a great dad. Kylie had done all right.

When the wedding party was announced, Paul carried Bree into the reception to great applause. Tom and Kylie danced well into the evening, and Kylie had such a good time she could not stay angry at her brother. But she would never forget what he had done.

***

We lost Pebbles shortly after Kylie's wedding. We were heartbroken again. The house was so empty. Paul had developed allergies to the dogs over the last few years, so we decided there would be no more animals for us. We would continue to spoil Keith's dogs as we always have, and we'd watch Tina's dogs whenever she asked, but we would not have any more ourselves. It was just too much for Paul.

It was during this time that we read about the fall of the real estate market in Florida. We were always looking for our next project home. Although we owned the house in Aruba, I didn't want to retire there. I told Paul on numerous occasions Aruba was great for now, but when we got older I wanted to be in our own country. He felt the same way, so in November we took a trip down to look at real estate in Southwest Florida.

Alex's mother lived down there, and Alex visited often. She raved about the area. Ironically, Cape Coral was one of the hardest places hit when the bubble burst. We couldn't believe how low the prices were. Armed with lists of bank owned properties for sale, we rented a condo for a week. We wanted to check out as many houses as possible in the time we were there.

Paul and I quickly learned the saying "you can't get there from here" was the case for most of Cape Coral. Once you figured it out, Cape Coral was well designed, but for a newcomer, it was a nightmare. There were so many canals that without a map you couldn't figure out how to get from one end of a street to the other. We mistakenly believed if a street ran across the Cape we could simply follow the street, but it couldn't be done. There were certain main roads, called parkways and boulevards, you could follow, but the numbered streets, avenues, places, and lanes were all cut up

239

by canals. By the end of the first day, Paul and I were barely speaking to each other.

But we were determined. That night we got out maps and the computer and wrote better directions to the properties we wanted to drive by. Paul had a list of fifty or so houses to look at. We didn't want to get a broker because that would take too long. We were just going to drive by, and if the house was vacant and no one was around, we did peek in a few windows. Paul was like a kid in a candy shop. He loved real estate, and to him this was a big sale. However, I wasn't sure I liked the area at first.

We were heading over to Orlando on our last day in Florida to see Paul's parents before going home. We had only a few more houses to look at and all were in the northwest section of the city. We planned to look at them on our way out of town. That's when I fell in love with Cape Coral.

We drove up what was called Old Burnt Store Road, a really odd name for a road, but it was a beautiful ride. Many of the houses on the west side sat on canals that went out to the ocean. The homes were beautiful with pools, tile roofs, pavered driveways, and palm trees. They were spread apart giving it a country feel. There were beautiful homes in the south, but they were packed in close together. The inexpensive homes we had been looking at were in neighborhoods that were spacious, but many were small, a lot were vacant, and rarely had anyone done any landscaping. I knew this was where I wanted to be.

When we crossed over to Burnt Store Road, from "Old" Burnt Store Road, we saw a for-sale sign on a house that was not on our list. We stopped to look around. Noticing no people in the area, and after making sure the home was vacant, we walked around and peeked in the windows. We had just found our first house in Florida.

I called the number on the sign when we got home and made an offer. It was a "short-sale," so it would take\ time. We waited patiently.

In the meantime, Christmas was coming. That year I had a six-year-old and two, two-year-old granddaughters. It would be fun. They had a Christmas pageant at the church the kids attended, and Renee was going to be singing with her class.

I couldn't persuade Paul to go, but I didn't want to miss it. Last Christmas we were barely speaking to James, and I missed seeing the girls. I left a bag of presents at their house but didn't stay to see them open the gifts. It's such a shame when the parents' actions affect the children.

I was hoping for a better holiday this year. The jury was still out on whether James was about to crash. I prayed it was only a minor bump in the road but had learned to be leery. I was meeting Kylie and Bree at the church. James would be there with his family, too.

The crowded church was filled with Christmas music played by the church band. The festive atmosphere immediately lifted my spirits as we found seats and waited for the children's performance. At just over two, Bree was still shy and very proper. She sat in her pretty holiday dress and quietly observed everyone and everything going on around her.

Suddenly, seemingly out of nowhere, little Gabby ran over squealing loudly and dancing around in a pretty new dress as well. I couldn't help but laugh. My two two's, as I had started calling them, were so very different. Bree was calm, quiet, pretty, and proper while Gabby was loud, curious, cute as a button, and always moving.

I looked around to find her parents. I knew from past

experience and Kylie's tattling they didn't always keep a good eye on their girls when they were at church. This time, however, James was not too far away. He scooped Gabby up in his arms and tickled her until she squealed again. One thing I was sure of, James loved his children and tonight it showed. He told us when Renee would be on stage and sat with Kylie and me for a while, taking Bree out of Kylie's arms. He loved his niece too.

I took a long look at James. He was clean in more ways than one. Not only was he drug-free, he was clean shaven and dressed in a clean white shirt and tie with black pants and shoes. I assumed the outfit was new. I had no doubt it would not look as nice again. But that night he looked great. He was confident, sure of himself, and attentive to his children and Lauren, as well as his mom, sister, and niece. That night he made me proud to have him as my son.

When the lights dimmed, James took Gabby back to his seat near the front with Lauren. The music started again with the first act of the nativity. The children were talented. They had been practicing for weeks and it showed. I was amazed at some of the soloists. They were so young, but their voices were clear and strong, showing the emotions of much more mature performers.

Renee was in the chorus in the second act. At six, she wasn't concerned with being perfect. She sang when she was supposed to, but in between songs, she yawned, looked at the ceiling, looked behind her, tied her shoe, and fidgeted. I laughed. She reminded me so much of James. She was adorable.

About that time, Gabby made her way back to us. James caught my eye, and I waved to let him know I would watch her. She was dancing in the aisle. It was a good thing we were in the back of the church because Gabby grabbed

Bree's hand, and now both my two's were dancing. It was so unusual for Bree to come out of her comfort zone in public. She usually hid behind Kylie and buried her head in her hands if anyone spoke to her. But now she and Gabby were dancing and giggling as only two-year-old girls can. Kylie and I laughed until we cried.

The pageant ended to a standing ovation. The kids had done a wonderful job, and the people who worked behind the scenes deserved just as much credit. They served coffee and desserts after the performance so the children could mingle with the audience. I visited with a few people but mostly just watched my children and granddaughters. They all looked great. They had come so far from their moments of despair and addiction. At this moment, they were happy, well adjusted, competent adults with families and friends. I was proud of them all. I was even thankful for Lauren. She had come through for Kylie at the wedding and had stuck with James during his worst. This was a night I would remember for a long time. Life was good. For now.

It continued to be good for a while. Christmas that year was indeed fun. I got all the girls clothes and toys, but they liked the dress up bride costumes the best and played "wedding" for hours. For some reason, everyone ended up at our house that year.

Late in the afternoon people just came by. Keith and Karen from next door with their three kids as well as Paul's older brother, Doug, and his three children. He was now living in the apartment over the garage. He had been going through a divorce after Kylie moved out and asked if he could stay for a couple of weeks. He was still there almost five years later.

Tina came over with Alex and their daughter, too. My

sister even stopped by. She usually had Christmas with her husband's family, but she and her husband were separated. Alex wanted to fix her up with Doug. We laughed a lot that day. One of those days you can't plan. They just happen. It was great.

It would be less than a month later when life fell apart again. James crashed hard this time. He slowly destroyed the brand new company truck he had been given, driving off the road a number of times and into a mailbox once. These accidents were happening late at night. He was looking thinner again and finally was accused of stealing an expensive new tool from the company he worked for. Richard and Keith tried to intervene and stop the fall, but he couldn't be stopped. He lost his job at the end of January.

James was different this time. He was smarter now. He showed up at the house one day asking for money.

"I need four hundred dollars for oil. I'm out and the kids are freezing," he said, making sure Paul was not around.

He knew how to corner me. He knew I wouldn't want the kids to be cold. This wasn't their fault.

"James, I can't afford to pay your bills." I tried, but I knew I would give him the money.

"I have one more check coming. I'll sign it over to you."

"I don't know, James." I didn't believe him for a second. And then he did something he had never done before. He got angry with me.

"I said I will pay you back. Just give me the money!"

I was shocked, a little scared, and very hurt, but I still gave him the money. I don't know why. Kylie once told me we give addicts money to ease our own conscience. Or just to make them go away. I'm not sure which category I fit into then, but I was positive the money I gave him would not find its way into their oil tank. For some reason, I gave it to him anyway.

After he left, I realized I was an enabler. It was so obvious. Why hadn't I seen it before?

Now I was angry. I resolved never to do that again. The next day, I asked Lauren if they had oil. She told me what I already knew, no, and she was done with James. He wasn't welcome back there. It would be a week before I saw or heard from him again.

We were heading for Aruba the next week. We were planning on spending at least a month this time. We had bought four huge suitcases after we purchased the house, and every trip down we stuffed them full of everything we could bring through customs. We slept on a blow-up bed we brought down on the first trip. We weren't sure how much furniture we would buy because we didn't know how long we would keep the house. We settled for a plastic table with two chairs, and of course, a couple of lawn chairs for the beach.

James showed up looking awful the night before we were scheduled to fly out. He was thinner than I had ever seen him and had shaved his head again. He had cuts on his face from a recent shave as well. I had a feeling he hadn't shaved in a while. I would never know why he shaved his head when he was at his worst. Maybe he was hot or itchy. I should find out sometime.

This time, Paul was there, and we sat in the kitchen and talked.

"What are you doing, James? Look at you. You're a mess." Paul tried to get through to him.

I was still angry about our last encounter, so I didn't

say much. We were never on the same page.

"I know."

"Look what you're doing to your family."

"I know."

"What are you going to do about it?"

"Richard's taking me to the *Teen Challenge* in Vermont this weekend," he told his father while trying unsuccessfully not to shake.

"Are you going to stay this time?"

"I have to. I'm going to lose Lauren and the girls if I don't."

"You never stayed before."

"I will this time. I'll make it work. I have nowhere else to go."

"Is that a good enough reason?" Paul didn't think he'd stay any more than I did.

"I want to get better."

I realized he was shivering. He was so thin his clothes hung off him. I pulled his favorite, big, soft, heavy blanket off our couch and wrapped it around him. I was angry, but I was still his mother.

"Can I sleep here tonight? I don't have anywhere to stay."

He was also in no condition to drive. I looked at Paul.

He answered, "Yes, you can stay. Only for tonight. We're leaving tomorrow."

"Thanks."

I followed James up to the spare bedroom and tucked my adult son, now twenty-six years old, into bed. We talked for a few minutes. My anger fading a little.

"Are you really going to stay this time?" I asked him. His eyes were starting to close. I didn't know when or where he had last slept.

"Yes. Don't you want me to?"

"Of course I do. I only hope your faith is strong enough."

I will never know why I said that to James that night. *Teen Challenge* is a faith-based organization, and although he had been going to church, I wondered if he was only going through the motions. He told me numerous times *Teen Challenge* wasn't right for him. I worried this time would be no different.

"I have to. Lauren's going to have another baby. You'll be a grandmother again." His words were slurred with sleep, and I wasn't sure I heard them correctly. But I was horrified!

"What did you say?"

My abrupt response must have scared him.

"No, I was just kidding."

He smiled and fell asleep.

We spoke very little the next morning. James was going to spend the next couple of days with my mother, hopefully staying clean. They had become close over the last few years, and she adored his children. James was her first grandchild, and although she has five others, there would always be a special place just for him in her heart.

We hugged goodbye and wished him luck. It was becoming a routine.

"Stay this time. I don't want to hear from you for thirty days." I said as we all left heading in different directions. I never asked about a baby. I didn't want to know. If it was true, I would find out soon enough.

It's hard to be excited about a trip to Aruba when one of your children is falling apart, but I tried. Paul and I didn't talk much about James on the long flight. I didn't mention a baby. Why get him upset if it wasn't true?

"He looks awful. Probably doesn't even weigh one-twenty. And why does he shave his head like that?" Paul asked out of the blue, somewhere over the Caribbean Sea.

"I don't know. I'm really worried. He looks sick, like he's near the end." Then I started to shake and the tears came without warning.

Paul took my hand and said, "I know, but we buried him a long time ago. He's on borrowed time."

"You're right, but that doesn't make it any easier." We didn't talk about it anymore.

Chapter Twenty

We kept tabs on James as best we could. He managed to stay clean and made the trip to Vermont with Richard. So far, so good for James.

Not so much for Kylie. She was not happy. She had managed to survive our one-week vacations and our last trip to Florida, but this was an extended stay with no return date booked. I had gotten her and Bree passports for birthday gifts, just in case, I told her. Flights to the island were expensive, but I had learned how to shop for the best deals. We were able to get flights the previous year for less than two hundred dollars round trip through a charter company that was only looking to fill a plane. It was last minute, but we were flexible. So I kept my eyes open for another good deal. We could get service on our laptop in the parking lot of the local Pricesmart grocery store, so we made the trip daily to check on things at home. The cell phones would only be used in an emergency. The cost per minute was outrageous.

We settled in for our nice, working vacation in warm, sunny Aruba, but our minds constantly drifted back to home and James. Within a week, we found out that Lauren was indeed pregnant again. She always wanted a boy, Lauren told Kylie. Needless to say, we weren't happy.

A few days later, we found out James had left the *Teen Challenge* and had taken the bus back to our area. They required bus fare before they let him stay this time. My mom picked him up at the bus stop, and he was staying with her.

Lauren didn't want anything to do with him.

James' excuse this time was he had stomach and chest pains. He saw his doctor when he got back, but the doctor could find nothing wrong.

James had taken to leaving his grandmother's house at night and wandering the streets. My mother would wake up to him being gone and would drive around looking for him. It was the middle of an incredibly cold winter, and she worried.

I was getting angrier every time I communicated with her. Tina had purchased a "magic jack" computer phone for us before we left for Aruba. I figured we would never use it but found myself spending a lot of time talking to my mother about James. The connection was bad, and sometimes I would only catch every other word, but Mom preferred the phone calls to e-mail.

Mom was noticing money missing from her wallet. Then someone had used her debit card, but the card was still in her possession. The amounts of money added up, but James always denied it was him. She was, however, loaning him money to help with Lauren and the girls. I wondered if they ever received it.

She told me about finding bent spoons. Two spoons bent at weird angles and one was all black. Burned. A few days later she found needles. And James was getting sicker. She took him to the emergency room at the local hospital in the middle of the night twice in one week. No one could find anything wrong.

During an e-mail chat with Kylie, she said she was sure James was doing coke again. The pain he felt in his chest was real, caused by the cocaine. Cocaine can damage the heart, she continued. It can kill you. He needs to stop, she wrote. I missed talking to her in person. My daughter helped me understand so much. She was still in counseling with Dr. Stevens, and he often asked about James.

Then one night a few days later, Mom found James in a snowbank. He had looked awful earlier in the day, so when he disappeared, she was even more worried than before. Mom was sure he had pneumonia, she told me. She had spent hours looking for him when she saw something that looked like a blanket on top of a snowbank. She stopped to check it out, and sure enough, it was James. He was barely conscious. It was after midnight as she drove him to the emergency room for the third time that week.

James had damaged a valve in his heart and was admitted to the hospital. The next day, Mom discovered checks missing from her checkbook. They cleared her bank to the tune of fifteen hundred dollars. She got copies of the checks. They were written to James and signed by my mother. It was James' handwriting.

By the time she got back to the hospital later that day, she was livid. My mother gave James a "tongue lashing" as she was known to say. Mom was done helping and didn't want to see him again. I learned all this over the magic jack phone that constantly cut out on me. I was sitting in the parking lot of the local grocery store. My son was in the hospital with a damaged heart, and I was in Aruba.

I was so angry I didn't even call James. So was my mother, but she kept in touch with the hospital about his progress and forwarded me the information by e-mail. He was where he needed to be. If he was in the hospital, he wasn't doing drugs or living on the street, and he wasn't stealing from anyone.

Every time I got online at the grocery store, I checked flights to Aruba. I hadn't mentioned it to anyone, but I was hoping to find a cheap flight for Kylie and Bree. I knew Tom couldn't come since he had a job. But Kylie worked from home, so I was sure she could take a last minute trip if I found one that was reasonable.

I found one a week after James was admitted to the hospital. I checked the charter company that we had flown with the previous year. They were advertising a round trip flight from Boston for ninety-nine dollars! That was unheard of. It was for the week after February school vacation. I reasoned they had to send a plane down to pick up all the people they had brought down for vacation week. They simply wanted to fill the plane. The flight would leave Boston in five days, and I hadn't mentioned my plan to anyone.

I quickly talked to Paul, and he was fine with it. He knew how much I missed her, and he wanted to stay another month. Kylie would not be happy with that, but a trip to Aruba would surely soften the blow. My problem was she would have to fly out of Boston with two-year-old Bree, alone, and she had never flown before.

I had another idea. I had been keeping in touch with my sister, Denise, more than usual since she separated from her husband. She worked at a large company but had been there for over twenty years. Could she get time off on such short notice?

She could. I e-mailed Kylie, and I think I heard her scream all the way in Aruba. We planned the trip. We bought two more blow up beds, and I told them both to bring sheets. They'd be roughing it, but they didn't mind.

I tried not to think of James. It didn't work. I worried about him constantly, but I was angry enough at him for stealing from my mother that I didn't call him. I wanted to pay Mom back somehow, but even though we owned a house in Aruba and were looking at houses in Florida we were not wealthy. We bought the homes to make a living, and we watched every penny. We no longer had a business that brought in a steady income. Our income now was sporadic, and we had to make it from one sale to the next. I'd think of some way to make it up to her.

It was a very early flight, but my sister managed to get all of them to the airport in Boston on time and in one piece. Kylie and Bree slept for most of the flight after getting up at two in the morning. When they finally arrived, they looked like they had just gotten out of bed.

I saw them at the airport in Aruba right away. Queen Beatrix Airport is small, and I knew where they would be. Bree saw me first as Denise and Kylie were looking in the wrong direction. Bree made her way around the stroller packed with suitcases, and to her mother's dismay she took off running. But Kylie quickly noticed she was running toward me.

"Mimi!" Bree yelled and ran straight across the terminal and into my arms as some of the passengers cheered and clapped. A "Hallmark" moment, I thought, on "One Happy Island," Aruba's slogan. I teared up. Bree was talking to me, but I needed a little extra cuddling before I could speak. It had been almost a month since I'd seen her. I hugged her mom and my sister too, all the time fighting off those tears.

Their vacation flew by as vacations have a way of doing. We went to the beach every day, loaded up with sunscreen. I was especially concerned about Bree. Although she looks so much like her mother, she has my fair skin, and I was determined not to send her home with a sunburn.

We walked on the beach to the time-share resort we

had stayed at on our first trip down. I remembered the cutest kiddie pool and playground. It became our favorite spot for the week. We could buy cocktails and sit by the kiddie pool while Bree played. I loved her reaction to the huge, multi-colored iguanas that roamed around the resort. She'd chase after one until it turned around, then she'd squeal and run back to us giggling. We laughed, joked, and talked for hours somehow avoiding any conversation about James.

I was surprised how much fun Paul was having with his daughter. It was the first time they bonded as adults. There's something about living under the same roof that made them see each other differently, or should I say the same. They were so much alike, now more than ever.

One night near the end of the week, Denise finally asked if I had talked to James. Everyone else was asleep. We were sitting on the lanai, drinking wine, enjoying the warm Aruba breeze.

"No," I said not wanting to go there.

"Aren't you concerned?" she pushed. Denise is my big sister by eleven months.

"Of course I'm concerned, but I'm also angry, hurt, and tired."

"Mom says he could die."

She was going somewhere with this conversation, but I didn't know where.

"Paul and I buried James years ago," I said in a whisper.

"How can you say that? He's your son." Denise began to cry.

"No, he's not. The person in that hospital bed is not my son. My son's been gone a long time. Sure, I see glimpses of him once in a while but that's it. My James would not steal from his grandmother who has done nothing but help him for years. He wouldn't bounce checks all over town and demand money from me and God only knows who else. My James wouldn't lose job after job and leave his family homeless, without heat and food. I don't know what else that stranger in that hospital bed may have done. But I do know he's not my son."

I didn't realize I had raised my voice, and I too started to cry.

Denise hugged me, and we cried together.

"There now, don't you feel better?" She smiled.

Denise had done what only a big sister could do. She let me vent. Without judgment. I couldn't have said those words to anyone else.

"I'm sorry. I didn't mean to ruin your vacation," I said as I wiped away my tears.

"I have something to tell you," Denise said, her eyes still wet from crying. "Alan got arrested a few weeks ago. He was shoplifting at the Hannaford Food Stores in the area to feed a drug habit. Oxys. No needles yet. He had six thousand dollars on him."

Alan is my sister's sixteen-year-old son.

"I'm so sorry." I didn't know what else to say right then.

"I don't know what to do." She cried some more.

We hugged again and talked well into the night, finishing two bottles of wine. Alan had a court date coming up soon. He was a juvenile. I told her those were good things. She would have more control to get him the help he needed.

We made plans to get together when I got back home in a month. I would send her some information and direct her to some good websites. I talked to her about Suboxone and warned her about methadone. I told her to confide in Kylie. She knows everything about drugs. After almost six years in counseling, she should. We went to bed late and

---

woke up with headaches, but that was okay. We needed the time together.

We spent their last full day at the beach and the kiddie pool. Bree said goodbye to all the iguanas, and then we all went to dinner that night at one of our favorite restaurants. We laughed a lot and took tons of pictures. It had been a great week, one that I will always remember.

They left at noon the next day. I called James at one.

We didn't talk much. The connection was bad, but I was glad I called. So was James. I said I would see him in a month. James spent six weeks in the hospital. It wouldn't be his last time.

Chapter Twenty-one

A month and a half later we flew home. Paul had gotten an extra two weeks out of me. I think he would have stayed longer, but we got an e-mail from the realtor in Florida. The bank had agreed to the short-sale and wanted to close on the house in two weeks. Sometimes, I wondered what we were doing, but for the first time in our married lives, we had no ties. No jobs, pets, or young children. We had to work, and our job was renovating neglected properties. We could go wherever the properties were. We had no problem roughing it. One good thing about working on houses for a living was you always had a place to sleep. Our lives had changed so much since the days of the oil company.

I checked on flights to Florida after I unpacked from Aruba. Then I checked on James. Kylie and Bree had picked us up from the airport, so I had already seen them. They always picked us up, getting there early to watch the planes come in. This time, Bree ran to me "just like in Aruba," she said.

James had been released from the hospital two weeks earlier and was staying with Lauren at someone's camp. Lauren had taken him back again.

I found out where the camp was and stopped by on my way to get groceries. The camp looked like every other house they had ever stayed at. I wondered what the owners would do when they saw it. But James and the girls looked good. Lauren looked pregnant. She was due the middle of August, she said. I did the math in my head and figured she got pregnant in late November or early December. James was doing well back then. I forgave her.

"How are you feeling?" I asked James when we were alone.

"Tired but okay. I'm on coumadin, a blood thinner. I might bleed to death if I cut myself shaving," he said with a shy laugh.

"You better stay away from drugs then. I've seen the way you shave when you're high." It wasn't funny. It was true.

James stopped by the house later that day. He hadn't talked to Paul since before we left for Aruba. He was nervous, having let his father down again.

"Hi, Dad," he said when he walked into the house.

I still got nervous and looked to make sure my pocketbook was safely hidden in the bedroom, in my closet, under a pile of clothes.

"Hi, James, what happened to you?" Paul asked.

"I had a heart valve problem." James proceeded to tell Paul about his hospital stay never mentioning his drug use was most likely the cause.

"You know we're heading to Cape Coral next week. We could use your help."

Was Paul really asking James to come with us? We were going to check out an unfinished house while we were there too, another project house.

"Sure. I'd love to go."

And so Paul told James about the unfinished house and how he could use his help figuring out the plumbing and HVAC system. We hadn't decided to purchase it yet. We made an offer but had ten days to do an inspection. Although I had no doubt Paul could figure things out, I knew Florida's buildings and code laws were very different from New England's. Aruba hadn't been a problem since the house we bought there had no heating or cooling systems. In fact, it only had cold water. Most older homes on the island were like that. If they had air conditioning at all, it was split units in the bedrooms only. Their constant trade winds cooled the homes during the day, and they never required heat. It just didn't get cold.

Owning a home in Florida would be different, and James had lived in Cape Coral. Paul was right. His son could help. So I booked flights for the three of us. I managed to get the same two bedroom condo we had stayed at before. We were going for a week.

James turned out to be a big help. We inspected and closed on the house near Old Burnt Store Road. The one we hoped would be our home base in Florida for a while. James helped with the inspection, and then after we had the power turned on, he helped us get the water going.

He showed Paul how to work the rather elaborate water systems they have in Cape Coral. This home had its own well, but the water was high in sulfur and had an awful rotten egg odor. Salt was added to a salt bin which was attached to a filter system. This process removed the sulfur content from the water, and the smell went away. Paul would never have known any of this without James.

Once again I saw James educate his father. It had been years, but I could see how proud James was. He always looked to Paul for approval. I knew James needed to be needed.

James continued to educate us the entire week. He

taught Paul about the HVAC systems, the new plumbing done with pex tubing, and the lawn watering system that is unique to Florida.

"If you water on the wrong day, you get fined. And you're only allowed to water your lawn two days a week."

"Even if you have your own well?" Paul asked.

"Yeah, something to do with the water table. All the wells are shallow, so they schedule your time to water by the house number in your address. That way you and your neighbor don't water at the same time."

"They have so many rules in Cape Coral you have to be careful," James continued. "I couldn't park my company truck in my own driveway. They'll fine you if you don't pull your trash cans up by your house within a day of having the trash picked up. And I heard you're not allowed to hang clothes on a clothesline outside."

I wondered what we had just bought into.

The week continued with the inspection on the unfinished house. We wanted to buy it, but James warned us about the hassles of dealing with the Cape Coral planning board and permitting department. We should have listened more closely. We did buy the house but sold it six months later in the same condition for very little profit. In the future, we would stick to already finished homes that didn't need permits and approvals.

Paul and I decided to go for a run in the neighborhood near the condo one morning a few days before our scheduled departure. Out of the blue, Paul asked James to join us.

I had started running shortly before I turned forty. I had always exercised intermittently but had never been fully committed. When you approach the big "4-0," you start to look at things differently. I began running to lose the few pounds I gained every winter, noticing they weren't just falling off in the spring anymore. I was not really overweight, but I was certainly not where I was in my twenties. If I didn't do something about it then, I knew it would be a losing battle.

That was why I started running, but I continued because it made me feel good. I loved the quiet. I never listened to music like so many people do. I got lost in my thoughts. I don't know how I would have survived the last few years without running. More often than not, if I left with a problem, I came back with a plan. I started many conversations with Paul saying, "You know when I was running I thought...." He began saying, "Did you figure it out? I know you just went for a run...." I would never admit to him those days back when we had the oil company, and he wanted me to come in fifteen minutes early, that I just couldn't give up my run. If it was too cold or the road was covered in snow, I ran on the treadmill I had asked Paul to buy for me. But if it was above freezing and the road wasn't completely covered, I ran outside.

When the drug issues began, I found myself talking to God during many of those runs. I prayed for His help, and for a while, I yelled at Him when He didn't. I soon realized James had to ask for help himself. I prayed he would do just that.

So on this morning in Cape Coral, Paul offered to go with me, and it was his idea to invite James along. We were in a newer section of mostly waterfront homes, a beautiful area with palm trees and tile roofs. The closer we got to the ocean the bigger the houses got. When you love real estate like we do, it was amazing to see the workmanship and intricate details on some of the homes we ran by. James turned around long before we did, but he put in a good effort.

In all my years of trying to find something that would work for James, I had read somewhere that drug addicts who

261

make regular exercise a part of their recovery succeed far more often than those who don't. I wondered if I could persuade him to give it a try again when we got home.

The trip was a great success. James helped us in ways we would have never known. We saw a glimpse of his old self. We watched him like a hawk afraid that he would find old contacts, but he never even tried. I think he was happy just to be alone with his mom and dad. We bonded again and forgave a lot. I wasn't sure if we would ever forget.

James spent time in Florida on our laptop applying for jobs back home. He had an interview with a big company in the city for the day after we returned. It was not in plumbing and heating like before. This job was for a delivery driver. Paul had taught him to drive the oil trucks, and James actually passed the driver's test. He had a class "A" license but had never really used it. Paul confided in me he doubted he would ever get this job, and if he did, as soon as they found out he didn't have much experience behind the wheel, they would fire him.

Paul was wrong. James got the job and kept it for almost a year before the red flags showed up.

In the meantime, James and his family got kicked out of the camp they had been staying in. I couldn't imagine why. But they needed a place to stay until James could make enough money to rent an apartment. For some reason, this time, Paul relented and let them stay with us.

They all moved into our upstairs bedroom.

One Saturday morning Paul challenged James to run with me on the dirt road we live on. The first mile is almost all up hill.

"I bet you can't make it halfway."

"You wanna bet? No problem, how much?"

"All the way to the top and back, and I'll let you stay at my house another night."

Not much of a bet, but it was all in fun, and James did indeed make it up and back. Then he discovered blood in his urine. We didn't ask him to run again. Maybe we'd try another time when he was no longer taking coumadin.

They stayed for two weeks. James finally found an apartment in the area. We ended up helping them with the first months rent and security again. And again, they promised to pay us back. We had learned not to hold our breath.

This job seemed a good fit for James at the time. There were no "on calls," so he couldn't use work as an excuse to leave the house at night. There was not much overtime, and the job was not stressful. They settled into their new home, and Lauren gave birth right on time in mid-August. It was the boy they had hoped for.

Matthew looked even more like James than Renee with the same brown eyes and blond hair his father had at that age.

The day Matthew was born, James stopped at our house to show us pictures. He was so proud. I was going to go to the hospital to see the baby the next day. That's when my son asked to borrow money again. They were out of propane, and James didn't get paid until the following day. The propane had to be ordered and paid for that day in order to have it when Lauren came home with the baby. He would pay me back in the morning, he promised, so I loaned him three hundred dollars.

I saw him at the hospital the next day and asked for my money back. He had some excuse, but I wasn't buying it this time. I was sure he had been clean for months, with a new job and now a new baby. But something didn't feel right. I was beginning to trust those feelings.

When I saw him later that day at his apartment, I confronted him again about the money. I think it was the first time I had raised my voice in a long time.

"You promised, and I know you got paid today!" I yelled. "Give it to me now!"

"I'll give it to you tomorrow!" James yelled back.

"I'm not leaving until you pay me back!"

"What is your problem!?"

"You are! You're lying to me!"

James took two hundred dollar bills from his pocket and threw them at me.

"I never want to see you again!" he screamed.

He was mad at me! I couldn't believe it!

"Good!" I yelled back.

I left him in the parking lot by his apartment, still sitting in his car.

Feeling awful and needing to know I had done the right thing, I told Kylie about our fight later that day.

"He wanted to celebrate, he just had a son. He would've talked himself into 'just this one time'... 'I deserve it'... and he'd go get high," she said.

"You probably kept him clean. Good for you," she continued. "You should yell more often."

A week and a half later James called and asked if I wanted to see Matthew. He could bring the baby over. I said I'd love to see my new grandson. He never apologized, and neither did I.

I stayed in touch with my sister, Denise, over the

summer. Her son Alan had been to court. He was sentenced to rehab, but she and her husband could pick the place. His record would be sealed if he stayed clean and out of trouble.

They sent Alan to a one-month program out of state for $10,000. He stayed and "graduated" from the program. I was happy for Denise. She could put this all behind her. But it didn't last.

Alan began doing drugs within a month. This time, she found a program that would take him for the entire school year. It was on a farm in northern Maine. Denise bought him everything on the list provided by the rehab facility and dropped him off unsuspectingly in the middle of the five hundred acre facility. Then she left. It was surrounded by woods, and he would easily get lost if he tried to leave. Denise told me it was the hardest thing she ever did. She had taken her son's senior year of high school away from him.

I told her it was the best thing she ever did. She learned from my struggles with James and took control while Alan was still a minor. Since he was on probation, he would have been arrested if he left. He stayed.

James made it through the next winter without a relapse.

We left in October and drove Paul's pick-up to Florida that year. The house was exactly as I remembered it. We had a plan. We went to the local Walmart and bought a blow-up bed and some pillows. I had packed sheets, blankets, and towels. I had also brought a few pans, dishes, bowls, cups, and silverware. It was minimal but would get us by until we knew what we were doing. The house had blinds on every window so privacy wasn't a problem. It had all the appliances except for a refrigerator which we picked up at

Lowe's. It even had a washer and dryer. We assumed the home had been lived in but for only a short time.

It wasn't a large home and didn't have a pool, but it was a start. We were anxious to fix it up. Paul immediately wanted palm trees. He loved landscaping and was excited about the warm climate. This was near where I wanted to be, but it was in an area with similar sized homes, and not many owners had bothered to landscape. Paul went crazy and ordered twenty-two palms in all different sizes. Then he added shrubs and fixed the lawn.

We went home to New Hampshire for Christmas, then flew to Aruba. Realizing it would be too hard to make a living on real estate in Aruba, we put the house up for sale so we could concentrate on Florida. Things just moved too slow in Aruba. By the time we got a house sold, the government would take three or four more months to complete the sale.

In Cape Coral, most homes were now bought and sold with cash. Closings often happened in less than two weeks. It would be a better place for us to make a living and stay warm at the same time. We headed back home to New Hampshire in the middle of April.

The red flags started right before summer.

Lauren and James were fighting a lot. There never seemed to be enough money. He hadn't asked to borrow money from me since our argument last summer, so I was surprised by his request one Sunday afternoon.

"Mom, I collected money from a 'cash only' customer on Friday, and Lauren spent it thinking it was mine. I have to turn it in tomorrow or I'll lose my job."

It sounded oddly familiar, but I wanted to believe him. He had been so good. I loaned him the money with an assurance I would have it back on Friday, payday.

266

This time, he did pay me back. But I spoke with my mother a few weeks later, and she confided in me he had asked her to do the same thing, twice. He also asked her to bring him gas late one night when he ran out on a long dirt road. She was getting concerned, but he denied anything was wrong. He "just needed time alone."

In the meantime, I had a long talk with my sister. Alan was getting ready to graduate. He was accepted into a college in Boston and was doing great. She e-mailed pictures of a smiling, clean-cut, seventeen-year-old boy I barely recognized. The farm/school he attended had been wonderful, and she had high hopes for his future. I was happy for her, not so much for me.

Those little warnings and gut feelings continued. I knew James had to submit to random drug testing, so I tried to overlook the signs this time. He wouldn't do this again. He was doing so well. He almost died last time, I reasoned. I didn't want to believe it.

But James had gotten smarter. He knew he could do cocaine on Friday and be clean for a drug test on Monday. He was trying to be a "recreational" drug user. Kylie again was the one who saw the signs. Friday was payday. He'd get high only on Friday night. The problem was James was an addict. He couldn't control it for long.

He began disappearing every Friday night. Lauren and James continued to fight constantly, and James stayed at my mother's every time they had an argument.

In early September, my mother called me at six o'clock on a Monday morning. James had called from the hospital, and she was headed in to pick him up. She'd call later to let me know what happened.

"I have James with me," she said when she called back after an hour. "He wants me to take him to work. He's going to tell them he was in the hospital and needs to go home, but he's afraid they'll fire him if he doesn't go right there in person since he didn't call in. He's okay now. I'll call you after I drop him off."

Another hour later, my mother called me again. She had just dropped James off at his apartment.

"Jess, James' heart stopped. He actually died. I talked to the nurse." Mom was surprisingly composed, but I couldn't speak.

"The nurse said someone dropped him outside the emergency room in the middle of the night," my mother continued. "He was unconscious and before they got him inside his heart stopped. They were able to resuscitate him, but she didn't know how long it took."

My mind raced. Was he going to be okay?

"How can they just let him go home after something like that? Shouldn't he still be in the hospital?"

"I asked the same question," my mother answered. "The nurse said that's what they do. As long as he's stable, he's not admitted."

"But his heart stopped. He died. Shouldn't he be kept for observation or something? Did they send him home because he was a drug addict?" I asked, knowing she didn't have the answer either but was probably thinking the same thing.

That was all the information I ever got. My son had died that night and was home the next morning. He told his grandmother he couldn't remember anything. He didn't know who had dropped him off.

I didn't believe him. I was sure drug addicts didn't turn in their suppliers. I knew then there was no doubt James was going to crash again, and we were powerless to stop it.

James was back to work the next day. Although I may have heard it before, a new realization came to me. I saw first hand that week that a functioning drug addict will do anything to hold on to his job. That was where the money came from, and without money, there would be no drugs. The few times James got clean was when he had no job. Without a job, he had no vehicle and no money. No way or means to get drugs.

Within a few weeks, Lauren got a job and kicked James out of the apartment. He stayed with my mother and tried to stay clean to win Lauren back. It wasn't working.

We left for Florida in the middle of October. The following week my mother called to say James was depressed and maybe suicidal. Lauren had asked for a divorce. As I talked to James trying to console him, he asked to come down for the weekend. Paul and I decided it would do him some good.

We picked him up at the airport, and he stayed for three days. He bought drugs right under our nose, not once, but twice in those three days.

"I need to go to the store for cigarettes. Can I use the truck?" James asked at almost dinnertime his second night in Florida.

"Let your mother drive you," Paul answered before I could think of a way to keep him from going.

I drove him to the store a few miles away and waited patiently in the truck. It took a long time for him to come back, but I didn't think anything of it until the next night.

Our house was on a sparsely populated street. The road crosses from one main street to another so there is traffic but no reason for anyone to stop. I woke to the sound of voices and car doors slamming at midnight. That's when I realized we'd been had. Twice. I told Paul what I thought the next morning, but we had no proof, and James would only deny it anyway. We were losing steam, or maybe we just didn't care anymore. He left the next day.

James returned to find out his boss knew about his drug use. Someone had turned him in. But this was a good company, and James was a likable guy. He was a hard and dependable worker. Sometimes those qualities are hard to find, so they put him on a six-week paid leave with substance abuse counseling.

Paul and I were speechless. What company did that for their employees? We had pretty much done the same thing for James when he worked for us, but he was family.

Once more he had a chance to get help and keep his job while still getting paid. We wondered how he got so lucky.

That luck wouldn't last, however. By January he was unemployed again. He never told us why, but I believe he knew he would not pass a drug test, so he just didn't go back. He went to all the counseling sessions, but having six weeks off with pay without worrying about drug testing, most likely made it way too difficult to stay clean.

James did try to go back to Dr. Stevens, but he was more addicted to cocaine now than opiates. He showed up for a urine test after two weeks and tested positive for cocaine. Once again he was sent away.

My son spent the winter at my mom's house and babysat his children there while Lauren worked. By spring Mom had had enough. If James wasn't borrowing money, he was borrowing her car, often without permission. He also developed a bad habit of going to the hospital with unexplained pains. His favorite ailment was kidney stones. Emergency workers automatically gave strong pain medicine when you presented with the symptoms of a kidney stone. James was not stupid.

My mother was calling me in Florida on a regular basis to update me and tell me what James had done this time. All I could do was tell her to ask him to leave. But she worried because she loved him. And she believed everything he said. She believed he would pay her back. She believed he was in real pain, and she believed he had to run to the store late at night when she was sleeping.

Chapter Twenty-two

In March, James got a job selling frozen meat off a truck. He made new friends and stopped bothering to go back to my mother's house. She called, worried and angry. We both knew what was going on, but it wasn't confirmed until James actually told me a few months later. They paid James with drugs right from the beginning. He would never say so, but I believed the company was only a front.

We came home in April, and within a few weeks, James started calling me.

"Mom, I'm in the hospital in Conway. I have another kidney stone."

"Why are you in Conway?"

"I drove here last night so I could head out early to work."

"Where did you stay?"

"At a friend's."

"In Conway?" I knew he was lying. It was so obvious. He had gone to a different hospital. A place where he wasn't known. "I thought you just passed a kidney stone a few weeks ago."

"I did but now there's another one. They found it on a cat scan."

Was that supposed to make me believe him? A doctor told me a while ago if you look hard enough you can find something wrong with anyone. They looked for the cause of

James' pain until they found something that might be causing it. I was simply waiting for him to get to the point.

"Mom, I need gas money to get back home. Can I borrow some until tomorrow?"

I knew it.

"No, I'm sorry. I'm not giving you a credit card number so you can put gas in a company vehicle. You'll have to call your boss. Or sell some meat or something."

I was getting stronger but not strong enough.

James called a week later. He wanted my help, again.

"Mom, I hate my life. I want to change. Can you take me to *Teen Challenge*?"

"You want to go?"

"Yes, I already called them, and I'm just waiting to hear back. They're not sure they want me." He chuckled a little at that.

"You'll stay this time?"

"Yes, I can't live like this. I haven't seen my kids in months. This job sucks. I can't make any money. All the money I make goes into the gas tank. I don't have any place to live. I'm staying with this guy I work with, but he's getting kicked out."

I couldn't believe what I was hearing. Was this another bunch of lies? Was he after something or had he hit that bottom they talk about? I had never taken him to rehab myself. If he wanted to go, I figured it was my turn to take him.

"You make the arrangements, and I'll take you."

"Can I stop over later?"

What now? I hadn't seen him since we returned from Florida, but he was asking for help.

"Okay."

273

"I'll be there in an hour."
Now what was I going to tell Paul?

Paul was fine. I was sure he wouldn't want me to drive him. I didn't think he even wanted to see James. We talked a lot in Florida over the winter and decided to be firm and stay out of his life. He had chosen this path, and we had helped enough! We'd be unwavering! Now we were both caving. The thought of him getting into treatment was too compelling.

James came over a short while later and asked if I could drive him to Augusta tomorrow. They were expecting him at the *Teen Challenge* that was just outside of the city. We made all the plans. Was he packed? Did he have everything he needed? What time tomorrow?

Then he went to find his father.

I should not have let him out of my sight. I knew how he could manipulate me and my mother. I would have been on guard. He manipulated Paul this time, and I never saw it coming.

"Jess, can you get my gun out of the safe?" Paul yelled from the driveway where he was standing with James.

We've had a gun for twenty years, and it hasn't been out of the safe in fifteen. We keep it in one of those little fireproof safes for important documents. I wasn't even sure I knew where the key was. The safe itself was buried in the back of my closet. What could he possibly want with the gun? I was sure he wouldn't use it on James, not now. Maybe in a year or two if he didn't straighten out. But not today, he was going to rehab.

"Why?" I looked out the door. "Is everything okay?"

"Everything's fine. I'll tell you later. Can you bring the gun out here? And the bullets are in my nightstand."

"Is he insane?" I said under my breath as I walked into the bedroom. I found the key in the top drawer of my nightstand and the bullets in the bottom drawer of Paul's. Then I dug through the bottom of my closet. I had purposely piled boxes and clothes on top of the safe to hide it. Not really very clever when you think about it, but we live in a small town at the end of a long dirt road. We've never had a problem with intruders, except our own son of course.

I brought Paul the gun, a nine millimeter semi-automatic. Paul had taught me how to use it a long time ago. I'm not sure I remembered anymore.

Paul made sure the gun wasn't loaded and handed the gun, bullets, and two full magazines to James.

He looked at me and said, "James thinks he can sell it. He needs to take care of a few things before he goes tomorrow. I said he could use the money and pay me back when he finishes the rehab."

"Are you sure that's a good idea?" I looked at both of them.

"Come on, Mom. What? Do you think I'm going to shoot someone?"

I saw his hands tremble. This was not good. I looked at Paul again, and he gave me that "it's okay" look. I gave him that "are you nuts?" look as I turned and walked away.

After James left assuring us he would meet me in the morning, Paul looked at me with a small smile.

"What's wrong?"

"Everything," I answered. "You just gave a drug addict a gun and bullets."

"He's going to sell it. I told him if he couldn't get $350 for it to bring it back. He remembered me saying I was going to sell it a couple of years ago. He's supposed to call in an hour and let me know what happened."

"The whole situation scares me. What is he going to

do with the money?"

"He owes money to the people he's been working for. He wants to go away with a clean slate. It'll be okay, Jess." He reached over and put his arm around me. "Don't worry."

I worried.

An hour later James called to say he could only get $200 for the gun.

"I don't want to sell it for that. Just bring it back," Paul told his son.

"Okay, I'll head back."

We waited. I called him after an hour had passed. He didn't answer, and he didn't show up.

I continued to call his cell phone every fifteen minutes over the next few hours as the pain in my stomach increased with each unanswered call.

Paul and I never slept that night. We worried about what could have happened to James. I wanted to be angry at Paul, but I couldn't. James had manipulated him and played on his emotions exactly like he had done to me so many times before.

I should have listened to those gut feelings and stood my ground. Now I feared the worst. Suicide... robbery... murder... accident.... What a stupid thing to do. And all we could do was wait.

I started calling James' phone again early the next morning. He finally answered shortly before eight.

"Hi, Mom, what time are you picking me up?"

"Where are you?" My emotions were in overdrive. I was so happy to hear his voice I wanted to cry, but I was so angry with him I wanted to hang up. He was obviously fine, probably high, and wide awake.

"I'm in the parking lot at work. Can you pick me up

here? I have to leave the truck."

"Where's Dad's gun?"

"I have it."

I knew he was lying even over the phone. At this point, I just wanted to get him to rehab and not worry about him for a year.

"I'll head out in a few minutes."

"Okay, drive around back. Don't go to the door."

So, he was in trouble at work. That was why he wanted to go. I didn't care why just so long as he stayed. I picked up Kylie and Bree on the way, and we all headed to *Teen Challenge*. One big happy family.

When I finally asked James for his father's gun, he informed me he had pawned the gun for $200. He gave me the slip. It would cost us $350 to get it back. Paul would be furious.

My first trip to the *Teen Challenge* in Augusta was an interesting one. James was well known in the organization by now. This was his third, maybe fourth, time attempting the challenge, to put it one way. He never made it, but I could hope this time would be the time he would at least try.

I brought Kylie with me to help encourage him. They talked most of the way. Actually, Kylie talked and James grunted every once in a while. I wondered what he was thinking and what he had done to abruptly want to go away. I had a feeling he wasn't running toward help but running away from trouble.

The program occupied a big old farmhouse on a hill with a massive green lawn and a gorgeous view overlooking a large lake across the street.

"James, this is beautiful! You'll love it here. You can fish and swim. Do they have a boat?" James had long ago given up all his favorite activities. Fishing, boating, and swimming were tops among those.

"No. You can't do any of those things. You're not allowed to leave the property," my son mumbled.

He was in a really bad mood by now. Reality was setting in.

"Well, it's a nice view anyway," Kylie remarked. There wasn't much else to say.

"You'll just have to make the best of it," I added.

I was still so angry, but I felt sorry for him too. The thought of spending more than a year in this place was a little creepy all of a sudden. But James had done this to himself, and it could be a lot worse.

He could be spending time in jail. I was sure that would be his next stop. It was only a matter of time. I was surprised he hadn't been arrested a long time ago. He had one misdemeanor, had spent three nights in jail, and had the one DUI in all these years. I didn't know how he had managed to avoid a much more serious charge.

Actually, I knew how he avoided the police. James stole from the people who loved him the most. We wouldn't turn him in. He learned just how far to push people. Then he would beg for forgiveness and promise to pay everything back. He learned to cash bad checks but rarely in the same place twice and always under $500. The police wouldn't pursue that small an amount. I was letting myself get angry again and push the sympathy away. It worked.

After we helped James get his things out of the trunk, we met everyone there. They were all very cordial since most of the men in the program had come begging, having no one left who cared.

"James is lucky to have you drive him here," the supervisor said. "He still has people who love and care for him."

I watched my son walk across the parking lot to be introduced to a nice looking young man who was mowing the lawn. Then I turned to the supervisor and said, "I don't think I care very much anymore."

A short time later we all said goodbye, and I told James not to call, I wouldn't answer.

On the long ride home, Kylie told me what I already knew, James was high. Cocaine, she said.

That's what he did with the money from the gun. I was sure now. You're not supposed to drop them off high, I knew that too. I just didn't care, I guess. I was tired. I hadn't slept last night.

Paul was furious about the gun, but he shouldn't have trusted a drug addict. I didn't say that, of course. I simply said I was sorry. And I was. Sorry for everything James had done to him, to my mother, to me, and every other unsuspecting person he had taken advantage of in the last six and a half years. Had it been that long?

The phone rang two days later. I recognized the phone number. *Teen Challenge.* I didn't answer. Five more times in an hour. I turned the phone off.

Five minutes later, Karen came over from next door with a phone in her hand. It was James. I shook my head and walked away. A week would go by before I picked up the phone when it rang with a local number I didn't recognize.

"Don't hang up!"

It was James. I shouldn't have answered.

"I don't want to talk to you, James."

"I just want to explain. I had pains in my side again. I had to go to the hospital up there. I left and they wouldn't let me back in."

I didn't believe him for a second. Actually, I believed he did go to the hospital. I didn't believe he had anything wrong.

"It's your life. I have to go now."

"I just wanted you to know it wasn't my fault. I tried."

"Not hard enough." I hung up the phone.

It would be another week before James called again. When James called the next time, he was crying.

"Mom, I need your help, please. I'm so sick."

"I'm sorry, I can't help you." I started to hang up.

"Wait! Just take me to the rehab in Portland. It's free and they'll take me. I already called them, but I need a ride."

Paul and I were sitting outside having just finished dinner. Paul was listening to my end of the conversation. He knew the last few weeks had been difficult for me. I could feel myself weaken. I covered the phone and told Paul what James said about the rehab.

"You're not driving to the city tonight. You can take him tomorrow if you want."

"Do you think I should?"

"It's up to you. I guess it couldn't hurt."

I uncovered the phone. "I can take you tomorrow."

"Can I sleep on the couch tonight?" James begged.

I had been firm for over two weeks, but he was wearing me down, again.

"Okay. But we're heading to rehab first thing in the morning."

I think James was shocked when I woke him up at

eight to leave. He made excuses about being tired and having to call them to make sure they would take him.

"You're not staying here, so they better take you. We're leaving now. You can call from the car."

I was back to being angry. He called from the car.

"They may have a bed for me in a couple of hours," James said. Then added, "I haven't seen my kids for a couple of months."

"Kylie's watching Matthew. We can stop by for a minute." I knew the girls were in school.

"Thanks."

Matthew ran to his father and didn't let go. It broke my heart that James couldn't be the father Matthew deserved. I knew Lauren was still struggling with her own issues, and these kids had no stability in their lives whatsoever.

An hour later, the rehab called to say they had a bed. We decided to take Matthew with us to give James more time with his son. James sat in the back with Matthew not wanting to lose the precious little time he had with him. I watched from the rear view mirror as father and son played and laughed. I knew James loved his kids, but why didn't he love them enough to get better?

We brought Matthew into the building and sat at the table for the intake. James sat across from me with his son in his lap. I felt like I was looking at James at that age. Matthew was looking more like his father every day.

"What's the baby's name?" Joe asked. He was the intake specialist. Matthew would be two in a few months but was small for his age.

"Matthew," James answered.

"He's your reason for being here. He will be your reason to succeed. The reason you turn your life around."

They seemed to make a connection. Joe was likable

with a quick sense of humor, but he didn't pull any punches. James would be required to attend three AA meetings a day as well as group meetings and meetings with counselors and therapists. It was a seven-day program to detox. They would help him find a longer program before he left. This was only the first step.

We said goodbye. James tickled and hugged little Matthew as he giggled and hung on tight. My heart ached as I watched this father and son moment. The boy so innocent, the father so broken.

Please, God, make this work this time, for the kids, I prayed.

I thanked Joe for his help, and little Matthew and I headed back to Kylie's.

Kylie and I talked while Matthew ran after her cat, sliding on the hardwood floors in his stocking feet. We laughed. He was such a sweet little kid. His parent's divorce was final. Lauren was living in the same apartment and still working. She never hired a full-time babysitter instead relying on family, friends, and acquaintances. She often called at the last minute to ask if we could watch the children, like she had forgotten she had to work. "She just doesn't process things the way normal people do," Alex told me on several occasions.

Lauren's housekeeping hadn't changed either. Someone finally called the state's Department of Health and Human Services. She was put on notice last winter.

The woman's group from church cleaned her house and filled dozens of trash bags to take to the dump. Once again Lauren was furious, but it had to be done. It's not that she didn't love her kids. She was just different. Lauren would rather do crafts than do dishes. Maybe she simply hadn't grown up yet. Maybe she never would.

Kylie also confided in me that day she had been trying to get pregnant for over a year.

"I wanted to surprise you."

"Didn't you say 'never again' after your awful experience with Bree's delivery?"

"I know, but after Matthew was born, Tom and I started thinking we'd like Bree to have a baby brother or sister. Bree will be five this year. I'm getting nervous it's taking so long."

"Have you been to the doctor? Maybe he can find out what's wrong."

"I made an appointment. I'm afraid I can't have a baby now that I really want another one."

"Sometimes, these things simply take a while. Do you know how many people get pregnant when they stop trying?"

"I know, but I don't want Bree to be all grown up before we have another baby."

Sometimes, there just isn't anything you can say that will make it better, that hasn't already been said before, that she doesn't already know. Sometimes, all a mother can offer is a hug and the unspoken truth that she'll be there when you need her.

I hugged Kylie. She got teary eyed but didn't cry. We both knew there was a good chance the damage done during her emergency cesarean could be irreversible. That there may never be another baby, another sibling for Bree.

Chapter Twenty-three

James called me that night. There had been none of the "you can't have contact for thirty days," so I answered the unfamiliar number on the phone.

"Hi, Mom, I'm still here."

"Good. Are you staying? You better because you're not coming back here."

"I'm staying. These guys are pretty nice, and they know a lot. It's a good place. I'll call again in a couple of days. I have to go to a meeting now."

"Okay, thanks for calling... I love you, James."

"I know, I love you too."

I slept well that night. Better than I had in a long time. I knew my son was safe.

James stayed for the entire seven days. It was the first time he'd stayed in any rehab for more than two days. I know seven days isn't a lot, but it was a giant first step.

I had been hoping he would stay at *Teen Challenge* for a year, but I settled for seven days at the free clinic. It's funny how our expectations change. How we learn to settle for baby steps instead of giant leaps. He completed the program, that was the important thing. He was officially drug-free. Now we had to keep him that way.

"I have an appointment at the Tranquility House. Can you take me there?" James asked the morning he was set to leave.

"The Tranquility House, isn't that where Tom went?"

"Yeah, that's the place. It's a ninety-day program. You can work after thirty days, and the kids can even visit anytime."

James sounded excited, having the children close by would help. That had always been a drawback with all the other programs. Maybe this one would work.

We made arrangements to meet after lunch since his appointment was at two. I loved the place right away. It was set in one of the older buildings in the city. It must have been four stories tall, very ornate, with a huge living room and kitchen on the first floor. We were directed down to the basement where there were three or four offices. We met the women in charge, Carol, for the intake interview. She was a heavyset woman close to my own age with a gentle smile. She put us at ease right away.

"He'll fit in good here," Carol said after the interview.

"So you'll take him?" I asked.

"Yes, but we don't have a bed until Friday."

It was Wednesday. What would we do until then? She read my thoughts.

"He has to stay clean. If possible, we like to take them right from the clinic to here. That way we know they've detoxed. Can you keep him clean?"

"I won't let him out of my sight."

What was I going to tell Paul? We had agreed he was not coming home.

"Great, we'll see you Friday," Carol said. Then she leaned over and whispered to me, "This is a good place. We'll take care of him."

I fought back tears. This was a woman who knew how I felt. She had told us earlier she had a son who was going through the same thing. She knew the heartache that came with every failed trip to rehab, every lost job, every late night phone call. She knew what it was like to have a son who was an addict.

I hung on to those words, "we'll take care of him," and called Paul.

"They'll take him Friday. He has to stay clean until then."

I waited for a response. He had been so frustrated with James since the gun incident. I promised I would leave him on the street if he had no place to go. I would not bring him home. I waited....

"Well, you can't leave him on the street if he's clean."

"Should I bring him home?"

"Yes, bring him home but only until Friday!"

My dreams of a newly rehabilitated son were dashed three days after he was admitted to the Tranquility House. He called in tears.

"Something's wrong, Mom. I need you."

"Slow down, James, and tell me what's happening."

"I like it there and want to stay, but something's wrong. I can't go back right now."

"Where are you?"

It was early, barely light out, his phone call had woken me up.

"I'm just walking around.... I want to die. I don't want to live anymore." His voice started to crack on the last few words.

"Tell me where you are. I'll be there as soon as I can. James, don't do anything, okay? Just sit tight."

I told Paul where I was going, not asking for his

approval. There are times when I just know I have to do something. Without question, this was one of them. I just didn't know what I was going to do. James was on the road to recovery, and I didn't want to lose him now.

I met James on a street corner, and he got in the car. I pulled into the nearest parking lot and stopped.

"Tell me what happened, James."

"I don't know. I thought I was fine. Then all of a sudden this feeling come over me. I can't describe it. I wanted to step in front of a car. It scared me so bad. I had to leave. Then I just wanted my mommy, like a little boy."

He was crying, almost hysterical, by the time he finished. I had never seen him like this, and I had seen him at his worst. I was thinking I needed to take him to the psychiatric hospital. I knew they would be able to help someone who was suicidal.

"Did you take any drugs?" I hated to accuse him of anything right then, but I needed to know.

"No! I only took the anti-anxiety meds they gave me."

I had an ah-ha moment. I remembered hearing somewhere, probably on TV, about suicidal thoughts being a side effect of some medication.

"What was it called?"

"I don't remember exactly. I'd know it if I heard it."

I called Kylie. She knew everything drug related. Besides, she would have her computer. Together we figured out what drug it was, and yes, one of the side effects was suicidal thoughts. I called the Tranquility House. Carol didn't answer, so I left a message and took James home. I would stay with him overnight until I was certain he was back to normal. I was sure Carol would understand.

She didn't.

"I'm sorry, Jess, those are the rules. He cannot leave unaccompanied for any reason for the first two weeks. He can reapply in thirty days. Then he has to wait for a bed to open up."

"But, Carol, it wasn't his fault. It was the medication your doctor prescribed," I begged.

"He should have come to me."

"It was way too early. Everyone was sleeping. Please. Can't you make an exception?"

"I'm sorry, Jess. Have him come see me in thirty days."

She hung up.

So much for "this is a good place, we'll take care of him" I thought as I stifled some not so nice names I wanted to call Carol. I realized after a few minutes it wasn't her fault, but I wanted to blame someone. I was so frustrated. We were so close. It just wasn't fair! Now what was I supposed to do with James?

That was the start of the summer of 2011. It didn't get much better. I was sure we were on the right track. James had asked for help this time and had stayed at the seven-day detox clinic. It wasn't his fault he didn't stay at the ninety-day program. Just listening to my own thoughts caused me to stop and ask myself what I was doing. I was making excuses. I was blaming myself and everyone else except the person I needed to blame, James. I vowed this would be it. This summer would be the last time I would put my life on hold to help my son.

But I would help him this one last time.

We kept James at home for a while, hiding any alcohol we had in the house. We realized James had an addictive personality. If he wasn't using drugs, he drank too much. If he didn't use drugs or alcohol, he ate too much. If he had all three of those under control, he worked too much. He was always addicted to something.

I didn't think we'd make it thirty minutes let alone thirty days. Paul was on edge. He wanted to help but was still angry, and he didn't want to turn his life upside down for James.

"Hasn't James messed up our lives enough?" Paul would say that to me over and over again that summer.

I looked into every rehab and sober living house in the area. I didn't want to sit back and wait for the Tranquility House only to find out there was a long waiting list. We found another one that took James after three weeks, only to kick him out after two days. James was on a mild, non-narcotic pain reliever for the constant pain he was in. The pain, if there was pain, was most likely caused by all the years of abuse his body had taken. He was allowed to bring the medication, but it would be locked up. James was given the bottle at the appropriate times to take the necessary number of pills. James took more than he was supposed to.

Again, I found myself angry at the rules of the rehab facility. He was there because he was a drug addict. Why give a drug addict the entire bottle of pills to take out only two? Why not just hand him two pills? You can't trust a drug addict with drugs! What was wrong with these people?

Next, we tried a Christian sober living house. James had been baptized last year along with Renee. This house expected the occupants to work, go to AA meetings, and Bible studies. There was a curfew, and no alcohol or drugs were allowed. Random drug testing was mandatory. The kids could visit, and even an occasional overnight visit once in a while was okay. We set up an appointment. I promised Paul I would have him out of the house soon. I crossed my fingers.

This home was on the outskirts of the city, on the bus route. It was a pretty house with white clapboard siding and black shutters. It sat on a corner lot with a large green lawn surrounded by other similar homes. The home blended into the neighborhood well. There were well-kept flower boxes and neatly trimmed shrubs keeping its true mission disguised.

Again, the people were very nice. James would fit in well, they said. "Maybe he can fix our furnace," one of them said after finding out what he did for a living. I was barely listening. I had heard it all before. I would not get my hopes up again. I would not fall in love with the place or the people this time. Just say "yes, we'll take him." That's all I wanted to hear. If they added "today," that would be even nicer.

Don't get me wrong, I still loved my son. However, this summer I was realizing this was James' addiction, and I couldn't fix it. I knew he had to be the one to do the work, but I had always felt if I could get him into the right program, he would do the rest. I was now learning he needed to find his own program. His own way to recovery. And I needed to save my sanity. And my marriage.

They did take him, not that day, but yes, they would take him. So it was another trip to the city a few days later with James and all the things he would need. He had a job within a week, and the kids were spending a lot of time there on the weekends. Lauren loved the time off. James loved seeing his kids. All was good.

It lasted about six weeks.

***

James didn't come home one night. He claimed he was in the hospital with side pains again, but he didn't call. They didn't believe him. I didn't blame them. I blamed James.

So James spent his thirtieth birthday at our house. There was no celebration. No cake. I was not going to reward him. It was an eye opener for me. If I was still taking care of him at thirty, would I be doing the same thing at forty, fifty, or even sixty? At one of the many rehab houses we visited, I talked with a nice older gentleman who was there with his fifty-year-old son. Would that be me?

I saw Alex a few days later. She had stopped asking about James a long time ago. But I mentioned he had just turned thirty.

"You know there's an age when many people feel addicts won't ever recover," she said over a glass of wine.

"What age is that?"

"Thirty."

I drank more wine.

"I wasn't going to say anything," Alex said.

"It's all right. I know he has to change soon, or he's going to end up dead. I need to get him out of here and on his own, or I'm going to end up the same way."

"I saw a 'rooms for rent' sign at an old farm not far from the center of town."

"That could be exactly what he needs, thanks."

Alex left a short time later. I was left with the thought that if James didn't change soon he may never make it. My mother recently mentioned one of the doctors at the hospital referred to James as a "lifer." Had my son just passed the point of no return?

James still had his job and by now use of the company vehicle. I told him about the sign. I was determined he was a grown up and could handle this himself. I was wrong.

"I stopped by, and no one was there. I think it was the wrong place. It looks like it's falling down."

I wasn't buying it. I called to set up an appointment, and we went together. It did look like it was falling down, but that was because they were doing some much-needed repairs. A nice older couple had just purchased the building that had once been an old nursing home. They were turning it into rooms for rent to people in transition. They would love to have James, the kids could visit, and maybe he could fix their furnace. I had heard it all before.

"We can have the room ready in a couple of days."

"Not today?" I whined under my breath, but I smiled and said, "That would be great, he'll take it."

We left six weeks later for Florida. James stayed in that room until he lost his job in January. He got caught stealing. The very nice lady he worked for didn't press charges. She realized James had a drug problem and hoped he would get the help he needed.

Chapter Twenty-four

James ended up back at his grandmother's house. He convinced her he was in constant pain. And now he had a new ailment, possibly his gallbladder. He was in and out of the hospital for one reason or another for months. I worried about my mother. Not James this time.

Paul and I came home early that spring. We bought a project home in the fall and ended up selling both the project home and the home we were living in within a few weeks of each other. We liked both homes, so we decided we would keep whichever home didn't sell. However, when we had offers on both homes within a week of each other, we took a chance and sold the two of them, putting everything we owned in Florida in storage.

"It's a chance to get a home on the west side of 'Old' Burnt Store Road," I told Paul.

"But I like this house," Paul whined.

"We can stay here, and I'll stop looking for the house with a pool that's off the main road you keep talking about."

"No, you're right. I would like to get off the main road."

"Well, we can't buy a better house in a better location if we don't sell this one first. What do you want to do?"

So we sold both houses and began a search for our next Florida home to live in. We had one under short-sale agreement before both closings took place. It wasn't where I wanted to be and didn't have a pool, but it would be a place to stay and a good project. Knowing short-sales take time, we headed home at the end of March, Paul kicking and screaming all the way. He hated the cold, he hated having his stuff in storage, and I think for a while he hated me. Everything was always my fault.

At times I wanted to scream, "grow up!" But I just let him rant, occasionally saying, "Paul, everything will be fine."

Truthfully, I didn't want to go home either. I loved our time in Florida, but we had to face reality. We were going to put our big house on the lake up for sale. Our plan was now to spend only the summer months in New Hampshire. The house was just too big and the taxes, insurance, and mortgage too expensive for a house that would be used for only three months. We had to get it ready. Paul always stayed up with repairs, but there was landscaping to be done, the dock had to be put in, and the inside cleaned up from not having been touched in months.

And I didn't want to deal with James.

Kylie still wasn't pregnant when we got back. She had decided to take a job outside the home since Bree was now in school. Of course within weeks of quitting her stay-at-home job and starting her new one, she found herself expecting. Tom and Kylie were thrilled. I was happy for them.

"I'm due the end of November. Will you be here?"

That was one of Kylie's biggest fears, that I would be in Florida when her baby was born.

"You couldn't keep me away if you tried," I said, and I meant every word. I just wasn't sure what I was going to tell Paul.

***

I was so happy for Kylie and at the same time, so angry with James. He was taking advantage of my mother, still. She was sending me e-mails and calling to tell me about James' latest episodes. I told her not to help, not to open her door. I even told her to get a restraining order against him. He was becoming more demanding. I knew what that was like. I had been there. Now that we were back from Florida I had to do something.

When I finally saw James in April, he didn't look well. I had only talked to him on the phone a few times over the winter. He had asked for money, and I had refused. After a few more attempts, he stopped calling.

"Hi, James, how are you?"

"Okay, I guess. I might need to have my gallbladder out."

"You can't stay at your grandmother's anymore. It's too much on her," I said, getting to the point quickly.

"I know. I'm going to stay with Lois for a while until I get back on my feet."

"Who's Lois?"

"Gram's friend. She has more room, and she loves the kids. Her husband died years ago. It's only her and her son who lives in the basement. She offered to let me stay with them for a while."

He added the last part when he saw the doubtful expression on my face.

"I've helped her a lot this past winter. She loves me like a son," James continued.

Was this another person he would take advantage of?

"It's only until I get a job, then I'll get my own place," he said, pleading his case while waiting for my response.

"You better not take advantage of her," I finally said. I should have been more blunt and said, "Don't steal from

295

her."
    "Don't worry, I won't."
    He did.

    Lois did indeed love the kids. She set up a bedroom for them with bunk beds and toys. Lauren had been asked to leave her apartment last fall and was bouncing from one friend or family member to another. The kids didn't have a room to call their own, so they loved it. Lois took them to softball games and picnics. But James was on a downward spiral that no one could stop, again.
    It wasn't long before he was taking Lois' medication and borrowing money he couldn't pay back. On a weekend in early May, he used her debit card to fill up her gas tank, but he failed to return the card right away. Then James disappeared. When Lois discovered her account was drained, she was devastated and called my mother. Mom called me. I told her to call the police. James had to be held accountable. They both filed police reports the next week.
    The police officer took the information but said since Lois had given James the card and her pin number there wasn't much they could do.
    He next looked at my mother and said, "Are you sure you want to press charges against your own grandson?"
    She didn't.

    No one heard from James for almost six weeks. We knew he had last been seen with some heavy-duty drug dealers and addicts, a rough crowd. This was new for James. He was usually a loner.
    I was so angry with him, but again I was also scared. He was not violent, and the people he left with had a very

bad reputation for violence. During all the years we had been dealing with his drug use, James was always close by. At times he would be gone overnight, but that was the extent of it. I worried more and more as the weeks went by. Kylie mentioned a couple of times that someone had seen him somewhere at some point, but he never called.

The second week of July, I received a call from the psychiatric hospital in Bangor. They had James and wanted to release him, but he needed somewhere to go. I talked to James and agreed to pay for a bus ticket, but that was all.

He wanted to go back to the seven-day free clinic. He called the next day. They didn't have a bed. Could he stay with me until they did? I said "no." We both knew there was a homeless shelter near the clinic. I was glad it was summer.

James called a few days later from the clinic.

"I just wanted to let you know I'm in the clinic. I'll be here for a week."

"Good."

"I'll call you in a few days."

"Okay."

Paul didn't want me to take his calls. But I just couldn't do that. I wouldn't offer any help or money. I wouldn't even offer advice anymore. He knew what he had to do. I wouldn't waste my time. But I still felt he needed to know someone was there. Someone would be there when he finally turned that corner.

The clinic was designed as a first stop, and they tried to find long-term help for those who were willing to commit. Weeks passed by with the occasional phone call to let me know where he was and what he was doing. He bounced from the clinic to one of the local hospitals, to the New Beginnings Rehab Center, to the homeless shelter, to a different hospital, and back to the seven-day clinic. He also spent a few nights on the street.

The hospital got wise and told him not to come back. The clinic found a place for him at the Salvation Army, a six-month program. I dared to hope, but it quickly faded. He would have to work, and his health issues barred them from allowing him to work. Get healthy, and you can come back, they told him.

He begged me to let him come home, just for a while, but I continued to say no. "This has to be his bottom," I told myself over and over. "Don't pick him up now. He's so close, but he has to do it."

Kylie saw James on the street when she went to a doctor's appointment in the city.

"I knew it was him by the way he walked," she said.

"Did he see you?" I asked.

"No. I wanted to stop, but I didn't. I feel so bad. He's so thin. He was wearing a backpack, and he was filthy. I wanted to bring him home, like a little lost puppy, but that won't help him. We have to stay strong! Right?"

"I know you're right. I'll stay strong this time. I promise."

But it was so hard.

It was an emotional roller coaster ride. I was angry, furious actually, at the way he had treated my mother and her friend. I hated him for not being a good father, and I felt sorry for him because I knew how hard it was to beat this addiction. Most of all I still loved him. He was my son, my first born, my baby. I still pictured the toddler with the little blond curls and the infectious laugh. I wanted my son back, faults and all. I would be strong. I was learning the only way to help was not to help at all.

***

While James was struggling in the city, Paul and I were preparing for a trip to Florida. The house we had under short-sale agreement had defective drywall. The drywall was loaded with sulfur and would all have to be removed. We decided not to buy that property and immediately began searching for another Florida home.

Finding good deals and watching the real estate market in Cape Coral had become almost a passion for me. I had lists of properties that would be good projects, list of properties I would like to move into, lists of properties coming up for foreclosure. I had a favorite website I used to keep track of sales and listings. I watched prices of homes by neighborhoods, square footage, and year built. I could mark as a favorite any property I wanted to follow. Then I could see price drops or increases and the final sale price. I had seen some amazing properties sell for unbelievably low prices. I was determined to find our next home. I didn't want to move again for a while.

Within a week of passing on the other home, one of my all-time favorite homes showed a drastic price drop. Still out of our price range, but.... It was on the west side of Old Burnt Store Road, my favorite area in all of Cape Coral. The area was sparsely populated and the home was on a dead end road with only three homes past it. Gorgeous waterfront homes were nearby. Every home in the area was nicely landscaped with lush lawns and palm trees.

I showed the listing to Paul.

"I'm dreaming, I know," I said.

"I guess you're dreaming. We can't afford that. It is nice, though."

"It's a short-sale, and they just dropped the price, maybe they'll go lower," I continued.

"Go ahead, make an offer but don't get your hopes up."

I did. I made the highest offer we could possibly swing, and it was still way below the asking price. I crossed my fingers and waited. The owner accepted the offer, but now the bank had to agree to take way less money than what was owed on the property. Banks could sometimes take months to decide. I waited, trying not to dream. It would most likely be denied.

A week later the bank accepted our offer and wanted to close in ten days. We were excited, to say the least, and made arrangements to fly to Florida, inspect the home, and close the next day. Then we planned on spending a week to move everything out of storage before heading back home. It was the end of July.

And that's when it happened. The last straw.

James stole from his father, not once, but twice in three days. Not that he hadn't done so in the past, but I had always softened the blow explaining he didn't mean to, he had no choice, he would pay it back, or I simply didn't tell him. I couldn't help James this time.

The first incident happened on Sunday morning. We were flying out the following Saturday. I checked our e-mails and saw one indicating a receipt for payment on Paul's Paypal account for $117. I asked Paul about it, but he had no idea what it was for. We looked further into it and discovered the charge was for a hotel room in the city. James....

We called Paypal and disputed the charges. Then changed our password.

The phone rang a little while later. It was James.

I didn't answer. Paul was furious! I was not to speak to James again! He continued to call all morning, finally leaving a message a little before noon.

"Please answer the phone, I'll explain. I have the

money to pay you back. I'll put it in your account on Monday. I just had to sleep and shower. Please answer the phone."

I knew he was getting a small unemployment check weekly. I wanted to believe him. I asked Paul to listen to the message. He calmed down a little, and I called James. He assured me the money would be in the bank the next day. I knew better.

On Wednesday, James did it again. Paul received a phone call from one of our credit card companies with a fraud alert. Someone used our card for a hotel room and dinner the night before and was trying to pull $200 cash off the card right then. They reversed the charges, and we changed the password on that account and every other account we had. Credit cards, store cards, e-mail accounts, bank accounts, everything that had a password had to be changed.

We didn't talk about James. There was nothing to say. We were done. I was done. James never called. He knew.

I'm not sure exactly why, but that day I knew I just couldn't help my son anymore. Everything my husband and I had done in the almost eight years since he had first asked for help, hadn't helped. All our time, money, and love hadn't made a difference. He was no better, in fact he was worse.

We had been dangling a lifeline to James. "When you're ready, just grab a hold of the line, and your father and I will pick you up, put you back on your feet, drive you to rehab, pay for an apartment, help your kids, feed your family, and even get you medication. Whatever it takes to make you better, we will do it when you're ready." James knew Paul and I would always be there when he turned the corner. He just had to reach for the lifeline, ask for help, and want to change. Paul had eventually let go, but I still held on to that line.

That day I let go of the lifeline. I prayed my son would swim, but I knew if he didn't, I couldn't save him.

Chapter Twenty-five

We left two days later for our trip to Florida. We absolutely loved the house, but during our inspection, Paul noticed some copper wires were black. He knew that was a sure sign of defective drywall. Knowing about the last house we had under contract, the broker had assured us this house was fine.

"Are you sure, Paul?" I wanted to scream, "No! Not again!"

"I wish I was wrong, but I'm not."

"The bank will want a formal inspection," the broker interrupted. "The owner lived here for six years until just last week, and there's no odor." Defective drywall homes usually, but not always, have a distinctive rotten egg smell.

"I'm not paying for an inspection. I know what I'm seeing," Paul told the broker.

"How about if I have the owner pay for an inspection? Maybe there's another reason the wires are black."

"If the owner wants to pay, I'll listen to what an inspector says. Let us know when, and we'll be here."

We met the inspector the next day. He started out rude and cocky.

"There's no defective drywall here!" the inspector said while looking behind the refrigerator.

"Check the wires in the master bathroom." Paul had seen the worst evidence on that side of the house. He unscrewed an outlet and pulled the wires out. They should have been copper, but they were very black.

"That's not black," the inspector said.

"What do you mean, that's not black?" Paul wiped the wire with his fingers showing the inspector the black residue it left.

"That's not black," he said again as he left the room to continue his inspection.

The broker and I spent the next hour trying to keep Paul and the inspector separated.

When he was done, the inspector gave us a long lecture about defective, aka Chinese, drywall before admitting the home was full of it. Not a very toxic kind, though, he said. Even so, the house would have to be stripped, all the drywall in the house would have to be removed, the house thoroughly cleaned, and new drywall hung. Then the drywall would all have to be mudded, textured, and painted before reinstalling all cabinets, sinks, moldings, and appliances. All electrical outlets and carpeting would have to be replaced. There was a good possibility the HVAC system would have to be replaced as well. A major job sometimes costing more than $100,000 which was why we passed on the other property. But we loved this home.

Fortunately, we had talked the night before and agreed on a price we would be willing to pay for the home. We were able to get a rough idea of what it would cost for a renovation in this type and size home. We also knew the stigma of having had Chinese drywall at one time would devalue the home if we decided to sell it in the future.

Paul told the broker our price. The broker said the bank would never go for it. We explained how we came up with it. The broker said he knew someone who would buy it just the way it was at the same price we had it under contract for. We said fine, thank you for your time, and we left.

The broker called the next day. His friend didn't want to buy the house, and he would submit our new offer to the bank. We headed home to wait with our things still in storage. I started searching for another property knowing there was only a slim chance the bank would agree to our new offer.

After we arrived back home, I found out my mother had given in and picked up James. She was the "weak-link" this time, as Kylie would say. He had a doctor's appointment in the next town and couldn't get there. She took him to the doctor's office and dropped him back off at the shelter but opened the door by saying "if you need anything, call."

Two hours later, he did.

Mom said he slept for two days straight on her couch. Then he began to look for a job, getting one within a week. I tried to talk to her. I needed to protect my mother from my son.

"Mom, he can't stay with you. You can't trust him."

"I know, but he has a job now."

"How's he getting to work?"

"I've been driving him. I told him this is temporary."

"Last May you filed charges against him, now you're taking care of him again."

"I know, I just want to help him get on his feet."

My sister stepped in a week later and had a long talk with James. Denise can be pretty scary when she wants to be. She gave James two weeks to find a place and get out of Mom's house.

He did.

While all this was happening, we got a call from the broker. The bank accepted our offer. Again they wanted to close in ten days. We booked flights and headed back to Florida. This time, we stayed for three weeks. We couldn't move out of our storage unit yet, but we grabbed the blow-up bed, a few dishes, towels, and other necessities for our stay. We used the guest bedroom and bathroom on the opposite side of the house from the master bedroom and bath. We met with a contractor and settled on a price. We swam in our new pool, drank cocktails on our pavered lanai, and watched the sunset over the mangroves. More than once Paul smiled at me and said, "You did good."

The renovation would take three months. The contractor would start in the middle of September, finishing the middle of December. Kylie's delivery, a planned cesarean this time, was scheduled for November 30. I would definitely be home and have two weeks to enjoy my new granddaughter, yes it is a girl, before leaving for the winter. Things were looking great. I tried not to think of James.

I received an e-mail letter from James at the end of October. He apologized for everything that had happened. He talked about his job and said he met someone. He wanted me to meet her. Maybe have lunch. "I've told her all about my past, and she's okay with it," he wrote.

I almost didn't respond, but I couldn't do that to him. I wrote him that I was glad he was doing well, but I wasn't ready to see him yet. He had a long way to go.

However, Bree was turning six in November, and Kylie rented a room at an event center with an indoor pool for the party. I've missed most of Bree's birthdays because we were away. I didn't want to miss this one.

Of course Renee, Gabby, and Matthew were coming. That meant James and his new girlfriend would be there too.

When I arrived at the party, the small parking lot was already full. I had no idea what vehicle James was driving, but I assumed he was already there.

He was sitting by the pool with a nice looking, well-dressed woman about his own age. Kylie saw me enter the building and immediately nodded her head towards James.

"He looks good," she said.

"Yes, he does. But we've seen it before. It's only been a few months."

I suddenly realized I hadn't actually seen James since the previous spring. I was still hurt and angry. Paul was upset I would even come to this party knowing James would be here. "I can't let him control my life," I told Paul. And Kylie had forgiven him. She was still guarded around him, but she had cautiously let him back in her life.

James hadn't noticed me yet, so I watched him for a few more minutes watching his children swim and holding his new girlfriend's hand. He hadn't had a woman in his life since Lauren. He was devastated when the divorce was final almost two years ago. Maybe this new relationship would make a difference.

James noticed me then, even though I hadn't entered the pool area. I was standing by the window just watching him and the children in the pool. What a great idea for a sixth birthday party in November in New England. The kids were having a great time.

James stood up with his girlfriend and smiled that shy, little boy, "do you still love me?" smile that always melts my heart. I didn't realize how powerful my emotions were just under the surface. My eyes immediately filled with the tears I desperately tried to hold back. I wanted to be angry. I didn't want to care. I didn't want to love this young man who was once so close to my heart. Who had done all those awful things to me, his father, his sister, his grandmother, and many, many others. I didn't want to let him back in my life.

But it was useless trying anymore. He walked tentatively toward me not sure of my reaction.

"You look good," I said.

"I am good," he answered, still smiling while he waited for my next move.

I hugged my son then. I couldn't help it. But I wouldn't cry, I told myself. The children saw me then and ran over soaking wet to hug me too. I hoped nobody noticed the tears.

As I turned to leave the pool area and help a very pregnant Kylie with the food, I caught her, Karen, and Alex watching me and James. They were smiling, too.

Was this a new beginning? Would it last? For how long this time? I had no answers. I could only enjoy this moment... right now... today.

I did.

Chapter Twenty-six

Two weeks later Kylie called me. It was Wednesday, November 28th, 2012. Her cesarean was scheduled for the 30th, a week before her actual due date. Dr. Gutenberg did not want Kylie going into labor. It had never been determined why Bree "got stuck" as he described it. He didn't want to take a chance that the same thing would happen again. "A nice quiet cesarean birth is what we want," he said to Kylie.

"Mom, I think I might be in labor. I'm not sure. I don't have a lot of pain, just cramps."

"Sweetie, you need to hang up and call your doctor right now. Call me back," I calmly responded, emphasizing every word slowly. I knew she was scared, but I also knew she would need to be checked at any sign of labor this close to her due date. I worried constantly about a repeat of last time.

Five minutes later, she called back.

"He wants to meet me at the hospital to check. He doesn't want me to go to his office, just straight to the hospital."

I could hear the fear in her voice. Kylie was petrified of the cesarean. As much as she begged to be put to sleep, it was not good for the baby. She would have to be awake. Last time was an emergency, Dr. Gutenberg told her. "This time, we'll do it right."

Jess Gallant

"Kylie, it's going to be fine. Is Tom with you?"

"Yes. Can you pick up Bree?" We had already made these arrangements.

"I'll get her from school, and you let me know as soon as possible if we should head to the hospital. You'll be fine, Sweetie."

Kylie was indeed in the early stages of labor, but there was plenty of time for a nice, calm cesarean.

She did great! By the time I arrived at the hospital with Bree, Kylie was being wheeled back into the room with tiny, little Kellynn all wrapped up in a pink blanket and looking beautiful. Kylie was smiling and Tom grinned from ear to ear like all proud fathers do.

He proceeded to explain every little detail of the procedure while Kylie tried not to listen as we all watched God's little miracle squirm and make those adorable faces that only newborns make. We took lots of pictures, especially of Bree with her new baby sister, then I headed home to leave this new family alone with their perfect, little addition.

But their new little addition wasn't perfect.

Overnight, the nurses in the newborn nursery noticed Kellynn struggled to suck. On further examination, it was discovered that Kellynn was born with a cleft in her soft palate.

A steady stream of doctors and social workers came to Kylie's room over the next few days. We learned more about what exactly a soft palate cleft is and how it's repaired.

The soft cleft palate happens when the roof of the baby's mouth doesn't develop normally during pregnancy,

310

leaving an opening or cleft in the palate that may go through to the nasal cavity. Occasionally, normal baby spit-up would come out Kellynn's nose.

Kellynn was recorded as having a birth defect with the state which was "mandatory for record keeping," we were told. No one knows exactly what causes these clefts, but Kylie wondered if it was caused by something she had done. She worried people knew of her past and thought that somehow she had caused Kellynn's birth defect.

She had stopped taking Suboxone a few years ago. She just kept forgetting to take it, eventually realizing she didn't need it anymore. Kylie was now twenty-nine and still haunted by those bad decisions made at nineteen. Would it ever end?

Kellynn would need surgery at nine months of age before she started to talk. She was lucky the hard palate and lip were not involved. That would have required more surgeries. For Kellynn, one surgery should be all that's needed. "One and done" was how one particular doctor described it. "She'll be fine," he said.

She wasn't.

Kellynn weighed just under six pounds at birth. We left for Florida two weeks later. She was still not even six pounds, but except for being tiny, she was healthy.

I hated to leave, but the house was done, and we were anxious to move our things from the storage unit into our new Florida home. The contractors did a nice job, not perfect, but nice. Paul would redo a lot of the finish work. That was just the way he was. Paul was also going to install bamboo floors in the bedrooms. We would not be using any carpet in this home because of Paul's newly developed allergies.

We were going to repaint the exterior and do some much-needed landscaping as well. It was fun to see it all come together, but my thoughts were back home on little Kellynn. Kylie and I talked almost daily. She also sent pictures and videos regularly.

By the end of February, we were getting concerned that at three months old, Kellynn was still not yet six pounds. Kylie fed her constantly, but her cleft made sucking a chore. Even with special bottles, Kellynn couldn't gain weight. She was burning too many calories just trying to suck. On the first of March, Kellynn's pediatrician insisted she be hospitalized. She called it "failure to thrive."

Kylie was upset. I was checking flights home. We both calmed down and talked.

"I know she only needs to eat, but I'm afraid they'll do all kinds of unnecessary tests. She was gaining weight in the last few weeks. Then Bree caught a cold at school and gave it to Kellynn. I know I can get her to eat more now that the cold is gone."

"What exactly did the doctor say they would do?" I asked when Kylie took a breath.

"GI testing, genetic testing, and most likely a feeding tube either through her nose or surgically implanted."

"Okay. She needs food. A feeding tube through her nose would be the best case scenario, right? You have to take her in, but you can plead your case to the doctors at the hospital. Then listen to them, and together you can decide what's best for Kellynn."

"Do you think they'll listen to me?"

"Yes, but you need to listen to them too. They're the experts. They won't want to do anything that's unnecessary."

"Okay."

"Call me as soon as you know anything."

Kylie told the doctor what she told me, and they

decided on a nasogastric or NG feeding tube, one that is placed through the nose. Kellynn didn't even wake up when it was inserted. She gained almost a half pound the first day.

Kylie was taught how to use it at home, and Kellynn was released from the hospital after two days with the feeding tube in place. Kylie would feed Kellynn for twenty minutes then the remainder of the bottle would be fed to Kellynn through the feeding tube.

It was important the baby not forget how to suck and to associate sucking and swallowing with feeling full.

After two weeks, Kellynn not only continued to gain weight, but she also gained enough strength to finish her bottles within the twenty-minute feedings. The feeding tube was no longer needed.

I missed them so much I was checking flight information as soon as I realized Kellynn no longer needed the feeding tube. I discovered that the first week of April was a good time to fly to Southwest Florida. It was after the high season of February and March but before April school vacation. There were some inexpensive flights.

"Kylie could sure use a break," I told Paul.

"You'd put the baby on a flight?" he asked.

"Sure, babies fly all the time. She'll be fine. It's the other passengers who might not like it."

"I've been on some of those flights."

"This will be two short flights. Not like going to Aruba," I continued pleading my case.

"Is Tom coming too?"

I knew that question would come up. Paul had warmed up to Tom, but could he handle living under the same roof with him for an entire week?

"Yes, Tom would come too." I waited for his

reaction. Paul was never keen on company, but he loved his daughter.

"Okay. I know it's been rough on her... and you."

"Thank you." I kissed him quickly. "I've got to call Kylie." I grabbed my phone to see if they could come. She screamed.

They could.

I picked them up at Southwest Florida Airport a week later. Bree saw me first again and ran for the usual hugs and kisses. We twirled.

"I'm soooo excited!" she screamed.

So much like her mom.

By the time I got to hug Kylie I was fighting back tears. She looked great. Happy, healthy, and thin again. When I let go of Kylie, Tom handed me little Kellynn. I couldn't hold back the tears anymore.

At four months old, she was only eight pounds, but she was adorable. She smiled at me, and I melted. She looked like a newborn but had the personality of a four-month-old baby.

"She entertained everyone around us on the plane," Tom said.

We laughed. It would be a great week.

It was.

In the car, I asked Kylie how James was doing. He had called a few times, but because Paul was still angry I never talked long.

"I think he's doing great. I saw him and Sara the other day. They're good together, but she has rules. She handles the money and knows where every penny goes. She

Mom, I Need Your Help

uses a GPS tracker on their phones, so she knows where he is all the time. I don't blame her. With his reputation, I'd do the same thing." I knew Kylie would.

"How are the kids?"

"Good. James and Sara have them every other weekend. James would like to get full custody now that he's better. They rented a big house. Lauren is, well, Lauren. She'll never change. The kids are bounced around with no place to call home. At least they have their own rooms at James' house, but they're not there as much as he'd like them to be."

"We're almost there," I answered Bree's question before she had a chance to ask. "Are you excited?" Bree loved swimming pools.

"Yes! Yes! Yes! Can I go swimming?" Even buckled in she was jumping out of her seat.

"Of course you can. You can swim as much as you want."

And she did.

Bree lived in the pool for the entire week except when her parents took her to the beach, water park, and to see the manatees. That's when I got a chance to watch little Kellynn, and Bree got a chance to be alone with her mom and dad.

Kylie fell in love with the frogs that lived in our shrubs and the three legged one she found in the mailbox. She spent hours looking in the canals around our home for manatees, turtles, and of course, the alligator she was determined to see.

Paul did well with the company, even bonding with Tom over tequila drinks in the evening. Paul still referred to him as "the convict," but Kylie and I assured Tom that it was a term of endearment.

"If he didn't like you, he would be really, really nice.

315

It's a privilege to be called names by my father."

It was a fun week that flew by way too fast.

They left after seven days. We planned on following a couple of weeks later, but it would be six weeks. We found another project house. We have to work when the work is there. So we stayed to get the home ready to market. Our home on the lake still hadn't sold. Money was tight. The dream of a smaller home on the lake was fading too. The homes we renovated took longer to obtain and even longer to sell. Instead of three a year we were lucky to do one or two, some years were worse. When we sold the oil company in 2005, the real estate market was booming and mortgages were easy to come by. We hadn't planned on the real estate bubble and the banking reforms.

When we finally made it home at the end of May, I was nervous about Paul and James. Paul continued to be angry.

"He's never gotten the help he needs," he told me on the flight home. "We've seen it all before. I don't want him showing up at the house. I mean it, Jess."

"I know. I won't invite him over."

I knew I could see him at Kylie's house, and I knew his kids were welcome at ours. As much as I hated to admit it, Paul was right. James had been better many times before only to crash again after a few months or even a year. Why would this time be any different?

"Maybe after he proves himself. But I'm talking five years at least. Then maybe I'll believe he's beaten it." Paul rambled on.

"You're right. He has a long way to go."

I didn't want to talk about it anymore. Every time I talked to James, he asked how his father was. He ended every conversation with, "Tell Dad I love him."

Paul hadn't talked to James in over a year. I knew Paul had every right to be angry, hurt, disappointed... you name it, Paul had a reason to feel that way towards his son. James had cost us our dreams, our company, our retirement, and a small fortune. How could I still love him? But on the other hand, how could Paul not love his own son?

When James was clean, he was a good person. It was the addict, the disease that was bad, not the person inside. Had I been able to separate the two? Could Paul eventually do the same?

The next day while Paul turned the water on to the house and checked for any damage, I headed into town for groceries. On my way home, Paul called me on my cell phone.

"Do you have James' phone number?" he asked.

"Yes, why?"

"He was next door at Keith's, and he just left. I was standing in the driveway, and he drove right by me."

"I thought that's what you wanted."

"Would you call and tell him to come back so we can talk?"

"Sure." I ended his call and quickly called James.

"Hi, James, are you still on our road?"

"Yeah, I just left Keith's."

"Did you see your dad?"

"I saw him, but I didn't stop. I know he doesn't want to see me."

"Well, he does. He just called. He wants you to go back so you guys can talk."

"Maybe I don't want to."

I could hear the smile in his voice.

"Get your butt back there now!"

"Okay, okay." He laughed.

Maybe Paul had just learned to separate the two, the boy from the disease.

It turned out to be a great summer until the middle of August when Kylie almost died.

Kylie had been feeling tired and had vomited a couple of times earlier in the week, but by Sunday she was feeling better. Probably the flu, she said. I knew she was nervous about Kellynn's upcoming surgery that was scheduled for right after Labor Day. Maybe she was just stressed. We took all the kids to lunch, all five of my grandchildren. Knowing we'd be leaving soon, I wanted to visit with them. It was fun but hectic. Kylie seemed fine when I left her at her house late that afternoon.

I was surprised to get a call from Tom early Monday morning.

"Jess, something's wrong with Kylie. She got up in the middle of the night to make Kellynn a bottle and passed out. When I tried to help her get back to bed, she vomited what looked like coffee grounds. She insisted she was fine, but she passed out again this morning. Will you talk to her?"

"Sure. Put her on the phone, Tom."

"Hi, Mom. I don't feel good, but I don't want to be like James and run to the hospital every time I get sick."

Kylie sounded weak, her voice trembling.

"Kylie, something's very wrong. You need to be seen by a doctor right away. I'm coming over to take the kids."

"I didn't want to wake them up during the night. So I just stayed still hoping I'd feel better this morning, but I don't."

"Okay, Sweetie. Put Tom on the phone." She did. "Tom, I don't know if she needs an ambulance or not, but she needs to go to the emergency room now. Maybe you should call your mother. She would know." Tom's mother used to work as a paramedic. "I'm going to get ready to leave, I'll be there soon."

"Okay, I'll call my mom."

I rushed to get ready and ran out the door, telling Paul I didn't know when I'd be back, but I'd stay in touch.

By the time I got to their house, there was an ambulance getting ready to leave. Tom was standing in the doorway holding Kellynn. As often happens in a small town, Tina had just driven by and called to see what was happening.

"I'll be right there. I'll take the kids. You go with Kylie," Tina said.

I didn't have to ask. I have an amazing family. I took one look at Tom still in pajamas trying to keep it all together.

"Tina just went by and saw the ambulance. She's turning around. She's taking the kids." It took me only a second to decide if I should wait for Tina or if Tom should. "I'm heading to the hospital. I'll see you there," I said.

I've known her longer. She's my baby, I didn't say.

The hospital is a forty minute ride with the rush hour traffic. It seemed like everyone called me during that drive. Small town news travels fast. I had no idea what was wrong. I'd stay in touch. Everyone asked what they could do. It was nice to know so many people cared.

Tom had told me the paramedics had never seen anyone's blood pressure so low. They started IV's and rushed her out.

I couldn't imagine what would be so wrong. Kylie was healthy. I automatically thought of the worst, cancer.

The "C" word as Alex had once described it. Then I pushed that thought from my mind. I said a prayer and vowed not to think that way.

Kylie was in the trauma unit when I arrived. They let me right in to be with her. She was talking and smiling. I couldn't believe it. I took her hand. It was ice cold and almost yellow.

"Your hand is freezing," I said.

"That happens when you lose a lot of blood," the ER nurse responded.

"Is that what's happened, she's lost a lot of blood?"

"Yes, she's presented as if she was in a major accident," she said to me, then looked back at my daughter, "So no pain, Kylie?"

"No, except for feeling weak, I feel fine."

Kylie answered the rest of the long list of questions even telling the nurse about the Suboxone she had been on when the question of medications came up. They seemed more concerned about the amount of ibuprofen she took than anything else.

"We won't know for sure without more testing, but it sounds like you're bleeding internally somewhere in your GI tract. That's why you vomited 'coffee grounds.' It's actually digested blood. The only strange thing is you have no pain."

I stayed with Kylie and tried to warm up her hands as they were arranging an upper GI endoscopy to look inside her stomach. They also ordered blood since she had lost almost one third of hers.

Tom and his mom showed up a little later, and James even stopped by on his lunch break. We all just waited together while a constant line of doctors came in, asking questions, looking at her chart, and leaving. Kylie asked one doctor if she could go home after the procedure.

"Do you realize you almost died?" he said with

genuine concern.

"No," Kylie answered, looking up at all of us standing around her.

"Well, you did. You'll be staying here for a while."

We were all silent, lost for words and in shock.

The endoscopy showed multiple large ulcers in Kylie's stomach. One had eroded through a blood vessel. They were able to cauterize it during the procedure and stop the bleeding, but Kylie needed a total of four pints of blood.

She went home three days later with no idea how someone her age and health, with no symptoms at all, could have all those ulcers. The most common cause for ulcers at that age is an "h-pylori" infection, but she tested negative for it. Could the years of methadone and Suboxone use have caused these ulcers? Had her past come back to haunt her again? I realized then that it will always be lurking just around the next bend in the road that is Kylie's life.

As Labor Day weekend approached, Kylie was getting Bree ready for first grade and trying not to stress about Kellynn's surgery while still recovering from the loss of blood.

At the same time, James was worried about his children too. Lauren had no place to call home and was now staying with a friend out of state. She had full custodial custody of the kids, so James' hands were tied. He had no idea where they would be going to school. Now clean for over a year with a good job, a girlfriend, and a home, he wanted to have the kids live with him. At least until Lauren settled down somewhere, but she wouldn't hear of it.

That was until Labor Day weekend, when she dropped all three of them off on his doorstep with only the clothes on their backs, and school was starting in a couple of days.

"You can have them for the school year," she told James and left.

"I'm glad they're here, but a little notice would have been nice," James told me over coffee the next day. "I just can't afford to take time off work to get them registered in school, and I have to find daycare for Matthew."

Stress is one thing a recovering addict doesn't need, but James had reconnected with the family, and with all of our help, he got through the next few weeks.

In the meantime, Kellynn had her surgery in Boston while Bree stayed with us. The surgery went well, but it was very traumatic for her parents.

Kylie called from the hospital a few hours after the procedure.

"Mom, it's awful! I can't believe I let them do this to my baby!"

"Is she all right? Was the surgery successful?" I said, trying to concentrate on the positive.

"I guess so, but she's covered in blood and quivering all over. She doesn't even know us."

I couldn't imagine what it was like to see your baby like that. "Is she on pain medication?"

"They just gave her morphine. They never told us it would be like this."

"The morphine will help, Kylie. She won't remember this. She'll be okay. You have to believe you did the right thing."

My heart was breaking for my granddaughter and my daughter. Tom was with them and his mother was there too. She would be a big help.

"I know, but I never expected it to be this bad."

Kylie started to cry again, and Tom took the phone.

"It's bad, but they assure us she'll be much better by tomorrow." He was on the verge of tears too.

We said goodbye, and he promised to have Kylie call first thing in the morning.

She did.

"Kellynn smiled at us this morning. She's so much better. We'll probably be home by dinnertime."

Kellynn smiled at me too when they picked up Bree. She was on pain medication but no longer needed morphine. It was obviously uncomfortable at times, but Kylie stayed on top of the medication schedule to try and keep the pain to a minimum. Within a week it wasn't needed anymore.

Two weeks later Kylie turned thirty. It had been over ten years since that day in June when she first asked for my help with her addiction. Ten years almost to the day since she entered the methadone clinic. She never wavered from that path to recovery. She never slipped up or fell back. She'll tell you now the methadone clinic was a mistake. But maybe it was right at the time.

Chapter Twenty-seven

We left for Florida at the end of September. James' kids were settled in school, Kellynn was improving, and Bree loved first grade. I wasn't too sad this time because Kylie, Tom, and the kids were coming to Florida in six weeks. They were even going to bring Hannah. A real family vacation. They had "volunteered" to drive Paul's parents' vehicle with their dog to Orlando. I wondered why....

It's November 5th, 2013. Nine o'clock at night. James called.

"Hi, Mom. Has Kylie and her gang made it there yet?" They were close again. It was nice to hear that in his voice.

"Not yet. The GPS shows they just got off I-75. They should be here in twenty minutes or so."

"Well, I'm glad they had a safe trip. I'm going to bed."

As I ended the call, I thought of how far James had come in the last year. It was at Bree's sixth birthday party that I had let him back into my life, again. Bree would be celebrating her seventh birthday here in Florida, in five days. She was counting. More than a year and no "red flags" yet. Would this be the time he made it? Maybe things were different this time. My mother had moved to Florida last year, and we were gone for eight months at a time now.

There would be no one to pick him up if he crashed. He has
full custody of his kids. Is that enough? Sara seems to be a
good fit. A real partner but not a pushover. Maybe all of
these things combined are keeping James on the right track. I
know nothing is certain. It was in the news again today. A
famous actor died of a heroin overdose, at forty-six. He had
been clean for twenty-three years. There were no guarantees,
only todays.

Paul had gone to bed too. The kids were running late.
They had dropped the van and Buddy, the Cocker Spaniel,
off at my in-laws' house in Kissimmee around dinnertime.
They were now in a rental car for the last leg of their trip, the
three-hour drive to our house in Cape Coral. Not as easy as
they thought making the trip from New Hampshire to Florida
with a soon to be one-year-old, a soon to be seven-year-old,
a pre-teen, and a Cocker Spaniel. But they had jumped at the
chance to come back to our house in Florida. I certainly
didn't argue. Their trip last spring had been a lot of fun. I
hope one day to have James and his family here for a
vacation too, but I worry about the triggers. Cape Coral had
not been good for James. And Paul wasn't quite ready for a
stranger under his roof. He barely knew Sara. It took him
years to warm up to Tom. I'd have to work on him.

I checked the GPS on my phone. I figure they're
about ten minutes away. Kylie had found the app for the
GPS on the way down. Tina was calling often to check on
their progress, when Kylie remembered Sara had a GPS on
her and James' phone. Now Tina, Kylie, and I are all
connected, maybe too connected. Kylie called me earlier
today when I was at the grocery store.

"Where are you?" She had a little laugh in her voice.

"I'm just leaving Publix. I picked up some more
'beverages,'" I told her.

She laughed again. "I knew it! I saw you on the GPS.

Can you pick up some formula and diapers so we won't have to stop?"

I laughed with her. I loved her....

I followed them on the GPS, so I could see their car lights when they turned off Old Burnt Store Road. I watched from the door as they drove in the driveway. As soon as the car stopped, I was outside.

I hadn't seen Kylie and her family in six weeks. Not a long time for some families, but for me, it felt like forever. It always did when we left, but this was our life now. I hugged my daughter as she got out of the car, and I choked back the tears that always came. I'd be fine in a second, so I held her a little longer. By now, Tom had Kellynn out of the car seat. He handed her to me as we walked to the house.

I hugged her hard as I fought back those tears again. She giggled. I melted.

"She's gained weight, and she looks great," I said plastering her with kisses as only a "Mimi" can do.

"I know. Now she's my 'Chunky Monkey.' " That's Kylie's sense of humor I love so much. Kellynn was still not even up to a normal weight.

"Don't you dare!" I chastised teasingly. "We LOVE chubby babies!" I squeezed her harder.

Kellynn squealed. We all laughed.

I hugged Bree, Hannah, and their dad. I loved them all so much. I was lucky to have them here. It would be a great week. Too short, I knew, but I'd take it.

The last ten and a half years have been a challenge navigating the tumultuous world of drug addiction and recovery. Was it finally over? I hoped so. I prayed it was.

Life was good, maybe great.

"Please, God, make it last."

Epilogue

I started writing my story on Christmas Day, 2013. After five days and thirty pages, I stopped where I was writing and wrote the last page. I wanted to make sure my story had a happy ending. I had learned to hope for the best but plan for the worst. My story, my book, ends happily on November, 5th 2013. Five months later as I finish this, it's still happy.

I have shared my story to try to encourage and bring a little bit of understanding to other mothers or family members in similar situations. I ask that you take from it what you will and hope it may have in someway enlightened you in your own struggles with the ones you love. At this point, I consider myself among the lucky ones to have both my children well, at least for now, as we all know things can change in an instant.

I, in no way, am an expert and did not intend to give advice or suggest you follow my path. In fact, please don't follow my path. Please learn from my mistakes and ignorance, then find your own way, but know you are not alone.

Remember also that not all advice or guidance works for everyone. Every child or addicted person is unique as is every situation. Both my children struggled with the same addiction, but their paths to recovery were very different. If I were to give any advice, it would be to keep your children close to your heart even when you have to let them go.

P.S.

Paul finished his book, but since I'm writing under an assumed name and my husband is not, I can't tell you the title. I haven't read it yet, but I think he said something about glasses of water and a car chase. Maybe, something like that, I wasn't really listening. I was writing my own book.

www.ingramcontent.com/pod-product-compliance
Lightning Source LLC
LaVergne TN
LVHW051110080426
835510LV00018B/1974